A Handbook
on
Contemporary Public International Law

Sunod Jacob

Copyright © 2020 Sunod Jacob

All rights reserved.

A Handbook on Contemporary Public International Law

To
Anna, Dechen and Tenzin

Acknowledgments

As cited throughout the book and tabulated thereafter, I have relied upon a wide range of sources, encompassing government, intergovernmental and non-governmental reports. I thank the numerous researchers who have contributed to producing insightful reference material. I have also drawn on my experience working with the academia and with the ICRC. I single out my brother for challenging and inspiring me to complete this book. Thanks *achacha*.

Preface

This handbook is written to give expression to a two-fold belief strengthened and reinforced by 15 years of experience as a researcher, teacher and practitioner of International Law. First, that International law is dynamic and secondly, that this dynamism is substantially guided by international relations and foreign policy. The book is divided into twelve chapters and topics therein are extensively covered and appended where appropriate with case studies. The handbook captures developments even as recently as the judgement of the International Court of Justice in the Jadhav case, the impact of the US-China trade frictions, the Covid-19 pandemic period etc. Select historical theories and concepts, are discussed, wherever they find relevance to the present-day global order. The correlation between International law and operational reality has been paid due attention. Relying on my experience in the South Asian region generally and India in particular, references to regional and local contexts have been suitably provided. The language is kept as simple as necessary to convey direct messages making it an easy read for academia and practitioners alike.

Sunod Jacob

A Handbook on Contemporary Public International Law

A Handbook on Contemporary Public International Law

Abbreviations

ACE Advisory Committee on Enforcement
AfCFTA African Continental Free Trade Area
AHWG Ad Hoc Working Group
AJIL American Journal of International Law
AP Additional Protocol
APEI Areas of Particular Environmental Interests
Arb. Arbitration
Art. Article
ASIL American Society of International Law
ATSM Automatic Trigger Safeguard Mechanism
BRI Belt and Road Initiative
CARU Administrative Commission of the River Uruguay
CBD Convention on Biological Diversity
CBD Convention on Biological Diversity
CCS Convention on the Continental Shelf
CDIP Committee on Development and Intellectual Property
CDM Clean Development Mechanism
CDM Clean Development Mechanism
CEDAW Convention on the Elimination of all Forms of Discrimination against Women
CFCLR Convention on Fishing and Conservation of the Living Resources of the High Seas
Ch. Chapter
CHS Convention on the High Seas
CITES Convention on International Trade in Endangered Species of Wild Fauna and Flora
CLCS Commission on the Limits of the Continental Shelf
CNIPA China's National Intellectual Property Administration
COPUOS Committee on the Peaceful Uses of Outer Space
CPA Comprehensive Peace Agreement

CPV Consular, Passport & Visa
CRC Convention on the Rights of the Child
CSO Civil Society Organization
CTS Convention on the Territorial Sea and the Contiguous Zone
DOS Department of Operational Support
DPO Department of Peace Operations
e.d. edited
e.g. example
ECHR European Convention on Human Rights
ECOSOC Economic and Social Council
edn. Edition
EEZ Exclusive Economic Zone
EIA Environmental Impact Assessment
EO External Office
EPA Environmental Protection Agency
EU European Union
FAO Food and Agricultural Organization
FAO Food and Agriculture Organization
FCC Federal Communications Commission
FTA Free Trade Area
FTZ Free Trade Zone
G-4 Group of Four
GATS General Agreement on Trade in Services
GATT General Agreement on Trade and Tariff
GC Geneva Convention
GDP Gross Domestic Product
GHG Green House Gases
GL General List
ICAO International Civil Aviation Organization
ICAO International Civil Aviation Organization
ICCPR International Covenant on Civil and Political Rights
ICESCR Covenant on Economic, Social and Cultural Rights
ICJ International Court of Justice

ICPO International Criminal Police Organization
ICTY International Criminal Tribunal for Yugoslavia
IGC Traditional Knowledge and Folklore
IHL International Humanitarian Law
IHRL International Human Rights Law
ILC International Law Commission
INGO International Non-governmental Organization
Int'l International
INT'L&COMP. L. Q. International and Comparative Law Quarterly
Intergovernmental Committee on Intellectual Property and Genetic Resources
IP Intellectual Property
IPCC Inter-Planetary Commission on Climate Change
IPR Intellectual Property Rights
ISA International Sea Bed Authority
ISA International Solar Alliance
ISS International Space Station
ITLOS International Tribunal on Law of Sea
ITU International Telecommunication Union
IUCN The World Conservation Union
Jan. January
JARPA Japanese Whale Research Program under Special Permit in the Antarctic
LDC Least Developed Countries
LDN Land Degradation Neutrality
LLDC Land Locked Developing Countries
Ltd. Limited
MCTR Missile Technology Control Regime
MEA Ministry of External Affairs
MFN Most Favoured Nation
NDC Nationally Determined Contributions
NIAC Non-International Armed Conflict

no. Number
NPT Nuclear Non-Proliferation Treaty
OECD Organization for Economic Cooperation and Development
OIA Office of International Affairs
OPSD Optional Protocol of Signature concerning the Compulsory Settlement of Disputes
ORF Observer Research Foundation
Ors Others
OST Outer Space Treaty
p. Page
P5 Permanent Five (UNSC members)
Para paragraph
PBC Program and Budget Committee
PBF Peacebuilding Fund
PCA Permanent Court of Arbitration
PCIJ Permanent Court of International Justice
PCT Patent Cooperation Treaty
PLO Palestine Liberation Organization
PoW Prisoner of War
pp. pages
R2P Responsibility to Protect
RCEP
REMP Regional Environmental Management Plan
Rep Report
Reps Reports
Res. Resolution
S. Section
SDGs Sustainable Development Goals
Sec. section
Ser. Series
SIDS Small Island Developing States
SoP Standard Operating Procedures
U.S.C Code of Laws of the United States of America

UDHR Universal Declaration of Human Rights
UDI Unilateral Declaration of Independence
UNCCD United Nations Convention to Combat Desertification
UNCLOS UN Convention on the Law of the Sea
UNCTAD United Nations Commission on Trade and Development
UNECE UN Economic Commission for Europe
UNEP United Nations Environment Program
UNESCO United Nations Educational, Scientific and Cultural Organization
UNHCR United Nations High Commission for Refugees
UNFCCC United Nations Framework Convention on Climate Change
UNGA United Nations General Assembly
UNIDO UN Industrial Development Organization
UNOOSA United Nations Office for Outer Space Affairs
UNSC UN Security Council
US United States
USA United States of America
USTR US Trade Representative's Office
v. versus
Val. U. L. Rev. University Law Review
Vol. Volume
WCT WIPO Copyright Treaty
WEF World Economic Forum
WIPO World Intellectual Property Organization
WPPT WIPO Performances and Phonograms Treaty
WTO World Trade Organization
WWII World War II

TABLE OF CONTENTS

   Acknowledgments   ii
   Preface   iv
   Abbreviations   vi

1 **Introduction to Public International Law**   1

Meaning and scope of Public International Law
Functions of International Law
Subjects of International Law
Relationship between International Law and Municipal Law
Limitations of International Law

2 **Sources of International Law**   16

International Conventions
International Customs
General Principles of Law
Case study of Estoppel in Public International Law
Judicial Decisions
Rebirth of International Criminal Law
Scholarly writings
Other sources
A hierarchy of sources/norms of public international law?

3 **State Recognition**   33

Theories of state recognition
Constitutive Theory
Declaratory Theory
Lauterpacht doctrine
Conditional Recognition
Individual and Collective Recognition
Recognition of Governments
De jure and de facto recognition
State policies on recognition of governments
Unilateral Declaration of Independence

Democratic Legitimacy and Recognition

4 **State Responsibility** 47

Evolution of State Responsibility Topic under the International Law Commission
Salient features of the Draft Articles of 1996
ICJ and State Responsibility
Responsibility of States for Internationally Wrongful Acts
Countermeasures
Principle of Proportionality

5 **Law of Extradition** 57

Obligation to extradite
Factors prohibiting extradition
Grounds for mandatory refusal
Grounds for discretionary refusal
Double Criminality
Rule of Specialty
Documentation required for extradition
Rendition
India's Extradition Act 1962
How may the Extradition process be triggered against an Indian national

6 **Law of Diplomatic Relations and Consular Relations** 73

Functions of a diplomatic mission
Appointment of Head of Mission
Categories of Heads of Mission
Diplomatic immunity
Diplomatic privileges
Vienna Convention on Consular Relations
Influence of the Instrument on Subsequent Legal Developments
Kulbushan Jadhav case

7   The Law of Sea   85

   Truman Proclamation
   Santiago declaration
   UNCLOS I
   UNCLOS II
   Montevideo Declaration
   The Lima Declaration
   The Declaration of Santo Domingo
   Patrimonial Sea
   UNCLOS III
   Dispute Resolution
   International Seabed Authority
   Commission on the Limits of the Continental Shelf
   Order in the Indian Ocean – A case study

8   Space Law   127

   The Outer Space Treaty
   The Rescue Agreement
   The Liability Convention
   The Registration Convention
   The Moon Agreement
   Important Space Law Resolutions
   Committee on the Peaceful Uses of Outer Space
   International Space Station
   ASAT
   Space weaponization

9   International Environmental Law   143

   Climate change
   UNFCC
   Kyoto Protocol
   Sustainable Development

Biodiversity
Trans frontier pollution
Marine pollution
Endangered species
Hazardous materials and activities
Cultural and Natural Heritage preservation
Desertification
Recent ICJ Cases

10 International Humanitarian Law   163

Relevance and scope of the term Armed conflict
Typology of Armed conflicts
Relevance of International Humanitarian Law during absence of hostilities
When International Humanitarian Law ceases to apply
Protection under International Humanitarian Law
Belligerent Occupation and effective control
Legal Consequences of Belligerent Occupation
Definition of 'combatants'
Combatant's privilege
Definition of civilians and civilian population
Fundamental Principles of Humanitarian Law
Prohibited means of warfare
Emblems
Prisoners of War

11 International Human Rights Law   199
Universal Declaration of Human Rights
International Covenant on Economic, Social and Cultural Rights
International Covenant on Civil and Political Rights
International Convention on the Elimination of all Forms of Racial Discrimination
Convention on the Elimination of all Forms of Discrimination

against Women
Convention against Torture and other Cruel, Inhuman or
Degrading Treatment or Punishment
Convention on the Rights of the Child
International Convention on the Protection of the Rights of all
Migrant Workers and Members of their Families
Overlap of IHL and IHRL in Situations of Armed Conflict
International Refugee Law

12 The United Nations   215

Overview of the UN Charter
Sovereign equality of states
Non-use of force in international relations
Domestic jurisdiction clause
Membership to the UN
Observer status in the UN General Assembly
General Assembly & GA Revitalization
Security Council & Security Council Reform
Economic and Social Council
Trusteeship Council
ICJ: Jurisdiction, pending cases, India in the ICJ
Regional Arrangements
Secretariat and Secretary General
UN Peace Keeping, UN Peacebuilding
World Trade Organization and WIPO: A case study
Are International Organizations withering away?
US-China IPR differences and its implications for India

Select Bibliography   279

1. Introduction to Public International Law

Topics covered
- Meaning and scope of Public International Law
- Functions of International Law
- Subjects of International Law
- Relationship between International Law and Municipal Law
- Limitations of International Law

Meaning and scope of Public International Law

The term *international law* made its appearance in legal literature when the English philosopher Jeremy Bentham used it during the late 18th Century.[1] He defined international law as the law on inter-State relations, and proposed ways to strengthen its role in preventing wars and improving inter-State relations. This term replaced the older terminology of the *law of nations*[2] which can be traced back to the Roman concept of *jus gentium*.[3] However, since the mid-twentieth

---

[1] Jeremy Bentham, **Introduction to the Principles of Morals and Legislation,** 1780; Subsequent version printed for W. Pickering and E. Wilson, London, 1823

[2] E. Vattel, **The Law of Nations: Or, Principles of the Law of Nature Applied to the Conduct and Affairs of Nations and Sovereigns,** 1758

[3] For more on Roman perspective on International Law see Christian Baldus, **Vestigia pacis- The Roman Peace Treaty: Structure or Event?,** (First edition, Cambridge University Press, 2004)

century, the traditional definition has become outdated with broadening of the scope of Public International Law and gradual legitimization of newer political entities. Currently, public International Law is accepted as a set of rules that regulate or oversee relations between formally endorsed subjects of International law. The current understanding of Public International Law goes beyond the outdated restrictive version which acknowledged only those normative rules applicable to *nation-states* in their conduct of relations with each other. Today, Public International Law or simply said International law encompasses, in addition to traditional issues, new topics, such as international organizations, trade, economy, development, human rights etc. The establishment of the United Nations in 1945[4] led to progressive development of International Law. During the post-World War II era, substantive progress in the evolution of International law can be attributed to the following two significant events:

a) enhanced membership of the international community
b) proliferation of international organizations

The decolonization movement and political recognition led to the creation of new states.[5] The proliferation of international organizations mainly began with the establishment of specialized agencies of the United Nations[6] and other international organizations.[7]

---

[4] **The San Francisco Conference** 1945

[5] In 1945, the UN had 51 member states. With the formal induction of Republic of South Sudan in 2011, there are at present 193 sovereign states and 2 observer states

[6] There are 17 Specialized Agencies operating under the aegis of the United Nations vide Arts. 57 & 63 of the UN Charter 1945

[7] Refer Chapter (10) on International Organizations. Note: For the purposes of this book, private societies having international operations such as INGOs and CSO have not been considered as they do not constitute a subject of International Law as yet.

Since the creation of the UN as a successor to the failed League of Nations, significant number of international treaties have been concluded, reflective of the growth of topics dealt under the purview of international law. Of particular interest in terms of contemporary international law are universal law-making treaties. Furthermore, the contribution of institutions such as the world courts i.e. International Court of Justice (and its predecessor, Permanent Court of International Justice), International Law Commission created in 1947,[8] the organs of the United Nations and its specialized agencies deserve due mention and attention in the evolution of Public International Law.

> Contemporary Public International Law defined: *"International law is that body of law which is composed for its greater part of principles and rules of conduct which states feel themselves bound to observe and therefore do commonly observe in their relations with each other and which includes also: The rule of law relating to the functioning of International Institutions and Organizations, their relations with each other and their relations with states and individuals and Certain rules of law relating to individuals and non-state entities so far as the rights and duties of such individuals and non-state entities are the concern of the international community"*[9]

To summarise, the evolution of meaning and scope of public international law has been most remarkable in the last seven decades. Going further back, it can be said that the fundamental basis of this branch of law has transformed over a period of five centuries from *coexistence of states* to that of *cooperation of states* and creation of inter-State organizations bestowed with international legal personality. While nation-states continue to retain their position as the principal unit of discourse, the induction of individuals as objects and subject-

---

[8] UNGA Resolution 174 (II) of 21 November 1947
[9] JG Starke, **Introduction to International Law** (10th Edition, Butterworth - Heinemann, 1989)

matter signify another important step in the evolution of International Law (see chapter on International Humanitarian Law and International Human Rights Law).

Limitations of Public International Law
Does International Law constitute law (Positivists): One of the major weaknesses of international law is its inability to enforce its policies, sanctions and actions in an efficient and potent manner. The Positivist school of thought tests the validity of International law through the lens of John Austin's perspective. He defined *law* as a *"command from a political superior a sovereign to a political inferior, and backed by a threat of evil in the event of non-compliance."*[10] Based on this premise he goes on to state *"usually styled the law of nations or international law ... consists of opinions or sentiments current among nations generally. It therefore is not law properly so called"*.[11] Consequently, positivists generally tend to identify international law with moral principles or *positive morality*.[12] Efficacy of International law depends on consent to take any course of action, as a result, fails to stand the scrutiny of the *Austinian handicap*[13] i.e. *"Is international law law?"*

Jurisdiction based on Consent: A significant lacunae of International Law is the inherent weakness in jurisdiction of courts and tribunals and enforcement thereof. For instance, states would have to necessarily agree to accept the court's ruling in order to allow it to

---

[10] John Austin, **Province of Jurisprudence Determined** (1832 Edited by Rumble W. E, Cambridge University Press, 1995)
[11] *Ibid*
[12] Positivists such as HLA Hart and Hans Kelsen have made conscious attempts to distance themselves from Austins' strict notion of command theory
[13] DJ Harris, **Cases and materials on International law** (5th edition, Sweet & Maxwell, London, 1998) p. 6

judge their problems.[14] Most recently the inability of the Permanent Court of Arbitration Tribunal in enforcing its ruling pertaining to the South China Sea case on the *nine dash mile* and *historical rights*[15] and the response by PR China[16] is illustrative of the weakness of the courts and tribunal systems in place. Since the principal, yet unstated goal of international law is cooperative facilitation of transnational activity, power is decentralized and the sovereign as a coercive enforcer is virtually non-existent.

Collective security and Sanctions: One of the main tools available at the disposal of the international community is the UN Charter-based sanctions system which legitimizes the resort to exert *economic and political* pressure on errant states.[17] Sanctions are non-military forms of coercion imposed, for a period of time aimed at another country or individuals of that country to observe the international rule of law. This power is vested in the Security Council and may take the form of comprehensive economic and trade sanctions or arms embargoes, travel bans, and financial restrictions etc. Such efforts have met with mixed results over the last seven decades of operation, often leading to questions about the efficacy of the sanctions system. The UN Security Council has also been vested with the power to resort to use of force where such action is imminently required or where non-military options have failed to produce the desired behavior. The *veto*

---

[14] Refer chapter on UN, ICJ and Art. 36 of the Statute of the ICJ
[15] *Philippines v. China* (PCA case number 2013–19)
[16] "With regard to the award rendered on 12 July 2016 by the Arbitral Tribunal in the South China Sea arbitration established at the unilateral request of the Republic of the Philippines (hereinafter referred to as the "Arbitral Tribunal"), the Ministry of Foreign Affairs of the People's Republic of China solemnly declares that the award is null and void and has no binding force. China neither accepts nor recognizes it" Statement of the Ministry of Foreign Affairs of the People's Republic of China on the Award of 12 July 2016 of the Arbitral Tribunal in the South China Sea Arbitration Established at the Request of the Republic of the Philippines
[17] Art. 41 of the UN Charter 1945

power vested in the permanent members of the UNSC,[18] military alliances with explicit right to resort to collective self-defense[19] and implicit power to exercise preemptive use of force[20] have often undermined the sanctions regime and the efficiency of collective self-defense under the UN Charter.

Respect for sovereignty: As per art. 2(7) of UN Charter, the organization is not competent to interfere in the domestic matters of member-states. International law cannot interfere in the domestic matters. This Westphalian concept worked well in a world that was not so interdependent. It served, both as a strength as well as a weakness in international law. The privileged states (P-5) have often been subjected to criticism for not acting in time (e.g. Rwandan Genocide 1991) and being selective in their action (e.g. UNSC Resolutions supporting R2P). In either case, respect for the notion of sovereign equality of states appears to wrest more on politics and less on law.

Evolving functions of International Law

An important characteristic of contemporary Public International Law is the steady expansion of its scope through the inclusion of new subject matters, participants and subjects. The initial aim of Public International Law has been to create an orderly system of international relations. However, modern developments have added another objective, i.e. ensuring *justice* in the relations of States and securing *justice* for states and individuals. Trials on war crimes before the Nuremberg Military Tribunals (1945) and *Tokyo Trials* driven by The International Military Tribunal for the Far East (1946)[21] as well as

---

[18] Art. 27 *Ibid*
[19] For e.g. see Art. 5 North Atlantic Treaty 1949
[20] Art. 51 *Ibid*
[21] *Neither the official position, at any time, of an accused, nor the fact that an accused acted pursuant to order of his government or of a superior shall, of itself, be sufficient to free such accused from responsibility for any crime with which he is charged, but such circumstances may be considered in mitigation of*

the establishment of International Court of Justice in 1945 indicates a new imperative.

> *Public International Law distinguished*
> The rules of Public International Law are legally binding and has to be distinguished from *international comity*. Comity is a friendly gesture or courtesy exercised by one State toward another without constituting a legal obligation.[22] An example of a comity is the *flag salute* at the sea. A comity also serves as a tool towards building and maintaining friendly relations among States.
> *Private International Law* (or conflict of laws as described in the common law countries) means a body of principles and rules applicable to private parties involving trans-border cases, having at least one foreign element in it,[23] leading to questions as to applicability of foreign law or the role of foreign courts. Consequently, private international law is almost entirely the result of judicial pronouncements.[24] Public International Law deals, in general, with the external relations of States.

Subjects and objects of International Law
Subjects of International Law are entities vested with international legal personality. In other words' entities that are capable of rights and duties under international law. *States* are the original subjects of International Law. All States, by virtue of the principle of sovereign equality, enjoy the same degree of international legal personality. (refer chapter 3 on State Recognition).

---

punishment if the Tribunal determines that *justice so requires*" art. 6 Charter of the International Military Tribunal for the Far East 1945

[22] For traditional view see Ulrich Huber, **De Conflictu Legum** (edited by Ernest G. Lorenzen 1919)

[23] Paras Diwan and Peeyushi Diwan, **Private International Law Indian and English** (14th edition Deep & Deep Publications, New Delhi, 1998)

[24] P.M. North and J.J. Fawcett, **Cheshire and North's Private International Law**, (12th edition, Butterworths, 1992) p. 14

International organizations also exercise legal capacity in a myriad of ways. These include (but are not limited to) exercising ability to convene track 1 conferences, conclude treaties, create military forces (subject to UN charter) and appear before courts to enforce institutional rights. The legal capacity of the United Nations was a question brought before the International Court of Justice. In its advisory opinion in the *Reparation for Injuries Case of 1949*, the Court held that the *United Nations was an international person, although not a State, and therefore not having the same rights and duties as a State.*[25] In effect the ICJ concluded that the United Nations had an international personality and that without the powers of international legal personality, cannot carry out its mandated functions. The UN can perform legal acts such as entering into agreements with member States and with other international organizations, concluding contracts and bringing claims before a court. Such capacity to perform legal acts is a prerequisite of international legal personality.

Non-State Entities are entities, short of attributes of statehood, granted a certain degree of personality, comprising of specified rights and obligations under International Law. Their capacity is defined by, the purpose it exists for, and the powers or functions it can perform. Entities that have been docketed as NSEs include the following:

Insurgents are individuals or groups who rebel against their own government.[26] For rebels to attain status of international legal personality they need to meet, at a minimum, the following criteria:
a) They need to have control over a considerable part of the territory
b) Most of the people living in rebel territory must support the rebels out of their own accord and not as a result of the coercive actions taken by the insurgents, and
c) Rebels must be able and willing to comply with international

---

[25] **Reparation** of **Injuries** Suffered in Service of the UN, Advisory Opinion, 1949 ICJ 174 (Apr. 11)
[26] There is no universal formally agreed definition under International law

obligations.[27]

Belligerents are a body of insurgents who by reason of their temporary organized government are regarded as lawful combatants conducting lawful hostilities, provided they observe the laws of armed conflict. Recognition of *belligerency* is usually subject to the following four criteria:
a) There should exist within the state, a *situation of armed conflict*
b) Insurgents must *administer and occupy significant territory*
c) Hostilities must be conducted in accordance with the *rules of war* and through organized armed forces acting under a responsible authority, and
d) *Recognition* of belligerency by other states.

Upon recognition, belligerents can enter into valid arrangements with States, international organizations, and other belligerents and insurgents. From an absolute obligatory perspective, belligerents are expected to observe International law relating to the conduct of hostilities.

National liberation movements: The UNGA formally recognized, international legal status of the Palestinian movement[28] and accorded them *observer status*, permitting participation in meetings[29] and conferences convened by organs and specialized agencies of the United Nations. Furthermore, the UNSC permitted the Palestine Liberation Organization to participate in its debates with rights, equal to that of UN member nations. International practice has also accorded political entities recognized as national liberation movements with a number of legal rights and duties. The most significant being, the capacity to conclude binding international

---

[27] S.K. Verma, **An Introduction to Public International Law** (Eastern Economy, 1998) p. 113
[28] UN General Assembly A/RES/3237 (XXIX)
[29] UN General Assembly A/RES/52/250

agreements with other international legal persons, the capacity to participate in the proceedings of the United Nations, and the rights and obligations of International Humanitarian Law. For example, in 2012 PLO was accorded *Permanent non-member observer status* and is currently categorized alongside the Holy See[30] vide United Nations General Assembly resolution 67/19.

Status of Individuals under Public International Law
Following the failure of the League of Nations, evolution of public international law demonstrated a tendency to support protection and responsibility on individuals. The significant number of civilian casualties in the second World War had a substantial effect on this trend. Direct responsibility on individuals for crimes committed against the peace and security was enunciated in the Charter of London of 1943.[31] This approach was reinforced by the Charter of the Nuremberg International Tribunal of 1945. The Nuremberg International Tribunal explained the logic of placing international legal responsibility on individuals in the following manner:

> "*international law imposes duties and liabilities upon individuals as well as upon states..(since)..crimes against international law are committed by men, not by abstract entities, and only by punishing individuals who commit such crimes can the provisions of international law be enforced.*"[32]

While the Charter of 1943 was applicable to a very limited number of States, the principles identified and acknowledged through the decisions of this tribunal achieved global consensus when they were

---

[30] UN General Assembly A/RES/58/314
[31] The Charter of 1943 was agreed by the then '*allied powers*' constituted individual responsibility in case of '*war crimes*', '*crimes against humanities*' and '*crimes against peace*'
[32] International Military Tribunal for Nuremberg, Judgment, 1 October 1946, p. 41

re-affirmed by the General Assembly in 1946.[33] This was followed by adoption of the Genocide Convention 1948 which once again re-affirmed individual criminal responsibility vis a vis the crime of genocide. 1949 was a seminal year in this context when the previous laws of war were revised to address, in addition to land warfare, naval warfare and air warfare, the protection of civilians and prisoners of war from grave breaches.[34] This development in contemporary public international law is particularly significant considering that the four Geneva Conventions of 1949 even today constitute the most widely ratified conventions in the world. Simultaneously, the discourse in International law showed greater concern for individuals from the perspective of human rights and fundamental freedoms. This was a welcome departure from the Covenant of League of Nations which reflected a very limited (labour conditions) reference to human rights in the following manner;

> "Members of the League......will endeavour to secure and maintain fair and humane conditions of labour for men, women, and children, both in their own countries and in all countries to which their commercial and industrial relations extend, and for that purpose will establish and maintain the necessary international organisations"[35]

Scholarly view suggests that, disagreement among the then great powers in according equal rights and fair treatment as partly the reason for restrictive relevance of human rights under the Covenant.[36] In stark contrast, the UN Charter provisions make explicit reference to human rights in the following manner:

---

[33] See General Assembly resolution 95 (1) of 11 December 1946 and General Assembly resolution 177(II) of 21 November 1947 (Formulation of the principles recognized in the Charter of the Nuremberg Tribunal and in the judgment of the Tribunal)

[34] Art 50, 51, 130,147 of 1949 Geneva Conventions I-IV respectively

[35] Art. 23 of The Covenant of the League of Nations 1919

[36] John Humphrey, "The International Law of Human Rights in the Middle Twentieth Century," (International Law Association, London, 1973)

> *"The Purposes of the United Nations……To achieve international co-operation in solving international problems of an economic, social, cultural, or humanitarian character, and in promoting and encouraging respect for human rights and for fundamental freedoms for all without distinction as to race, sex, language, or religion."*[37]

> *"The General Assembly shall initiate studies and make recommendations for the purpose of….promoting international co-operation in the economic, social, cultural, educational, and health fields, and assisting in the realization of human rights and fundamental freedoms for all without distinction as to race, sex, language, or religion."*[38]

> *"With a view to the creation of conditions of stability and well-being which are necessary for peaceful and friendly relations among nations based on respect for the principle of equal rights and self-determination of peoples, the United Nations shall promote…..universal respect for, and observance of, human rights and fundamental freedoms for all without distinction as to race, sex, language, or religion"*[39]

> *"The Economic and Social Council may make or initiate studies and reports with respect to international economic, social, cultural, educational, health, and related matters and…. may make recommendations for the purpose of promoting respect for, and observance of, human rights and fundamental freedoms for all."*[40]

Art. 76 of the UN Charter also makes reference to human rights, within the functioning of the Trusteeship Council. However, given

---

[37] Art. 1 (3) of the UN Charter 1945
[38] Art 13 (1)(c) *ibid*
[39] Art. 55 (c)
[40] Art. 62 (2)

the irrelevance of the Council[41] in contemporary international affairs, the provision is mentioned here for purely academic reasons. UN GA resolution of 1950 on Human Rights i.e. UDHR and subsequent conventions like the International Covenant on Civil and Political Rights of 1966, and the International Covenant on Economic, Social and Cultural Rights of 1966 have further solidified the position of the individual as an actor in international law. However, the status stops short of international legal personality which only states or other entities discussed earlier possess. Contemporary International Law considers individuals as participants and *subjects* of law.

> Individuals have a sort of legal personality under International Law. They are granted rights and subject to obligations directly under International Law. Consequently, the position of individuals under International Law can be summarized in this manner. It is applicable in case of relations between states and individuals and to interrelations of individuals *where such relations involve matters of international concern.*

Relationship between Public International Law and Municipal Law
Public International Law and municipal / domestic /national law are two different legal systems. The latter governs the internal relations of recognized actors within a state. Whereas, the former is principally concerned with the relations between States, international organizations and certain entities. With greater interaction between states at various levels, more so with globalization, the relationship between national laws and International Law warrants attention for addressing the many practical problems, including:
- What is the status of International Law before a national court?
- What is the status of municipal law before an international court?
- Which rule prevails in a case of conflict between the two?
- How does International Law take effect in the national law?

---

[41] The last Trust territory i.e. Palau in 1994 was delinked from council and later recognized as an independent member of the UN as the Republic of Palau

These questions have sought to be addressed on the lines of two divergent theories, namely the *monist* and the *dualist* theories.

Theories on Relations Between International Law and National Law
The *dualist theory* considers that International law and domestic law are two distinct legal systems. Both systems operate independently of each other, regulate different subject matters, function on different levels, and *most importantly each is dominant in its respective sphere. Consequently, municipal law cannot create or alter International law or vice versa.* Hence, where a country's legal framework mandates a specific formal process of adoption of international law into its domestic rules, the national law has supremacy over International Law. In case of a conflict between International Law and national law, a national court would apply national law. *Monists,* on the other hand uphold unity of all laws, by alluding to the proposition that International Law and municipal law constitutes a singular legal order. Consequently, both laws are founded on: *the regulation of conduct and the welfare of individuals*. However, monists assert the supremacy of International Law over national law even within the national sphere; i.e. *in event of a conflict between the two laws, International Law is supreme*. It is notable that positions taken by both these theories is a reflection of their respective ideological backgrounds. The dualist theory adheres to *positivism*, while the monist theory follows *natural law* thinking and liberal ideas of a world society.

> Because the above opposing theories, in reality, do not adequately reflect actual State practice, legal scholars tend to pay less attention to these theoretical views. Actual state practice of various countries leads to the following conclusions:
> a) most countries accept the operation of customary rules within their own jurisdictions, provided there is no conflict with existing laws
> b) in some countries, treaties operate automatically (self-executing) while others require a process of internal legislation.

> c) some countries allow treaties to supersede all national laws, whether made earlier or later than the treaty, while others allow treaties to supersede only ordinary laws and only that made earlier than the treaty. Others adopt opposite positions.

Indian Practice: According to the Indian Constitutional scheme, making of international treaties is an executive act. A Treaty is concluded with the approval of the Union Cabinet. It is not placed before the Parliament for discussion and approval. However, were the performance of treaty obligations to entail alteration of the existing domestic law or requires new enactment, it would accordingly require legislative action.[42]

---

[42] For more on Indian practice see MEA document titled, *Guidelines/SoP on the conclusion of International Treaties in India;* https://www.mea.gov.in/images/Revised-SOPs-with-forwarding-letter-02042018.pdf; website accessed on 18 March 2020

2 Sources of International Law

> **Topics Covered**
> - International Conventions
> - International Customs
> - General Principles of Law
> - Case study of Estoppel in Public International Law
> - Judicial Decisions
> - Rebirth of International Criminal Law
> - Scholarly writings
> - Other sources
> - Is there a hierarchy of sources/norms of public international law?

Art. 38 of the Statute of the International Court of Justice identifies the sources of international law. It essentially mentions the following;
(a) international convention,
(b) international custom,
(c) the general principles of law,
(d) judicial decisions and scholarly writings and
(e) *ex aequo et bono*[43]

---

[43] In terms of sources of international law, the Permanent Court of International Justice (predecessor of the ICJ) was guided by similar art. 38 of the PCIJ statute which read as follows:
The Court shall apply:

A Handbook on Contemporary Public International Law

> **Art. 38 of the ICJ Statute**
> 1. The Court, whose function is to decide in accordance with international law such disputes as are submitted to it, shall apply:
> a. international conventions, whether general or particular, establishing rules expressly recognized by the contesting states;
> b. international custom, as evidence of a general practice accepted as law;
> c. the general principles of law recognized by civilized nations;
> d. subject to the provisions of Art. 59, judicial decisions and the teachings of the most highly qualified publicists of the various nations, as subsidiary means for the determination of rules of law.
> 2. This provision shall not prejudice the power of the Court to decide a case ex aequo et bono, if the parties agree thereto.
> **Art. 59 of the ICJ Statute**
> The decision of the Court has no binding force except between the parties and in respect of that particular case.

As has been pointed out by Judge Antonio Augusto Cançado Trindade,[44] when the Court exercises its advisory function it takes

---

1. *International conventions, whether general or particular, establishing rules expressly recognized by the contesting States;*
2. *International custom, as evidence of a general practice accepted as Law;*
3. *The general principles of law recognized by civilized nations;*
4. *Subject to the provisions of Art. 59, judicial decisions and the teachings of the most highly qualified publicists of the various nations, as subsidiary means for the determination of rules of law. This provision shall not prejudice the power of the Court to decide a case ex aqua et bono, if the parties agree thereto.*

The decision of the Court has no binding force except between the parties and in respect of that particular case. (Art. 59)

[44] United Nations Audio Visual Library of International Law, Lecture by J.Antonio Augusto Cançado Trindade on *Statute Of The International Court Of Justice*; https://legal.un.org/avl/pdf/ha/sicj/sicj_e.pdf; website accessed on 17 March 2020

into account the list of *formal sources* found in Art. 38 of its Statute (custom, treaties, general principles of law, jurisprudence, doctrine, equity). That list is not exhaustive, but rather illustrative. Such formal sources amount to the certain methods whereby international law manifests itself, not excluding other methods (e.g., unilateral juridical acts of States, resolutions of international organizations). It may be recalled that the list in Art. 38 of the Statute dates originally from 1920, when the Advisory Committee of Jurists of the League of Nations prepared it for the PCIJ. Ever since, international law has evolved considerably.

International conventions

According to Art. 2 (1) (a) of the Vienna Convention on the Law of Treaties[45]

> *" (A) treaty means an international agreement concluded between States in written form and governed by international law, whether embodied in a single instrument or in two or more related instruments and whatever its particular designation."*

Further Art. 5 states;

> *"The present Convention applies to any treaty which is the constituent instrument of an international organization and to any treaty adopted within an international organization without prejudice to any relevant rules of the organization."*

Strictly speaking a treaty is not a source of law so much as a source of obligation under law[46] and as such the obligations are binding only on States that are high contracting parties. Hence, treaties are agreements drawn between consenting states in a written form,

---

[45] Signed at Vienna 23 May 1969, Entry into Force: 27 January 1980
[46] United Nations Audio Visual Library of International Law, Lecture by J. Christopher Greenwood on Sources of International Law: An Introduction; https://legal.un.org/avl/pdf/ls/greenwood_outline.pdf; website accessed on 17 March 2020

akin to written contracts drawn between individuals under domestic law. In principle, states have a choice to sign up to a treaty and consent to be obliged to comply with what they have signed up to. Treaties have often constituted the formal articulation of informal rules and practices e.g. the fundamental principles of treaties governing the laws of war are drawn from historic practices followed by belligerents during battles. Likewise, treaties arrived with near universal consensus may also indicate opinion juris and feed into the formation of customary international law. Based on the number of states involved, treaties may be categorized as *bilateral treaties* (between two states) and where it is signed up by multiple states, *multi-lateral treaties*. Treaty of Peace and Friendship Between the Government of India and Government of Nepal of 1950 is an example of a bilateral treaty. Even, if a third state has legitimate interests but is not a party, the treaty is still a bilateral treaty and does not automatically create obligations on interested states. E.g. Agreement on the Maintenance of Peace and Tranquility along the Line of Actual Control in the India-China Border Areas 1993. For academic reasons Multilateral treaties can be further categorized as *regional treaties*, such as the Agreement on South Asian Free Trade Area 2004 and *multi-regional treaties*, such as the Washington Treaty of 1949. Treaties may also be described as *law making treaties* if a new rule is adopted by a significant number of states, such as the United Nations Convention on the Law of the Sea 1982. Where a treaty provision is not intended to be modificatory but rather is an innovation designed to change the rule, it can become part of customary law if it is accepted in practice. See, e.g., the North Sea Continental Shelf cases (1969):

> "Although the passage of only a short period of time is not necessarily, or of itself, a bar to the formation of a new rule of customary international law on the basis of what was originally a purely conventional rule, an indispensable requirement would be that within the period in question, short though it might be, State practice, including that of States whose interests are specially affected, should have been both extensive and virtually

> uniform in the sense of the provision invoked; - and should moreover have occurred in such a way as to show a general recognition that a rule of law or legal obligation is involved."[47]

Treaty formation normally involves the following steps: negotiations leading to an agreement, followed by signature by representative,[48] ratification (consent through due domestic process of signing state) and entry into force (usually based on the date pre-determined and minimum number of ratifications in case of multilateral treaties). States that have signed and are yet to compete ratification process are still obliged by the object and purpose of the treaty (stopping short of all other provisions of the treaty). The general rule is that treaty obligations are absolute, however the exception is that treaty obligations would be considered void if it contradicts with a higher inviolable norm i.e. *jus cogens* norms.[49] These norms are of such authoritative value, that no derogation from such norms are permissible. A treaty may be terminated by withdrawal, denunciation or supersession, usually subject to its exit clauses.

The nomenclature *treaties* are synonymously used with certain other terminologies, albeit with minor variations in its usage. For instance, the term *convention* is also used to denote a treaty. Conventions are treaties which are drawn under the auspices of an International organization.[50] Yet another description of treaty is the word *charter* which is associated with treaties leading to the creation of an international organization.[51] The term *protocol* is used

---

[47] ICJ Reps, 1969, p. 43
[48] The State Representative may sign a treaty *ad referendum*, i.e., under the condition that the signature is confirmed by his state. See Art.12 (2) (b), Vienna Convention on the Law of Treaties 1969
[49] Art. 53 *Ibid*
[50] Treaties adopted under the auspices of the UN General Assembly are illustrations of Conventions
[51] E.g. UN Charter 1945

to denote a written instrument that is created subsequent to a treaty to supplement it.[52] A protocol does not constitute a stand-alone treaty and hence cannot exist in the absence of the original treaty. In conclusion, treaties are *written* agreements between subjects of international law, created by *states or institutions vested with treaty making power* establishing *binding rights and obligations* and is *governed by international law*.

International custom
International customs, simply put, are un-written rules having authoritative value. Some of the early examples can be identified in the requirement of States to grant immunity to a visiting Head of State. International customs have two elements namely *state practice* and *opinio juris*. Applying the same example, i.e. States exhibit a *widespread* and *consistent* practice of according immunity to a visiting Head of State. Secondly, States must accord immunity because they believe they have a legal duty to do so, in other words i.e. *opinio juris*, is *a belief in legal obligation*.[53] Consequently, for a new rule of customary international law to emerge, it has to satisfy the existence both of these elements. State practice is the objective or material element and *opinion juris* is the subjective element. Practice alone is not enough (see *SS Lotus case*[54]) and likewise a rule cannot be created only on the basis of *opinion juris* without any evidence of actual practice. (see ICJ advisory Opinion on Nuclear Weapons)[55] Over time, the weightage given to each of these two elements have varied and hence require closer examination. To meet the test of state practice, a usage has to be *consistent* and *uniform*.[56] State

---

[52] E.g. Additional Protocol to the Child Rights Convention
[53] United Nations Audio Visual Library of International Law, Lecture by J. Christopher Greenwood on *Sources of International Law: An Introduction*; https://legal.un.org/avl/pdf/ls/greenwood_outline.pdf; website accessed on 17 March 2020
[54] *France v. Turkey* PCIJ (ser. A) No. 10 (1927)
[55] ICJ GL No 95, [1996] ICJ Rep 226, ICGJ 205 (ICJ 1996), 8th July 1996
[56] Columbian Peruvian Asylum Case 1950 ICJ

practice, includes not just the practice of the government of a State but also of judgments rendered in municipal courts, laws enacted by parliament, statements made during parliamentary sessions, statements made at inter-governmental and multilateral forum etc. And indeed, traditionally, it continues to include what States actually do. The difference between the latter and state articulations have been distinguished by the latter being described *as benign state practice*. Also, practice needs to be carefully examined for what it actually says about law. The fact that some (perhaps many) States practice torture does not mean that there is not a sufficient practice outlawing it. To quote from the ICJ's decision in the Nicaragua case:

> *"In order to deduce the existence of customary rules, the Court deems it sufficient that the conduct of States should in general be consistent with such a rule; and that instances of State conduct inconsistent with a given rule should generally have been treated as breaches of that rule, not as indications of the recognition of a new rule."*[57]

Opinio juris, given the abstract nature of its definition i.e. a belief in obligation[58] it is hard to quantify and hence not uniformly perceived. Criticism of this description can be attributed to the fact that such a description does not account for the various rules that are permissive in nature (e.g. aspects regarding sovereignty such as rights over continental shelf, fishing rights etc.) In such circumstances, *opinio juris* as a belief wrests not on an obligation but on a right. Secondly, it might be better to consider *opinio juris* as the *assertion* and not merely the *acknowledgment* of a legal obligation. Once there is sufficient practice together with *opinio juris*, a new rule of custom will emerge. Subject only to what is known as the *persistent objector* principle the new rule binds all States. This principle allows a State which has persistently rejected a new rule even before it emerged as such to avoid its application.

---

[57] ICJ Reps, 1986, p. 3 at 98
[58] see, e.g., the North Sea Continental Shelf cases (1969)

> "*General Assembly resolutions, even if they are not binding, may sometimes have normative value. They can, in certain circumstances, provide evidence important for establishing the existence of a rule or the emergence of an opinion juris. To establish whether this is true of a given General Assembly resolution, it is necessary to look at its content and the conditions of its adoption; it is also necessary to see whether opinion juris exists as to its normative character.*" (Legality of the Threat or Use of Nuclear Weapons, Advisory Opinion 1996)[59]
>
> In its advisory opinion in the Legal Consequences of the Separation of the Chaos Archipelago from Mauritius in 1965, the ICJ observed on 25 February 2019 as follows: "*although resolution 1514 (XV) is formally a recommendation, it has a declaratory character with regard to the right to self-determination as a customary norm, in view of its content and the conditions of its adoption. The resolution was adopted by 89 votes with 9 abstentions...The wording used in resolution 1514 (XV) has a normative character, in so far as it affirms that "all peoples have the right to self-determination". Its preamble proclaims "the necessity of bringing to a speedy and unconditional end colonialism in all its forms and manifestations" and its first paragraph states that "the subjection of peoples to alien subjugation, domination and exploitation constitutes a denial of fundamental human rights [and] is contrary to the Charter of the United Nations."...The nature and scope of the right to self-determination of peoples, including respect for "the national unity and territorial integrity of a State or country", were reiterated in the Declaration on Principles of International Law concerning Friendly Relations and Cooperation among States in accordance with the Charter of the United Nations. This Declaration was annexed to GA resolution 2625 (XXV) which was adopted by consensus in 1970. By recognizing the right to self-determination as one of the "basic principles of international law", the Declaration confirmed its normative character under customary international law.*"[60]

---

[59] ICJ Reports 1996 (I), pp. 254-255, para. 70
[60] ICJ GL No 169, ICGJ 534 (ICJ 2019), 25th February 2019

It is to be noted that international customs can be localized practices restrictively applicable to certain states as law does not insist on a threshold in terms of number of states for constituting a custom. Such customs are described as *local customs* and cannot be made applicable to states who do not practice such habits. *Right of passage* is illustrative of local custom[61] whereas the principle of *non-refoulement* is illustrative of a universally applicable customary international law. The crystallization of customs in international law as opposed to customs under domestic law is attempted to be expedited. Successful attempts are generally described as *instant customs*, where in lesser weightage is given to the longevity of the practice and greater emphasis place on *opinion juris*. With the advent of technology, International law has expanded its scope into hitherto unknown domains such as space and cyber. In such a scenario, the traditional view of slow crystallization of customs is seen to be increasingly clumsy.

General Principles of Law

The third source listed in the Statute of the International Court of Justice are the *"general principles of law recognized by civilized nations."*[62] While, use of the words *civilized states* are being debated at the UNGA in terms of its relevance, especially post de-colonization, the more appropriate description in contemporary times, would be general principles of law recognized by the community of states. So, what are these general principles? Where are they derived from? When and how does a general principle get recognized as a principle of international of international law?

General principles constitute foundational principles upon which concrete laws are established. These principles are unwritten and these principles must be applied by significant number of states in their respective legal systems. Consequently, verification of application of the principle in individual legal systems becomes a

---

[61] *Portugal v India* Right of Passage over Indian Territory ICJ 1960
[62] Art. 38 (1) (c) Statute of the ICJ,1946

pre-requisite and cannot be based on presumptions derived from majority of states. Due to its abstractness and inherent limitations, the ICJ has preferred to principally rely upon treaties and customs and where both these sources fail to provide solutions, general principle have been resorted to, to plug the lacunae.

This is not to say that general principles are to be ignored. Bilateral arbitral tribunals have used general principles more when compared to international courts. Over the years, the world court has acknowledged the following as general principles of international law;

  a) Personality of corporations (e.g. in the Barcelona Traction Co. case)[63]
  b) Considerations of equity such as estoppel[64]
  c) One cannot take advantage of ones' own misdoings (Meuse case)[65]
  d) Obligation to pay reparations (Chorzow factory case)
  e) Practicing ones' obligations in good faith[66]
  f) Proportionality between gravity of crime and punishment[67]
  g) Equality and non-discrimination[68]
  h) *Res judicata*[69]

Case study of Estoppel in Public International Law: Estoppel, is a principle which prevents states from acting inconsistently to the detriment of others. International estoppel is based on good faith.

---

[63] Case Concerning Barcelona Traction, Light, and Power Co., Ltd (*Belgium v. Spain*) [1970] ICJ 1

[64] *Temple of Preah Vihar* case ICJ Reports (1962); see also *Eastern Greenland* case (1933), PCIJ, Ser. A/B. no. 53

[65] Diversion of Water from the Meuse Case (*Netherlands v. Belgium*) [1937], PCIJ (Ser. A/B) No. 70

[66] Nuclear Test cases ICJ Rep. 1974

[67] Blaskic, (ICTY Trial Chamber) IT-95-14-T. 3 March 2000

[68] South West African Cases

[69] Judgment in the Application of the Convention on the Prevention and Punishment of the Crime of Genocide case

Originally, application of estoppel in the sphere of International Law was confined to disputes involving contested territorial claims. International estoppel requires satisfaction of three elements;

First, statement creating estoppel must be clear and unambiguous;

Secondly, such statement must be voluntary, unconditional, and authorized and

Thirdly, reliance upon such a statement either to the detriment of the relying party or to the advantage of the party which states so.

It is to be noted that the third element has been a subject of frequent debates. Claims of estoppel in international law have often emerged in two circumstances, namely, when a unilateral declaration has been made by a state and acceptance thereof. A state may act unilaterally in one of two ways: it may make a unilateral promise or it may make a unilateral statement of fact. Either may give rise to an estoppel. In case of the latter, i.e. acquiescence or acceptance, estoppel may also arise out of a state's acquiescence to the declaration of another state or to existing circumstances. If all three elements of estoppel are met, even silence binds the acquiescing state. The value of general principles as a source of public international law can best be described in the following manner; Lord Lloyd-Jones, Justice of The UK Supreme Court in a speech[70] on 16 February 2018 quoted from South-West Africa case;

> "The way in which international law borrows from this source is not by means of importing private law institutions "lock, stock and barrel" ready-made and fully equipped with a set of rules. It would be difficult to reconcile such a process with the application of "the general principles of law." In my opinion, [he said] the true view of the duty of international tribunals in this matter is to regard any features or terminology which are reminiscent of the

---

[70] https://www.supremecourt.uk/docs/speech-180216.pdf; website accessed on 17 March 2020

> *rules and institution of private law as an indication of policy and principles rather than as directly importing these rules and institutions."*

In conclusion, general principles remain an ambiguous source of international law and is premised on recognition.

Judicial Decisions

Art. 38(1)(d) refers to judicial decisions as *subsidiary means* for the determination of rules of law. Common law countries religiously apply a system of hierarchy of courts and doctrine of binding precedent. However, in the domain of Public International Law *stare decisis* is of no authoritative relevance. The Statute of the ICJ expressly provides that judgments of ICJ are not binding on anyone except the parties to the case, that too only in respect of that particular case.[71] Nevertheless, the ICJ refers frequently to its own past decisions and most international tribunals make use of past cases as a *guide*. In other words, subsidiary sources have persuasive value and should not be read synonymous with insignificant. The world courts' practice and reliance on judgments indicates a greater reverence to ICJ and PCIJ judgments in comparison to domestic court judgments. At this juncture it would be instructive to note that Art. 38(1)(d) does not distinguish between decisions of international and national courts. The utility of the domestic courts judgment and position can be viewed in light of its evidentiary value in identifying state practice leading to formation of customary international law.

Re-birth of International Criminal Law: In a keynote address titled, *Reflections on International Law in Changing Times* at the 60th Anniversary Symposium of the Harvard Law School on 9 March

---

[71] Art. 59, Statute of the ICJ

2019, ICJ Justice Nawaf Salam[72] said, *"In my opinion, the most significant development in international law since the end of the cold war remains the re-birth (if I may use this term) of international criminal law. When I graduated from HLS, the existence of international criminal law was confined to the legacy of the Nuremberg and Tokyo tribunals, as no progress in this field had since been made. And let me add that while the establishment of these tribunals has indeed represented a historical milestone in the journey of international criminal law by holding individual leaders responsible for their crimes, one should not forget that they had also been criticized as representing "victors' justice." It is only owing to a revitalized Security Council at the end of the Cold War that the idea of resorting anew to international criminal tribunals to address situations of widespread atrocities such as the one that erupted in the former Yugoslavia could materialize. Hence, the International Criminal Tribunal for the former Yugoslavia ("ICTY") was established in 1993 pursuant to a unanimous Security Council resolution, to be shortly followed in 1994 by another resolution establishing the International Criminal Tribunal for Rwanda ("ICTR"). In addition to providing a framework for trying the individuals accused of perpetrating atrocities in Rwanda and the former Yugoslavia, the establishment of these two tribunals undoubtedly heralded a new era of putting an end to impunity. Several international or internationalized tribunals were subsequently created jointly by national governments and the United Nations: The Special Panels and Serious Crimes Unit in East-Timor, the Special Court for Sierra Leone, the Extraordinary Chambers in the Courts of Cambodia, the Regulation Panels in the Courts of Kosovo, and The Special Tribunal for Lebanon. Moreover, for the first time in human history, a universal criminal court, the International Criminal Court, was created to help end impunity for the perpetrators of the most serious crimes of concern to the international community, namely genocide, crimes against humanity, and war crimes. Established pursuant to the Rome Statute of 1998, which*

---

[72] https://harvardilj.org/wp-content/uploads/sites/15/1_Salam_60.2.pdf; website accessed on 11 May 2020

> *entered into force in 2002, it has now a membership of 122 states.*
>
> *There important contributions of the jurisprudence of these tribunals to the development of international criminal law:*
>
> *One: In the Tadic case, the ICTY held that the notion of 'war crimes' also applied to serious violations of international humanitarian law rules in internal armed conflict and so was not limited to inter-state conflicts. Likewise, in the 2003 Had Hasanovc & Kabure case, it held that the notion of 'command responsibility' also applied in time of internal armed conflict.*
>
> *Two: International criminal tribunals developed an important body of case law regarding sexual violence in situations of armed conflict. For example, while the crimes of rape were not prosecuted and punished at the Nuremberg and Tokyo Trials, the ICTY was the first international criminal tribunal to enter convictions for acts of rape as constituting a form of "torture," and for sexual enslavement as a "crime against humanity." In a number of cases it also examined charges of sexual assault against men. As to the ICTR, it held that rape can be an underlying act of genocide in the famous Takayasu case. The ICC handed down its first conviction for rape as a war crime and as a crime against humanity in March 2016 in the Bemba case, based on Bemba's failure to exercise control properly over the militia he commanded.*
>
> *Three: Based on the doctrine of command responsibility, a superior may be convicted not only for crimes that he ordered, but for crimes committed by his subordinates which he either failed to prevent or failed to punish after they had occurred. The jurisprudence of the international criminal courts and tribunals contributed to clarify and develop this important doctrine, by applying it not only to military actors, but also to paramilitary actors and civilians in positions of command, whether de jure or de facto."*

Scholarly Writings

The writings of international lawyers may also be a persuasive guide to the content of international law but they are not themselves creative of law and there is a danger in taking an isolated passage from a book or writing and assuming that it accurately reflects the content of international law.

Other Sources

Art. 38 of the Statute of the ICJ has been often criticized on grounds of it being incomplete. This criticism is to a large extent premised on its silence vis a vis actions of different organs of the United Nations. However, based on operational history, this criticism is gradually being put to rest. Contemporary public international law has witnessed significant contributions by UN organs and agencies in evolving public international law. For example, UNGA is not vested with power to legislate for the international community; that is to say, its resolutions are not legally binding. They are recommendatory or persuasive in nature.[73] However, many of those resolutions have an important effect on law-making process. For instance, some of these resolutions are part of the treaty-making process. In some other instances, General Assembly resolutions given their endorsement by states is evidence of state practice. A series of similar resolutions passed with widespread acceptance by the States may embody a rule of customary international law.[74] The UDHR 1948 and the ILC Articles on State Responsibility adopted in 2001 are good examples of UNGA in contributing to law making process. In contrast the status of resolutions of United Nations Security Council is higher in terms of creating binding legal obligations. Decisions taken by the Council under Chapter VII of the Charter and framed in mandatory terms are legally binding on all States.[75] Art. 103 of the UN Charter establishes the duty to carry out a decision of the Council and such UNSC decisions prevail over

---

[73] Art. 13, UN Charter 1945
[74] e.g., The discussion of the resolutions on nuclear weapons in the Legality of the Threat or Use of Nuclear Weapons, Advisory Opinion, ICJ GL No 95, [1996] ICJ Rep 226
[75] Art. 25 of the UN Charter 1945

treaty obligations in case of a contradiction.[76] It is to be noted though, that the UNSC is not considered a legislature, as it does not create new laws but rather obligations in relation to specific issues.[77]

Is there a hierarchy of sources/norms of public international law?
This is a long-debated question in the UN General Assembly. As such Art. 38 makes no explicit mention of the word *hierarchy* or for that matter any word to denote the existence of any hierarchy among the norms. However, such a hierarchy is discernible in certain respects.[78] The universally accepted norms that have achieved the status of *jus cogens* constitute the highest of the norms. These include prohibition on piracy, genocide,[79] slavery[80] and torture.[81] Thus, when any norm of international law including treaty law and general customary international law contradicts with a peremptory norm, the former is considered void.[82] Cases of conflict between the general norm and the peremptory norm are very rare and any suggestion that such a conflict exists should be carefully scrutinized.[83] Hence, no country is permitted to agree to

---

[76] see Questions of Interpretation and Application of the 1971 Montreal Convention arising from the Aerial Incident at Lockerbie (*Libyan Arab Jamahiriya v United Kingdom*) [1992] ICJ Rep 3
[77] see the decision of the ICTY in *Prosecutor v. Dusko Tadic* (Appeal Judgement), IT-94-1-A
[78] https://legal.un.org/avl/pdf/ls/greenwood_outline.pdf; website accessed on 11 May 2020
[79] *Bosnia and Herzegovina v Serbia and Montenegro* [2007] ICJ 2
[80] Rome Statute of the International Criminal Court, 2002
[81] *Prosecutor v. Furundžija*, ICTY, 121 International Law Reports 213 (2002)
[82] Art. 53, Vienna Convention on the Law of Treaties, 1969
[83] See e.g. the rejection both by the ICJ – Case Concerning the Arrest Warrant of 11 April 2000 *(Democratic Republic of the Congo v. Belgium)* ICJ Reports 2002, p. 3– and the English courts – *Jones v. Ministry of Interior Al -Mamlaka Al -Arabiya AS. Saudiya (the Kingdom of Saudi*

waive a peremptory norm. In case of a conflict between a treaty norm and a general customary norm, the treaty shall prevail vis a vis the parties to the treaty. However, such treaty will not affect the rights of States that are not party to that treaty and in their relations *inter se*. In conclusion it would suffice to say that barring *jus cogens* there is no rigid hierarchy of norms and all norms are based in the principle of consent.

Arabia) [2006] UKHL 26– of the suggestion that the law on sovereign immunity conflicted with the prohibition of torture.

3 State Recognition

Topics Covered
- Theories of state recognition
- Constitutive Theory
- Declaratory Theory
- Lauterpacht doctrine
- Conditional Recognition
- Individual and Collective Recognition
- Recognition of Governments
- De jure and de facto recognition
- State policies on recognition of governments
- Unilateral Declaration of Independence
- Democratic Legitimacy and Recognition

The Uruguay Convention on the Rights and Duties of States of 1933, popularly called as the Montevideo Convention, identifies four criteria to be met for statehood. These are as follows;
(a) a permanent population;
(b) a defined territory;
(c) government; and
(d) capacity to enter into relations with the other states.[84]

---

[84] Art. 1 of the Montevideo Convention of 1933

The Convention of 1933 further goes on to state;

> "*The political existence of the state is independent of recognition by the other states. Even before recognition the state has the right to defend its integrity and independence, to provide for its conservation and prosperity, and consequently to organize itself as it sees fit, to legislate upon its interests, administer its services, and to define the jurisdiction and competence of its courts.*"[85]

According to Art. 6 of the same convention, "*The recognition of a state merely signifies that the state which recognizes it accepts the personality of the other with all the rights and duties determined by international law. Recognition is unconditional and irrevocable.*" Since the end of the second great war of the twentieth century, provisions of the UN Charter relating to membership, have been a guide towards nation states attaining international recognition and acceptability. The relevant provision i.e. Art. 4 of the UN Charter states;

> "*Membership in the United Nations is open to all other peace-loving states which accept the obligations contained in the present Charter and, in the judgment of the Organization, are able and willing to carry out these obligations. The admission of any such state to membership in the United Nations will be effected by a decision of the General Assembly upon the recommendation of the Security Council.*"

In terms of contemporary developments in this front, South Sudan and Montenegro are relevant. For instance, the Republic of South Sudan became the 193rd member of the United Nations on 14 July 2011.[86] South Sudan's independence from the rest of Sudan was the result of the *January 2011 referendum* held under the terms of the 2005 Comprehensive Peace Agreement (CPA) that ended the decades-long civil war. Prior to South Sudan, in 2006, Montenegro

---

[85] Art. 3 *Ibid*
[86] *UN welcomes South Sudan as 193rd Member State*, **UN News**, dated 14 July 2011; **https://news.un.org/en/story/2011/07/381552**; website accessed on 17 March 2020

after attaining independence from Serbia became the 192nd member State of the United Nations.[87]

Theories of State Recognition

Views on state recognition and statehood under Public International law, traditionally fit into two theories namely, the *constitutive theory* and the *declaratory theory*. The third view, which is contemporary and in line with actual practice can be attributed to Lauterpacht. All these three views attempt to decode the logic of answering the questions as to how and when an entity is recognized as a state. According to the *constitutive theory*, a state or government does not exist for the purpose of international law until it is recognized.[88] Thus the constitutive theory maintains that explicit recognition by other states is what constitutes the pre-requisite for an entity to be described as a subject of international law. In other words, the act of recognition by other states creates a new state and endows it with legal personality. The constitutive view is largely dominated by legal positivists.[89] Kelsen,[90] Anzilloti,[91] Triepel,[92] Wheaton,[93] and Oppenheim[94] can be cited in support of it. Oppenheim in support of the constitutive theory opined that *"state is and becomes an international person through recognition only and exclusively."*[95] Consequently, a new state is vested with rights and

---

[87] UN General Assembly Resolution A/RES/60/264
[88] https://sheir.org/edu/theories-for-state-recognition/
[89] *Recognition in International Law: A Functional Reappraisal*, **The University of Chicago Law Review**, Vol. 34, No. 4 (Summer, 1967), pp. 857-883
[90] Hans Kelsen, Principles of International Law, 206-207 (1952)
[91] Dionisio Anzilotti, Cours de droit international (1929), 407–8
[92] Heinrich Triepel, **Volkerrecht und Landesrecht**, (By. Leipzig: C. L. Hirschfeld, 1899; reprint by Scientia Antiquariat Aalen, 1958) p. 102
[93] Henry Wheaton, Elements of International Law; edited with notes by Richard Henry Dana (8th edition, Little, Brown and Company, Boston, 1866)
[94] Oppenheim, **International Law: A Treatise** (1905)
[95] *Ibid*

duties only when existing states formally recognize it. According to the proponents of constitutive theory, emphasis is on the formal act of recognition (as opposed to any factual basis). In effect, even if an entity possesses all other attributes of statehood, it still would not have a legitimate claim to participate in international law until a formal act of recognition has been made by the remainder of states. This proposition leads to a complication which has frequently been witnessed in contemporary times. For instance, when a few states recognize an entity with statehood whereas other states refrain from according formal recognition. The more serious objections to the theory are based on its moral implications. Non-recognition of a state means that the citizens of that state may not be protected by international law, either in war or in peace. Thus, the two basic criticisms of the constitutive theory are that it is logically unsound and morally objectionable.

> Writing in 1941, Hans Kelson[96] from Harvard University argued, *"The term 'recognition' may be said to be comprised of two quite distinct acts: a political act and a legal act. The political act of recognition of a state or government means that the recognizing state is willing to enter into political and other relations with the recognized state or government, relations of the kind which normally exist between members of the family of nation...The political act of recognition, since it has no legal effect whatsoever, is not constitutive for the legal existence of the recognized state or government. Political recognition presupposes the legal existence of a state or government to be recognized. If one wishes to indicate the negative fact that an act has no legal consequences by saying that the act is only 'declaratory,' then the political act of recognition can be characterized as "declaratory."... The legal act of recognition is the establishment of a fact; it is not the expression of a will. It is cognition rather than re-cognition. It has the same character as the establishment*

---

[96] Hans Kelsen, *Recognition in International Law: Theoretical Observations*, **The American Journal of International Law**, Vol. 35, No. 4 (Oct., 1941), pp. 605-617

> *of a legally relevant fact by a court. Its effect is that the recognized community becomes in its relation with the recognizing state itself a state, i.e., a subject of rights and obligations stipulated by general international law. Before recognition, the unrecognized community does not legally exist vis-á-vis the recognizing state. Only by the act of recognition does it come legally into existence in relation to the recognizing state. Only its legal existence, its existence as judged by international law, not its natural existence."*

The *declaratory theory* of recognition is supported by writers who have less commitment to the consistency of legal dogmatism than to the efficacy of a legal order.[97] Brierly[98], Moore,[99] Chen,[100] Kunz,[101] and Briggs[102] can be listed in support of this theory. The basic tenet of this approach is that, international law is an objective system, which dictates the conditions upon which a state becomes a member of the international community. When a state has fulfilled these conditions, it automatically becomes subject to the rights and duties of international law, without any formal action on the part of the other members of the international system. Consequently, in line with the Montevideo Convention of 1933, a State is deemed as a person in international law if it meets following four criteria,

---

[97] *Recognition in International Law: A Functional Reappraisal*; **The University of Chicago Law Review**, Vol. 34, No. 4 (Summer, 1967), pp. 857-883

[98] James Leslie Brierly, **The Law of Nations**, (6th edition revised by Sir Humphrey Waldock, Oxford: Clarendon Press, 1963) p. 140

[99] John Basset Moore, **International Law Digest** (Washington, 1906)

[100] Chen Ti-chiang, **The International Law of Recognition**; Edited by L.C. Green (Stevens and Sons, 1951)

[101] Josef L. Kunz, "*Identity of States Under International Law,*" **AJIL** Vol. 49, Issue 1, Jan 1955, pp. 68-76

[102] Herbert W. Briggs, "*Recognition of States: Some Reflections on Doctrine and Practice,*" **AJIL** Vol. 43, Issue 1 Jan 1949, pp. 113-121

(reiterated by Badinter Arbitration Committee)[103]
1) a defined territory
2) a permanent population
3) a government
4) a capacity to enter into relations with other states

Thus, statehood is self-evident and untrammeled by the motivations of other states, thereby limiting the role of the international community to mere articulation of an existing status. The declaratory theory was developed during early to mid-20th century, subsequent to the constitutive theory giving the benefit of hindsight to the supporters of the declaratory theory. This theory addressed the two limitations of the constitutive theory. However, an important limitation is that what declaratory theorists perceived as a mere political function of acknowledging facts did not meet reality. During the second half of 20th century, the world witnessed a significant rise in the number of nation states and actual practice fell somewhere in between the two theories.

Lauterpacht Doctrine
Some attempts have been made to combine the best features of both these approaches to the problem of recognition and perhaps the most pragmatic attempt is the Lauterpacht doctrine. The doctrine commences from a constitutive basis, and departs to establish an obligation to recognize upon each of the existing members of the international community. According to Lauterpacht, the duty is triggered off when the objective elements of statehood (population, territory, government and sovereignty) are met, thereby importing the declaratory attributes.

Conditional recognition
This modus of recognition is archaic and is not of relevance to

---

[103] Also see generally Arbitration Commission of the Peace Conference on Yugoslavia 1991

contemporary international law and practice. During the 19th century, there have been instances when a nascent state's recognition has been subject to conditions or strictures in addition to meeting the accepted 4 elements of statehood. This provides the state imposing additional barriers an option to withdraw recognition if such additional condition(s) was not met. However, this practice is no longer relevant today post-Montevideo Convention of 1933.

Individual and Collective recognition
When a political entity is formally recognized by one state, such circumstances are described as individual recognition and has by itself no legal consequences on other states who are yet express similar sentiments. However, when a significant number of states together formally recognize a political entity as a state, such method of recognition is called as collective recognition. Such singular act of recognition is often witnessed in global multilateral forums, especially, membership to the United Nations. It is to be noted that recognition at a regional forum or for that matter a multilateral forum with limited threshold of states does not lead to collective recognition. PLO's membership to numerous multilateral forums is illustrative of such a scenario.

Recognition of Governments
Existing states do enjoy considerable discretion when it comes to recognition of foreign governments. Such discretion is not prohibited under International law. There are usually two discernible circumstances when recognition of governments come into play. The most common situation is one where there has been a constitutional change of government. For instance, in the case of constitutional republics or democratic republics, the governments are elected for a fixed duration. As the tenure comes to a close, elections are again conducted and a new government may be established. This is routine and other states symbolically recognize the new government by extending a congratulatory message,

usually to the new head of the state. A government established by a constitutional coup is also recognized as *routine* and falls under this category. The second circumstance is one, where a government has replaced an existing government by extra-constitutional means, such as a *military coup* or *civil revolution*. In such circumstances, State practice has not been uniform and discretion has been exercised by the recognizing or non-recognizing states. Such discretion has been usually based on domestic policy. For instance, UK pursued the Lauterpacht doctrine during the Cold War,[104] however, the UK refused to recognize the Tinoco government (1917-1919) of Costa Rica[105] which is a case in point in terms of inconsistency.

The most commonly cited reason for refusing recognition is that the new government did not demonstrate *effective control* over its territory and population. US practice differs from that of the UK and in 1976 the former noted, "*In the view of the US, international law does not require a state to recognize another entity as a state.*"[106] So, it reflected the fact that states grant or withhold recognitions at their discretions. In the absence of consistent state practice, some questions require attention. These include the following:

> What is the scholarly view on recognition of government?
> What are the factors considered for recognition of government?
> What is the distinction between *de jure* and *de facto* government?
> What have been the various state policies in contemporary legal history that has led to inconsistency in state practice?

---

[104] This position by the UK was usually attributed to fend off US criticism of UK for having recognized communist government of China.

[105] See generally The Tinoco Arbitration Award (*Great Britain v. Costa Rica*) 1 U.N. Rep. Int'l Arb. Awards 369 (1923) Note: Non-recognition does not impair de facto existence of government

[106] Digest of the United State Practice in International Law, 1976, pp. 19-20

According to Malcolm Shaw, *"Recognition of an entity as the government of a state implies not only that this government is deemed to have satisfied the required conditions [of governance] but also that the recognizing state will deal with the government as the governing authority of the state and accept the usual legal consequences of such status."*[107] Juristic account of state practice indicates that the following four factors are considered by states while choosing to give or refuse recognition of a foreign government:
1) Effective control
2) Obedience of population
3) Stability and permanence
4) Respect for international obligation

De jure and de facto recognition

Recognition *de jure* implies that in the view of the recognizing state, the state or government recognized formally fulfils the requirement laid down by international law for effective participation in the international community.[108] In contrast, *de facto* recognition is where, in the opinion of the recognizing state, provisionally and temporarily, the state or government recognized has factually satisfied the requirements but is yet to evidence prospects of satisfying one of the factors, say, effective control or respect for international obligation.[109]

> The challenge of determining the differences between *de jure* recognition and *de facto* recognition was seen clearly in the case of Israel.[110] The British Mandate over the area that was to become the Jewish state of Israel was to end on May 14, 1948. That morning

---

[107] Malcolm N. Shaw, **International Law** (Eight edition, Cambridge University Press, 2017)

[108] JG Starke, **Introduction to International Law** (Tenth Edition, Butterworth -Heinemann, 1989) P. 125

[109] *Ibid*

[110] Charles L. Cochran, *De Facto and De Jure Recognition: Is there a Difference?*, **The American Journal of International Law**, Vol. 62, No. 2 (Apr., 1968), pp. 457-460

> the Provisional Government of Israel sent a note to US President Truman assuring him that the government had been *"charged to assume the rights and duties of government"* for that state and to discharge its international obligations. President Truman replied to the note that same day announcing that: *"This country recognizes the Provisional Government as the de facto authority of the new State of Israel. When a permanent government is elected in Israel it will promptly be given de jure recognition."* The statement definitely appears to indicate something less than the traditional concept of *de jure recognition*. However, Philip Jessup, the Deputy United States Representative in the Security Council said in December, 1948, "*the United States extended immediate and full recognition to the state of Israel as a de facto authority of the new state.*" The extension of "full recognition" indicates the traditional concept of "de jure recognition," while de facto authority describes the type of power the government enjoyed. Further uncertainty was caused by a White House Press Release which announced that "de jure recognition" had been extended as of January 31. The release read:
>
> *"On October 24, 1948, the President stated that when a permanent government was elected in Israel, it would promptly be given de jure recognition. Elections for such a government were held on January 25... The United States Government is therefore pleased to extend de jure recognition to the Government of Israel as of January 31."*

State policies on recognition of governments

Tobar doctrine was propounded by the Foreign Minister Tobar of Ecuador which dictates not to grant recognition to any Government coming into existence by revolutionary means *so long as the freely elected representatives of the people have not constitutionally recognized the country*,[111] i.e., until such a government has been recognized by its own people in a constitutional manner. In other words, the state

---

[111] Jorge Castaneda, **Mexico and the United Nations** (First Edition, Manhattan Publishing, 1958) p. 185

of Ecuador would not provide any recognition to Governments that come into existence after applying force. In contrast, Estrada, Foreign Minister of Mexico, in 1930, stated that there is a duty of states to continue diplomatic relations with the states without regard to revolutionary change in a country.[112] Estrada's view flagging Mexico's policy places emphasis on the factual existence of effect control. Sometimes Estrada doctrine is known as *doctrine of effectiveness* and *non-intervention*. In 1931, a dispute near the Chinese city of Mukden (Shenyang) precipitated events that led to the Japanese conquest of Manchuria. In response, U.S. Secretary of State Henry Stimson issued what would become known as the *Stimson Doctrine*, stating that the United States would not recognize any agreements between the Japanese and Chinese that limited free commercial intercourse in the region.[113]

Unilateral Declaration of Independence (UDI)
The UDI is a relatively recent process of state creation. Contemporary international relations show that such declarations have been resorted to by subjugated entities for cessation leading to creation of an independent state. The Unilateral Declaration of Independence was a statement adopted by the Cabinet of Rhodesia on 11 November 1965, announcing that Rhodesia, having governed itself since 1923, regarded itself as a sovereign state, independent from the United Kingdom.

> "That it is an indisputable and accepted historic fact that since 1923 the Government of Rhodesia have exercised the powers of self-government and have been responsible for the progress, development and welfare of their people...That the people of Rhodesia fully support the requests of their government for

---

[112] Palacios Trevino, Jorge. **La Doctrina Estrada y el Principio de la No-Intervención** (1937)

[113] *The Mukden Incident of 1931 and the Stimson Doctrine*, US Office of the Historian Release, https://history.state.gov/milestones/1921-1936/mukden-incident; website accessed on 17 March 2020

> *sovereign independence but have witnessed the consistent refusal of the Government of the United Kingdom to accede to their entreaties...That the Government of the United Kingdom have thus demonstrated that they are not prepared to grant sovereign independence to Rhodesia on terms acceptable to the people of Rhodesia...That in the belief that procrastination and delay strike at and injure the very life of the nation, the Government of Rhodesia consider it essential that Rhodesia should attain, without delay, sovereign independence"*[114]

This move was considered illegal by Great Britain and the United Nations[115] and was unprecedented in the history of the United Nations. Rhodesia continued as unrecognized until it reconstituted itself as Zimbabwe after which the government revoked the Unilateral Declaration as part of the Lancaster House Agreement of 1979. In the case of Kosovo, upon a referral by the UN General Assembly,[116] the ICJ gave an advisory opinion on the question, *Is the unilateral declaration of independence by the Provisional Institutions of Self-Government of Kosovo in accordance with international law?* In its Advisory Opinion delivered on 22 July 2010, the Court concluded that *the declaration of independence of Kosovo adopted on 17 February 2008 did not violate international law*.[117] It noted that State practice during the eighteenth, nineteenth and early twentieth centuries *points clearly to the conclusion that international law contained no prohibition of declarations of independence*. Subsequently, the UNGA adopted a resolution to the effect of acknowledging the opinion of the Court.[118]

---

[114] Rhodesia's Unilateral Declaration of Independence, 1965
[115] UN Security Council Resolution 216 and 217 S/RES/216 (1965)
[116] UN General Assembly Resolution RES/63/3 (A/63/L.2) of 8 October 2008
[117] Accordance with International Law of the Unilateral Declaration of Independence in Respect of Kosovo, Advisory Opinion, ICJ Reports 2010, p. 403
[118] UN GA Resolution 64/298

> *Democratic Legitimacy and Recognition*
> In recent times, there has been increased interest in the role of *democratic legitimacy* as a distinct criterion for the legal recognition of governments.[119] In the 1990s, Haiti and Sierra Leone generated much debate in the backdrop of an ousted yet legitimate government (i.e. one lacking effective control) in order to impose democracy against an incumbent but illegitimate government. In the period of 2010-2020 the same logic was stretched even further. In Ivory Coast, the incumbent Alassane Ouattara, who won the electoral battle was recognized as the new head of state by the international community and an international coalition forcefully removed his predecessor Gbagbo from power who refused to relinquish his powers. A similar situation occurred in The Gambia in 2017. Following these instances, this view has gained considerable traction.

An important question of international law relating to state recognition could have been considered at the ICJ in respect of the US decision to shift its capital to Jerusalem. However, that remains inconclusive.[120]

Self-determination and state recognition
Post-world war 2 decolonization was resisted by the erstwhile great powers and its manifestation was clearly discernible during the adoption of the UNGA Resolution in 1960.[121] Powers which wished to retain the colonial status quo abstained from the Resolution.

---

[119] http://opiniojuris.org/2019/07/18/recognition-of-governments-legitimacy-and-control-six-months-after-guaido/; website visited on 6 April 2020

[120] Relocation of the United States Embassy to Jerusalem (*Palestine v. United States of America*) 2018 see https://www.icj-cij.org/en/case/176; website visited on 6 April 2020

[121] Declaration on the Granting of Independence to Colonial Countries and Peoples; General Assembly resolution 1514 (XV) of 14 December 1960

However, soon after this momentous resolution many of the erstwhile great powers acknowledged the change in status quo and accepted the rule of law by expediting the decolonization process. With the exception of Spain and Portugal, which retained their colonial possessions until the end of the 1960s and 1970s, respectively, the other states had given up their claims and acceded to claims of right to self-determination leading to the creation of newly independent states. By hyphenating state recognition to the principles contained in the UNGA resolution of 1960, it became clear that, in the opinion of the community of states, these principles had become positive international law applicable to every state. Observance of right of self-determination is not strictly speaking a new criterion of statehood in terms of international law. However, this right is seen from the enhanced perspective over the traditionally accepted criteria of the ability and willingness of the new state to abide by international obligations.

4 State Responsibility

> **Topics covered**
> ➢ Evolution of State Responsibility Topic under the International Law Commission
> ➢ Salient features of the Draft Articles of 1996
> ➢ ICJ and State Responsibility
> ➢ Responsibility of States for Internationally Wrongful Acts
> ➢ Countermeasures
> ➢ Principle of Proportionality

State responsibility constitutes a central tool in the system of international order and international law. The law of state responsibility encompasses a variety of issues, including;

a) circumstances under which a state's action can be deemed to have breached its international obligations as well as corresponding legally permissible justifications
b) consequences of such breach/breaches i.e. in particular, the obligation to make full reparation, as well as ending continuance of internationally wrongful acts
c) Manner and means of implementation of (b) above, including legally permissible countermeasures.[122]

---

[122] https://www.oxfordbibliographies.com/view/document/obo-9780199796953/obo-9780199796953-0031.xml; website accessed on 6 April 2020

> *Chorzow Factory Case:* It is a principle of international law that a breach of an engagement involves an obligation to make reparation....Reparation is indispensable...Reparation must, as far as possible, wipe out all the consequences of the illegal act and reestablish the situation which would, in all probability, have existed if that act had not been committed. [123]

Evolution of State Responsibility topic under the International Law Commission (ILC)

Work on State responsibility began in the ILC as early as 1956. Originally, the ILCs work focused on State responsibility for injuries to aliens and their property leading to six reports between 1956 and 1961. There was lack of consensus derailing discussions on the proposals made by ILC. In 1962 it was proposed to enhance the scope of the topic to include *"definition of the general rules governing the international responsibility of the State."*[124] Consequently, State responsibility vis a vis diplomatic protection and other fields was also discussed. These discussions focused on identifying the framework of rules of responsibility, breach and consequences thereof. The next year, ILC approved this reconceptualization of the topic and over the next two decades produced eight reports and provisional adoption of 35 articles constituting a part of the proposed draft articles.[125] Exhaustive work on rules pertaining to attribution and justifications for breaches played a pivotal contribution towards crystalizing the concept of state responsibility. Art. 19 of the Draft Articles on State Responsibility of 1980 which contributed to the concept of responsibility towards

---

[123] Factory at Chorzow, *Germany v Poland*, Judgment, Claim for Indemnity, Merits, Judgment No 13, (1928) PCIJ Series A No 17

[124] UN ILC Special Rapporteur R Ago, *'Report on State Responsibility'* [1963] para. 5

[125] https://opil.ouplaw.com/view/10.1093/law:epil/9780199231690/law-9780199231690-e1093#law-9780199231690-e1093-div1-2 website accessed on 6 April 2020

crimes was severely debated.[126] Between 1980 and 1986, ILC submitted seven reports in all, encompassing *content, forms, degrees of International Responsibility* and *settlement of disputes*. From amongst these submissions, five articles were provisionally adopted, by far the most significant being, the provision defining an *injured State*.[127] During 1988 to 1995 seven reports were prepared, enabling the ILC to adopt the text with commentaries in 1996. Thus, the evolution of state responsibility, courtesy ILC, can be broadly categorized in three phases, namely, part 1 (1971 to 1980), a few articles in Part 2 (1980 to 1986) and the rest (reparations, countermeasures, consequences of international crimes, and dispute settlement (1992 to 1996).[128] There was no reconsideration of earlier articles at any point.

Salient features of the Draft Articles of 1996
a) Part One of 1996 Draft was not limited to obligations to States, as distinct from obligations to non-State entities.
b) No distinction was drawn between treaty and non-treaty obligations: international law draws no distinction between responsibility *ex delicto* and *ex contract*.
c) No separate requirement of *fault* or *wrongful* intent to constitute an internationally wrongful act.
d) No requirement of *harm* to another State for responsibility to arise.
e) No *a priori* limit on the content or scope of international obligations
f) The existence of injury, harm, or damage is relevant in terms of extent of reparation
g) Arts 19 and 40 (3) 1996 Draft Articles - notion of

---

[126] See also International Criminal Law generally and typology of obligations in Arts 20 to 26 1980 Draft Articles.
[127] Art. 40 of the Draft Articles
[128] For a table showing the evolution of the first reading text see Crawford [2002] 315

international crimes of States. These were defined as breaches of an international obligation *so essential for the protection of fundamental interests of the international community that its breach is recognized as a crime by the community as a whole.*[129]

h) Art. 19 (3) of the 1996 Draft Articles provided examples of international crimes *on the basis of the rules of international law in force.*

ICJ and State Responsibility

In the second phase of the South West Africa Cases,[130] Ethiopia and Liberia attempted to justify their claim on the basis of *public interest* (see also Mandates). However, the International Court of Justice refused to accept the logic of this argument on grounds that the claim did not involve rights of individuals of Ethiopia and Liberia.[131] This restrictive approach posed a serious lacuna, especially in circumstances, when the direct beneficiary of an international obligation is not a subject of international law.[132] Another dimension that emerged out of the long-held approach was that consequences of a breach were automatic by law. Such an approach holds well where reparations were the only remedy to the breach. This was followed in the Case concerning the Factory at Chorzow (*Germany v Poland*) (Claim for Indemnity)[133] and German Interests in Polish Upper Silesia Cases.[134] However, consequences such as countermeasures do not automatically follow. While

---

[129] Art. 19 (2) of 1996 Draft Articles
[130] *Ethiopia v South Africa* & *Liberia v South Africa* ICJ Reports 1966, p. 6
[131] See also South West Africa/Namibia [Advisory Opinions and Judgments]
[132] This was sought to be redressed by the ICJ in the Barcelona Traction case
[133] **Claim for Indemnity, Merits,** Judgment No 13, (1928) PCIJ Series A No 17, ICGJ 255 (PCIJ 1928),
[134] *Germany v. Poland* PCIJ Series A. No 7

responsibility entails reparation, the claims process requires opting for choices depending on the factual circumstances.

> *Corfu Channel Cases:*[135] Mines were exploded in the Corfu Channel as a result of which British warships suffered damage and crew members had died. The explosion had taken place in Albanian waters that had been previously demined. About a year later in 1947, UK approached the ICJ accusing Albania of having laid or allowed a third State to lay mines. The Court found that Albania was responsible under international law for the explosions. While not finding that Albania had itself laid the mines or that it was done with the connivance of Albania, the ICJ observed that the mines could not have been laid without the knowledge of the Albanian Government. The exclusive control exercised by a State within its frontiers might make it impossible to furnish direct proof of facts incurring its international responsibility. The State which is the victim must, in that case, be allowed a more liberal recourse to inferences of fact and circumstantial evidence; such indirect evidence must be regarded with special weight when based on a series of facts. Albania counter-claimed that the UK had violated Albanian sovereignty by sending warships into Albanian territorial waters and of carrying out minesweeping operations in Albanian waters after the explosions. The Court held that UK had exercised the right of innocent passage through international straits. However, the mine-sweeping operations was construed as a violation of Albanian sovereignty, as it was carried out against the will of the Albanian Government. The ICJ rejected the assertion of *self-help* raised by UK in its defense.

---

[135] *United Kingdom of Great Britain and Northern Ireland v. Albania* ICJ Reports 1948, p. 15; Corfu Channel case, Judgment ICJ Reports 1949, p. 4; Corfu Channel case, Judgment ICJ Reports 1949, p. 244

In the ICJ case relating to the Bosnian Genocide, the question was whether Serbia was responsible for genocide committed by Bosnian Serb insurrectional movement. ICJ held that Genocide Convention impliedly imposed state responsibility for genocide, including complicity in genocide.[136]

Responsibility of States for Internationally Wrongful Acts
The salient features and provisions are provided hereunder;
- ➢ *'General Principles'* (Articles 1 to 3): *"Every internationally wrongful act of a State entails the international responsibility of that State. There is an internationally wrongful act of a State when conduct consisting of an action or omission: (a) is attributable to the State under international law; and (b) constitutes a breach of an international obligation of the State.*
- ➢ *The characterization of an act of a State as internationally wrongful is governed by international law. Such characterization is not affected by the characterization of the same act as lawful by internal law."*
- ➢ Art. 12 states, *"There is a breach of an international obligation by a State when an act of that State is not in conformity with what is required of it by that obligation, regardless of its origin or character."*
- ➢ Articles 30 to 32 state that *"The State responsible for the internationally wrongful act is under an obligation: (a) to cease that act, if it is continuing; (b) to offer appropriate assurances and guarantees of non-repetition, if circumstances so require. The responsible State is under an obligation to make full reparation for the injury caused by the internationally wrongful act. Injury includes any damage, whether material or moral, caused by the internationally wrongful act of a State. The responsible State may not rely on the provisions of its internal law as justification for failure to comply with its obligations under this part."*

---

[136] *Bosnia and Herzegovina v Serbia and Montenegro* [2007] ICJ 2

In terms of reparation, Articles 34 to 38 apply.
- Full reparation for the injury caused by the internationally wrongful act shall take the form of restitution, compensation and satisfaction, either singly or in combination.
- Obligation to make restitution, that is, to re-establish the situation which existed before the wrongful act was committed
- Such restitution should not be: (a) materially impossible; (b) a burden disproportionate to the benefit deriving from restitution instead of compensation.
- State responsible for an internationally wrongful act is under an obligation to compensate for the damage caused thereby, insofar as such damage is not made good by restitution.
- Compensation shall cover any financially assessable damage including loss of profits insofar as it is established.
- State responsible to give satisfaction when it cannot be made good by restitution or compensation. Satisfaction may consist in an acknowledgement of the breach, an expression of regret, a formal apology etc.
- Interest on any principal sum due shall be payable
- Serious breaches of obligations under peremptory norms of general international law are covered in Art. 40
- A breach of peremptory norms is serious if it involves a gross or systematic failure by a State to fulfill the obligation.

Most recently in early 2020, the world court, while giving provisional measures in the Application of the Convention on the Prevention and Punishment of the Crime of Genocide,[137] observed that, irrespective of the fragile ground situation in Rakhine State, Myanmar being a party to the Genocide Convention is

---

[137] *The Gambia v. Myanmar* 23 Jan 2020 General List No. 178

> obliged to observe the provisions of the said convention. By virtue of Art. 1 of the said Convention, Myanmar has confirmed its willingness to consider genocide as an international crime and is obliged to prevent and punish independently of the prevailing context *of peace* or *of war*.[138]

Countermeasures constitute exceptional measures that may be resorted to by the wronged state against the State committing an internationally wrongful act. The scope of such exceptional measures extends to *cessation* and *safeguards for non-repetition* i.e. prevention. It is also widely accepted in international law that countermeasures when permissible have to be proportionate.[139] While the principle of proportionality does help in safeguarding legitimacy and restraint of countermeasures, the precise content, context, and contours are subject to debate. One view is that proportionality is to be tested in light of injury suffered. Another view is that proportionality has to be premised on the nature of the infringed rule. The third view, is that proportionality must be addressed in the context of seriousness of the breach. *Proportionality* in relation to countermeasures was the subject of examination of an Arbitral Tribunal established with the agreement of the US and France.[140] The dispute broke out between the parties when France refused to allow a Pan American aircraft travelling from the US to Paris with change of gauge in London to disembark its passengers and freight. France argued that the decision of Pan American

---

[138] See also Application of the Convention on the Prevention and Punishment of the Crime of Genocide (*Bosnia and Herzegovina v. Yugoslavia*) Preliminary Objections, Judgment, ICJ Reports 1996 (II), p.615, para.31

[139] Federica Paddeu, **Countermeasures, in Justification and Excuse in International Law: Concept and Theory of General Defences** (Cambridge University Press, 2018) pp. 225–284

[140] Case Concerning the Air Services Agreement of 27 March 1946 (*US vs France*) 1978 Volume XVIII pp. 417-493

Airlines to use smaller aircraft for the route from London to Paris was in violation of their 1946 Agreement. In response the US ordered two French airlines to file the schedule of their flights and soon prohibited Air France from operating certain flights to the US. In assessing the lawfulness of the US action, the Tribunal noted that it would have to rely its conclusions on the aim actually pursued and whether that was confined to reciprocity, quicker settlement of the dispute, or prevention of future violations by other States. The Tribunal re-affirmed the rule that countermeasures should be equivalent to the breach although it acknowledged that proportionality could be assessed only by approximation. It also added that,

> "In the Tribunal's view, it is essential, in a dispute between States, to take into account not only the injuries suffered by the companies concerned but also the importance of the questions of principle arising from the alleged breach."[141]

In this context, what mattered was the proportionality with respect to the effects sought to be achieved by the countermeasures. Thus, the test of proportionality does not merely measure the breach and the response but the purpose aimed at and the means used in order to achieve it.[142] Viewed in this context the Tribunal did not find that the US response was disproportionate in comparison with the French measures. The principle of proportionality was also examined in the *Case Concerning the Gabcikovo-Nagymaros Project between Hungary and Slovakia*.[143] Under an agreement signed between them in 1977, Hungary and Czechoslovakia decided the construction and operation of a system of barrage and locks on that part of *the Danube* shared by them as an international river boundary. In the year 1989 Hungary, citing environmental

---

[141] *Ibid*
[142] E.Zoller, **Peacetime Unilateral Remedies: An Analysis of Countermeasures** (Transnational Publishers, New York, 1984) p. 131
[143] Gabcikovo-Nagymaros Project, *Hungary v Slovakia* ICGJ 65 (ICJ 1997)

concerns, suspended and eventually abandoned all of the works. To this, Czechoslovakia responded by diverting the waters of the river Danube within its boundaries. Czechoslovakia justified its response citing it as a measure of *approximate application* of the 1977 bilateral agreement. Assessing the lawfulness of Czechoslovakia's response, ICJ reaffirmed the principle that countermeasures should be commensurate with the injury caused. Highlighting the significance of international water resources, the ICJ noted that Czechoslovakia's response was amounting to interference on a shared legal right, depriving Hungary of its right to *an equitable and reasonable share of the natural resources of the Danube.*[144] According to the Court, this action was disproportionate. It is to be noted that it is in this framework that Art. 51 of the 2001 ILC Articles is drafted. Accordingly, what matters for purposes of proportionality is not only the injury suffered and the losses, usually material, caused as a result, but also the significance of the interests protected by the infringed rule and the seriousness of the breach.

Given the existence of multiple legitimate tools of self-redressal available to states, emphasis must be given on the basis of the function each response fulfills such as retributive, coercive or executive. Consequently, for each tool of countermeasure, measurement of proportionality would necessarily be varied. Proportionality is not a fixed and inflexible notion applicable to all situations. Rather, it evolves on a case-by-case basis. The emphasis is guided by timeliness, objectives and the appropriateness of the adopted measures in the light of the result they want to achieve.

---

[144] *Ibid*

5 Law of Extradition

> **Topics covered**
> - Obligation to extradite
> - Factors prohibiting extradition
> - Grounds for mandatory refusal
> - Grounds for discretionary refusal
> - Double Criminality
> - Rule of Specialty
> - Documentation required for extradition
> - Rendition
> - Ongoing extradition proceedings
> - India's Extradition Act 1962
> - How may the Extradition process be triggered against an Indian national living

Introduction

Extradition is the formal process of one state surrendering an individual to another state for prosecution or punishment for crimes committed in the requesting country's jurisdiction.[145] It is typically enabled by a bilateral or multilateral treaty. Some states will extradite without a treaty, but those cases are rare. Treaties

---

[145] https://www.cfr.org/backgrounder/what-extradition; website accessed on 6 May 2020

signed in recent decades tend to take a *dual criminality* approach, classifying as extraditable all crimes that are punishable in both jurisdictions. Older extradition treaties, by contrast, tend to list covered offenses. For instance, the treaty between Albania and the United States, signed in 1933, includes an inventory of more than two dozen crimes, including murder, rape, arson, and burglary. Many extradition treaties only allow extradition for crimes that carry a punishment of more than one year. Treaties also define instances when extradition is to be denied. For instance, authorities generally cannot extradite individuals for military or political offenses, with exceptions for terrorism and other violent acts. Some states will not extradite to jurisdictions with capital punishment or life imprisonment under any circumstances, or unless the requesting authority pledges not to impose those penalties. Other common provisions deal with nationality (many states will not extradite their own citizens, or will only do so on a limited basis), double jeopardy, statutes of limitations, administrative expenses, legal representation, and transfer of evidence.

> In *R v Evans and Bartle; Ex Parte Augusto Pinochet Ugarte*,[146] extradition was defined as the formal name given to a process whereby one sovereign state, *the requesting state*, asks another sovereign state, *the requested state*, to return to the requesting state someone present in the requested state, 'the subject of the request', in order that the subject of the request may be brought to trial on criminal charges in the requesting state. The process also applies where the subject of the request has escaped from lawful custody in the requesting state and is found in the requested state. Extradition for international crimes is based on the general principle of *aut dedere, aut judicare*. In terms

---

[146] Unreported, UK Court of Appeal, Lord Bingham CJ, Collins and Richards JJ, 28 October 1998 (High Court proceedings)

> of this principle the state from which extradition is requested has a duty to either prosecute the individual sought or to extradite him. The question whether this rule has achieved the status of customary international law has been a subject for debate because some treaties (but not all) impose extradition or prosecution as an obligation. However, Bassoon contends that obligatory extradition or prosecution can be seen as a general principle, and that states that default on this rule fail to meet their obligations in terms of international law.

Obligation to extradite: Art. 1 of the UN's Model Treaty on Extradition[147] acknowledges an *obligation to extradite* and states that *"Each Party agrees to extradite to the other, upon request and subject to the provisions of the present Treaty, any person who is wanted in the requesting State for prosecution for an extraditable offence or for the imposition or enforcement of a sentence in respect of such an offence."*

United States law: According to the United States Department of Justice,[148] international extradition is the formal process by which a person found in one country is surrendered to another country for trial or punishment. The process is regulated by treaty and conducted between the Federal Government of the United States and the government of a foreign country. It differs considerably from interstate rendition, commonly referred to as interstate extradition, mandated by the Constitution, Art. 4, Sec. 2.[149]

---

[147] https://www.unodc.org/pdf/model_treaty_extradition.pdf; website accessed on 7 May 2020

[148] https://www.justice.gov/jm/jm-9-15000-international-extradition-and-related-matters website accessed on 7 May 202

[149] According to Art. IV, Sec. 2 of the US Constitution, *"The citizens of each state shall be entitled to all privileges and immunities of citizens in the several states. A person charged in any state with treason, felony, or other crime, who shall flee from justice, and be found in another state, shall on demand of the*

Generally, under US law, extradition may be granted only pursuant to a treaty.[150] However, some countries grant extradition without a treaty, and of those that do, most require an offer of reciprocity. Further, 18 U.S.C. 3181 and 3184 permits the United States to extradite, without regard to the existence of a treaty, persons (other than citizens, nationals or permanent residents of the United States), who have committed crimes of violence against nationals of the United States in foreign countries. A list of countries with which the United States has an extradition treaty relationship can be found in the Federal Criminal Code and Rules, following 18 U.S.C. 3181, but in each instance the Criminal Division's Office of International Affairs (OIA) has to be consulted to verify the accuracy of the information. Because the law of extradition varies from country to country and is subject to foreign policy considerations, prosecutors must consult OIA on any matter relating to extradition before taking any action in such a case, especially before contacting any foreign official. If the fugitive is not subject to extradition, other steps may be available to return him or her to the United States or to restrict his or her ability to live and travel overseas. If a fugitive is apprehended only after a long delay, a prosecutor may have to litigate a motion alleging a constitutional speedy trial violation if extradition has not been sought or the Government has not been actively pursuing other steps to return the fugitive to the United States. All decisions to pursue or not to pursue extradition or other measures to obtain custody of the fugitive should be documented to prepare for any eventual speedy trial motion.

Factors prohibiting extradition
A country to whom an extradition request has been sent has to first convince itself if there are factors whose presence constitute an

---

executive authority of the state from which he fled, be delivered up, to be removed to the state having jurisdiction of the crime..."
[150] 18 USC 3184

essential hindrance for complying with the request. For instance, under the 2013 Extradition Treaty between India and Thailand, Art. 4 deals with the *grounds for mandatory refusal*. Accordingly:

> **Art. 4 Grounds for Mandatory Refusal**[151]
> Extradition shall not be granted under this Treaty in any of the following circumstances:
> 1. *The Requested State considers the offence for which the request for extradition is made by the Requesting State as a political offence. Reference to a political offence shall not include the following:*
> *(a) taking or attempt to take the life or an attack, or an attempt to attack on the person or deprivation of liberty of the Head of State or the Head of Government of the Requesting State or a member of his or her family;*
> *(b) any acts or omissions which are punishable as a criminal offence according to the obligations under multilateral treaties to which both Contracting States are party;*
> 2. *The Requested State has substantial grounds for believing that a request for extradition for a criminal offence has been made for the purpose of prosecuting or punishing a person on account of that person's race, religion, nationality or political opinion or that the position of the person sought may be prejudiced for those reasons;*
> 3. *The offence for which the request for extradition is made is exclusively an offence under the military law of the Requesting State and does not constitute an offence under the criminal law of the Requesting State;*
> 4. *The prosecution or the enforcement of a sentence in respect of the offence for which extradition is requested has become barred by lapse of time according to the laws of the Requesting State; or*
> 5. *There has been a final judgment rendered against the person in the Requested State in respect of the offence for which the person's extradition is requested.*

---

[151] https://mea.gov.in/Images/CPV/leta/Thailand.pdf; website accessed on 7 May 2020

The same treaty also has Art. 5 dealing with *grounds for discretionary refusal* and comprises instances where (a) the Requested State has jurisdiction over the offence for which extradition is requested; (b) the Requested State is in the process of proceeding against the person sought in respect of the same offence; and (c) in exceptional cases, the Requested State while taking into account the seriousness of the offence and the interests of the Requesting State deems that, because of the age or health of the person sought, the extradition would be incompatible with humanitarian considerations. Art. 6 dealing with *extradition of nationals* clearly states that, "*Each Contracting State shall have the right to refuse extradition of its own nationals.*" Further, if extradition is not granted the Requested State shall, at the request of the Requesting State, submit the case to its competent authority for prosecution. For this purpose, the Requesting State shall furnish relevant evidences.

> *Double criminality:* In *Factor v. Laubenheimerl* case,[152] Factor's extradition was requested by Great Britain on a charge of receiving certain sums of money, aggregating GBP 458,500, fraudulently obtained. On the complaint of a British consul, Factor was taken into custody in Illinois, and a US Commissioner in Illinois issued a warrant for his commitment pending surrender. On a return to a writ of habeas corpus, the District Court ordered his discharge from custody, but this order was reversed by the Circuit Court of Appeals. Both the District Court and the Circuit Court of Appeals seem to have regarded extradition as possible only if the offense charged was a crime both by the law of Great Britain and by the law of Illinois; the District Court held that receiving money known to have been fraudulently obtained was not a crime by the law of Illinois, but the Circuit Court, relied chiefly on *Kelly v. Griffin*,[153] thereby taking the contrary view.

---

[152] *Factor v. Laubenheimerl*, 290 US 276 (1933)
[153] *Kelly v. Griffin*, 241 US 6 (1916)

Rule of specialty: Specialty is a principle of International law that is included in most extradition treaties, whereby a person who is extradited to a country to stand trial for certain criminal offenses may be tried only for those offenses and not for any other pre-extradition offenses. Once the asylum state extradites an individual to the requesting state under the terms of an extradition treaty, that person can be prosecuted only for crimes specified in the extradition request. This doctrine allows a nation to require the requesting nation to limit prosecution to declared offenses. US courts have been divided on accepting the doctrine when the other nation has not explicitly or implicitly protested certain charges.

A person who has been brought within the jurisdiction of the court by virtue of proceedings under an extradition treaty, can only be tried for one of the offences described in that treaty, and for the offence with which he is charged in the proceedings for his extradition, until a reasonable time and opportunity have been given him, after his release or trial upon such charge, to return to the country from whose asylum he had been forcibly taken under those proceedings.[154]

Documentation required for extradition
Art. 5 of the UN Model Treaty on Extradition states, "*A request for extradition shall be made in writing. The request, supporting documents and subsequent communications shall be transmitted through the diplomatic channel, directly between the ministries of justice or any other authorities designated by the Parties.*"[155]

---

[154] *United States v. Rauscher*, 119 U.S. 407 (US 1886)
[155] https://www.unodc.org/pdf/model_treaty_extradition.pdf; website accessed on 7 May 2020

A request for extradition shall be accompanied by the following:
(a) In all cases, (i) As accurate a description as possible of the person sought, together with any other information that may help to establish that person's identity, nationality and location;
(ii) The text of the law creating the offence or, where necessary, a statement of the law relevant to the offence and a statement of the penalty that can be imposed for the offence;
(b) If the person is accused of an offence, by a warrant issued by a court or other competent judicial authority for the arrest of the person or a certified copy of that warrant, a statement of the offence for which extradition is requested and a description of the acts or omissions constituting the alleged offence, including an indication of the time and place of its commission;
(c) If the person has been convicted of an offence, by a statement of the offence for which extradition is requested and a description of the acts or omissions constituting the offence and by the original or certified copy of the judgment or any other document setting out the conviction and the sentence imposed, the fact that the sentence is enforceable, and the extent to which the sentence remains to be served;
(d) If the person has been convicted of an offence in his or her absence, in addition to the documents set out in paragraph 2 (c) of the present art., by a statement as to the legal means available to the person to prepare his or her defense or to have the case retried in his or her presence;
(e) If the person has been convicted of an offence but no sentence has been imposed, by a statement of the offence for which extradition is requested and a description of the acts or omissions constituting the offence and by a document setting out the conviction and a statement affirming that there is an intention to impose a sentence.
3. The documents submitted in support of a request for extradition shall be accompanied by a translation into the language of the requested State or in another language acceptable to that State.

Rendition

After the 9/11 terror attacks, the United States' reported programme of *extraordinary rendition* gained worldwide attention and criticism. The United States has never acknowledged such renditions, but the CIA's activities have been extensively studied and documented by European and other governments, as well as organizations that monitor human rights violations.[156]

Extraordinary rendition may be a new term, but it is not a new practice. For instance, after England outlawed torture in 1640,[157] she practiced *forced transportation* of prisoners to Scotland to be tortured.[158] Scotland outlawed torture later in early 18th century.[159] Until then, England relied on using Scotland for circumventing this legal obligation. Secret prisons are not a recent invention either. Britain ran such a camp holding Nazi prisoners at Bad Nenndorff Interrogation center in Germany during 1945-1947.[160] Evidence of cruelty was kept secret for 60 years. In an official document that was made public, the torture methods used here was stated to include the following:

> *"(1) insufficient clothing; (2) intimidation by the guards; (3) mental and physical torture during the interrogations; (4) they were kept in solitary confinement for long periods with no exercise; (5) they were confined to punishment cells, not for any offence, but simply because the interrogator was not satisfied with*

---

[156] https://www.icij.org/investigations/collateraldamage/post-911-renditions-extraordinary-violation-international-law/; website accessed on 11 May 2020

[157] Jardine, David. **A Reading on the Use of Torture in the Criminal Law of England** (Baldwin and Cradock, London, 1837) pp. 10–12.

[158] Jeffrey M. Perl, "*A Dictatorship of Relativism?*" 2007 **Common Knowledge**, Vol. 13, Issue 2-3) p. 276

[159] Sec. 5 of (Scottish) Treason Act 1708

[160] Stephens, Lt. Col. RGW Hoare, Oliver (ed.). *Camp 020: MI5 and the Nazi Spies: The Official History of MI5's Wartime Interrogation Centre.* Public Records Office (2000)

their answers; (6) in the punishment cells, during the bitter winter, they were deprived of certain articles of clothing, had buckets of cold water thrown into the cell and were forced to scrub the cell floor for long periods, and were assaulted and manhandled; (7) medical attention was grossly inadequate; (8) food was insufficient; (9) discharge of prisoners was unnecessarily delayed; (10) personal property of the prisoners were stolen."[161]

The US maintained a confidential post World War II camp known as *PO Box 1142* at Fort Hunt just outside of Washington DC. Its premises were used to extract information from German prisoners (combatants and non-combatants).[162] Declassified documents indicate that more than 3,400 Nazi prisoners were kept *off the books* in violation of the Geneva Conventions while they were interrogated about technical intelligence.[163] Similar practices with variations were adopted during 1980s, 1990s and post- 9/11. Suspects overseas were either *rendered* to US or to a third country to face trial. The CIA's extraordinary renditions reported to have occurred after 9/11 are quite different. What makes them extraordinary is absence of judicial proceeding or due process.

India's Extradition Act 1962
The Government of India applies the Supreme Court of India definition of extradition.

> *"the delivery on the part of one State to another of those whom it is desired to deal with for crimes of which they have been accused or convicted and are justifiable in the Courts of the other State."*[164]

---

[161] *Ibid*

[162] Dvorak, Petula, "World War II secret interrogators break their silence," **Washington Post**, dated 20th August 2006

[163] Ullstein, Berlin, **Tapping Hitler's Generals: Transcripts of Secret Conversations, 1942-1945** (Frontline Books, 2007)

[164] https://www.mea.gov.in/extradition-faq.htm; website accessed on 11 May 2020

An Extradition request for an accused can be initiated in the case of under-investigation, under-trial and convicted criminals. In cases under investigation, abundant precautions have to be exercised by the law enforcement agency to ensure that it is in possession of prima facie evidence to sustain the allegation before the Courts of Law in the Foreign State. The Extradition Act 1962 provides India's legislative basis for extradition. To consolidate and amend the law relating to the extradition of fugitive criminals and to provide for matters connected therewith, or incidental thereto, the Extradition Act of 1962 was enacted. It consolidated the law relating to the extradition of criminal fugitive from India to foreign states. The Indian Extradition Act, 1962 was substantially modified in 1993.[165] Sec. 2(d) of Extradition Act 1962 defines an Extradition Treaty as a Treaty, Agreement or Arrangement made by India with a Foreign State, relating to the Extradition of fugitive criminals and includes any treaty, agreement or arrangement relating to the Extradition of fugitive criminals made before the 15th day of August 1947. Extradition treaties are traditionally bilateral in character. The following five principles are a staple feature of bilateral treaties:

- First, the principle of *extraditable offences*. This principle lays down that extradition applies only with respect to offences clearly stipulated as such in the treaty;
- Second, the principle of *dual criminality*. This principle requires that the offence for which extradition is sought has to be an offence under the national laws of both requesting and requested country;
- Third, the requested country must be satisfied that there is a *prima facie* case made out against the offender/accused;
- Fourth, is the *rule of specialty*. the extradited person can be engaged only on the offence for which extradition was requested;
- Finally, the principle of *fair trial*. (this is of course part of international human rights law now).

---

[165] Act 66 of 1993

The Consular, Passport, Visas Division of the Ministry of External Affairs is the Central/Nodal Authority that administers the Extradition Act. It processes all Extradition Requests. Requests by India can only be made by the Ministry of External Affairs. The MEA formally submits such requests to the relevant State through diplomatic channels. Extradition is not facilitated on private requests. India's treaty partners have obligations to consider India's requests. In the absence of a treaty, it is a matter for the foreign country, in accordance with its domestic laws and procedures, to determine whether the country can agree to India's extradition request on the basis of assurance of *reciprocity*. Similarly, any country can make an extradition request to India. Extradition is possible from the non-Treaty States under Section 3(4) of the Indian Extradition Act, 1962. A request for provisional arrest may be transmitted through diplomatic channels through CPV Division of Ministry of External Affairs. The facilities of INTERPOL may also be used to transmit such a request through the CBI. Each extradition treaty specifies the documents required for a provisional arrest request and specify the means by which a provisional arrest request must be made. The Police/Law Enforcement Agency concerned in India, prepares the request for a provisional arrest and sends it to the MEA, which in turn forwards the same to the concerned authority of the foreign country through diplomatic channels.

Recent extradition cases: The most interesting extradition case in the last decade is the on-going proceedings in Canada concerning the senior Huawei executive Ms. Meng Wenzhou. The US wants Ms. Meng to stand trial on charges including fraud linked to the alleged violation of US sanctions against Iran. The indictment alleges Huawei misled the US and a global bank about its relationship with two subsidiaries, Huawei Device USA and Skincom Tech, to conduct business with Iran. A second indictment alleges Huawei stole technology from phone company T-Mobile used to test smartphone durability, as well as obstructed justice and committed wire fraud, which Huawei says was settled in a civil case filed in 2014. Ms. Meng, who was arrested in late 2018 in Canada, denies any wrongdoing. In March 2019, Canada's Department of Justice authorized Ms. Meng's extradition process to begin, though that decision was an early step in the process. If a judge is satisfied with the evidence presented during the extradition hearing, he or she will authorize the individual be committed for extradition. The Canadian justice minister then decides whether to surrender the person to the US.

Another equally gripping case pertains to the former boss of Nissan, Carlos Ghosn who escaped from Japanese custody and landed up in his country of birth-Lebanon. Lebanon does not typically surrender its citizens but Japan says it can request his extradition. According to reports, Mr. Ghosn walked out of his house on 29 December 2019 before boarding a bullet train to Osaka. He was then reportedly smuggled out of the country in a flight case, usually used to transport musical equipment.[166] Mr. Ghosn, who ran Nissan until he was arrested on charges of financial misconduct in November 2018, was banned from seeing his wife while on bail. But, in the final days of 2019, he skipped bail to board a private jet that took him to Turkey before he travelled on to Lebanon, where he is a citizen and where his wife was waiting. Security cameras caught the 65-year old walking out of his house in Tokyo alone at around 14:30 local time on 29 December 2019, according to Japanese media. He reportedly then met two men at a Tokyo hotel who escorted him to the city's Shinagawa station where they caught a train to Osaka, Japan's second city.

In India, the case of Nirav Modi has captured national headlines for years. Nirav Modi is wanted for his role in alleged bank fraud

---

[166] Carlos Ghosn: Japan presses for ex-Nissan boss's extradition from Lebanon, https://www.bbc.com/news/business-51010128; website accessed on 5 March 2020

amounting to approximately two billion dollars. A warrant against him was issued by the UK home office at the behest of India. The extradition trial of Nirav Modi has been fixed, as of now, from May 11 to 15, 2020. India and the UK have an Extradition Treaty, signed in 1992 and in force since November 1993. According to the Government of India, *"India can make an extradition request to any country. While India's treaty partners have treaty obligations to consider India's requests, in the absence of a treaty, it is a matter for the foreign country to consider, in accordance with its domestic laws and procedures, whether the country can agree to India's extradition request on the basis of an assurance of reciprocity. Similarly, any country can make an extradition request to India. The legal basis for Extradition with States with whom India does not have an Extradition Treaty (non-Treaty States) is provided by Section 3(4) of the Indian Extradition Act, 1962."*[167]

How may the Extradition process be triggered against an Indian national living in India: Extradition is triggered by a request submitted through diplomatic channels by a foreign country. In India, it proceeds through Ministry of External Affairs and may be presented to an Extradition magistrate to order to determine whether the request is in compliance with an applicable treaty, whether it provides sufficient evidence to believe that the fugitive committed the identified offense(s), and whether other treaty requirements have been met. If so, the magistrate certifies the case for extradition at the discretion of the External Affairs Minister. Except as provided by treaty, the magistrate does not inquire into the nature of foreign proceedings likely to follow extradition. India adheres to the principle of extraditing its own nationals.

The *Memorandum on Extradition* submitted by the Government of India to the Asian-African Legal Consultative Committee at its Third Session (Colombo, 1960), leaves no doubt on this matter. However, in practice, India follows dual system, by extraditing

---

[167] https://mea.gov.in/leta.htm; website accessed on 7 May 2020

nationals on the basis of reciprocity. If the other treaty State does not extradite, India also bars extradition of own nationals. The following table lists the countries to which extradition of Indian Nationals is barred by the bilateral Extradition Treaty.

- France (shall not be extradited)
- Germany (shall not be extradited)
- Spain (shall not be extradited)
- UAE (shall not be extradited)
- Saudi Arabia (may not be extradited)
- Bahrain (may not be extradited)
- Belarus (may not be extradited)
- Bulgaria (shall not be extradited)
- Hong Kong (may not be extradited)
- Republic of Korea (may not be extradited)
- Kuwait (shall not be extradited)
- Mongolia (may not be extradited)
- Nepal (may not be extradited)
- Poland (shall not be extradited)
- Russia (shall not be extradited)
- Tunisia (may not be extradited)
- Turkey (shall not be extradited)
- Ukraine (shall not be extradited)
- Uzbekistan (shall not be extradited)
- Vietnam (shall not be extradited)

6 Law of Diplomatic Relations and Consular Relations

> **Topics covered**
> - Functions of a diplomatic mission
> - Appointment of Head of Mission
> - Categories of Heads of Mission
> - Diplomatic immunity
> - Diplomatic privileges
> - Vienna Convention on Consular Relations
> - Influence of the Instrument on Subsequent Legal Developments
> - Kulbhushan Jadhav case

The Vienna Convention on Diplomatic Relations was adopted on 14 April 1961 by the United Nations Conference on Diplomatic Intercourse and Immunities held at Vienna, Austria, from 2 March to 14 April 1961. The Conference also adopted the Optional Protocol concerning the Acquisition of Nationality, the Optional Protocol concerning the Compulsory Settlement of Disputes, the Final Act and four resolutions annexed to that Act. The Convention and two Protocols were deposited with the UNSG and the Final Act deposited in the archives of the Foreign Affairs ministry of the host nation.

Functions of a diplomatic mission

The establishment of diplomatic relations between States, and also the establishment permanent diplomatic missions is on the basis of mutual consent between the sending state and the hosting state. The role of a diplomatic mission comprises of, subject to international law;

(a) representing the sending State in the receiving State
(b) protecting interests of nationals of sending state
(c) negotiating with the Government of the receiving State
(d) ascertaining conditions and developments in the receiving State, and reporting that to sending State
e) promoting friendly relations between sending and receiving State
f) developing economic, cultural and scientific relations

> *Case concerning Certain Questions concerning Diplomatic Relations*[168]
> Set in the backdrop of political instability in Honduras, the Ambassador of Honduras to the Netherlands filed in the Registry of the International Court of Justice, an application instituting proceeding against Brazil vis a vis a dispute pertaining to legal questions concerning diplomatic relations and the principle of non-intervention in domestic matters. It was alleged that Brazil had breached its obligations under Art. 2 (7) of the UN Charter and the 1961 Vienna Convention on Diplomatic Relations and the Court was requested *"to adjudge and declare that Brazil does not have the right to allow the premises of its Mission in Tegucigalpa to be used to promote manifestly illegal activities by Honduran citizens who have been staying within it for some time now and that it shall cease to do so."* For the purpose of jurisdiction, Honduras invoked Art. XXXI of the American Treaty on Pacific Settlement 1948 and, under the terms of Art. LX thereof.[169] By a letter dated 28 October 2009,

---

[168] *Honduras v. Brazil*, Order of 12 May 2010, ICJ Reports 2010, p. 303

[169] officially called the ***Pact of Bogota***, ratified without reservation by Honduras in 1950 and by Brazil in 1965

> Honduras informed the Court, inter alia, that the Ambassador of Honduras to the Netherlands was not the legitimate representative of Honduras before the Court and that *"Ambassador Eduardo Enrique Reina is being appointed as the sole legitimate representative of the Government of Honduras to the International Court of Justice."* The Court decided that, given the circumstances, no other action would be taken in the case until further notice. Later Honduras, informed the Court that the Honduran Government was *"not going on with the proceedings initiated by the application"* and that it *"accordingly withdraws this application from the Registry"*. Consequently, the Court ordered that the case be removed.

Appointment of Head of Mission: The sending State must make certain that the agreement of the receiving State has been given for the person it proposes to accredit as head of the mission to that State.[170] Two or more States may accredit the same person as head of mission to another State, unless objection is offered by the receiving State[171] (this is also called concurrent accreditation). The head of the mission is considered as having taken up his functions in the receiving State either when he has presented his credentials or when he has notified his arrival and a true copy of his credentials has been presented to the Ministry for Foreign Affairs of the receiving State, or as per local practice.[172]

Categories of Heads of Mission: Heads of mission are divided into three classes, namely:

(a) Ambassadors, *nuncios* (term applicable to Holy See), heads of mission of equivalent rank

(b) envoys, ministers and internuncios [(a) and (b) are accredited to the Head of State]

(c) *charges d'affaires* accredited to Ministers for Foreign Affairs.[173]

---

[170] Art. 4 of the Vienna Convention on Diplomatic Relations 1961
[171] Art 6 *Ibid*
[172] Art. 13
[173] Art. 14

The class to which the heads of their missions are to be assigned on mutual consent of both sending and receiving states.[174] If the post of head of the mission is vacant, or if the head of the mission is unable to perform his functions, a *charge d'affaires ad interim* shall act provisionally as head of the mission.[175] The mission and its head shall have the right to use the flag and emblem of the sending State on the premises of the mission, including the residence of the head of the mission, and on his means of transport.[176]

Diplomatic immunity
The person of a diplomatic agent shall be inviolable.[177] He shall not be liable to any form of arrest or detention. The receiving State shall treat him with due respect and shall take all appropriate steps to prevent any attack on his person, freedom or dignity. The private residence of a diplomatic agent shall enjoy the same inviolability and protection as the premises of the mission.[178] A diplomatic agent shall enjoy immunity from the criminal jurisdiction of the receiving State.[179] He shall also enjoy immunity from its civil and administrative jurisdiction, except in the case of:

> (a) a real action relating to private immovable property situated in the territory of the receiving State, unless he holds it on behalf of the sending State for the purposes of the mission
>
> (b) an action relating to succession in which the diplomatic agent is involved as executor, administrator, heir or legatee as a private person and not on behalf of the sending State
>
> (c) an action relating to any professional or commercial

---

[174] Art. 15
[175] Art. 19
[176] Art. 20
[177] Art. 29
[178] Art. 22
[179] Art. 31 (1)

activity exercised by the diplomatic agent in the receiving State outside his official functions.

A diplomatic agent is not obliged to give evidence as a witness.[180] The immunity of a diplomatic agent from the jurisdiction of the receiving State does not exempt him from the jurisdiction of the sending State.[181]

> *Commonwealth of Dominica v. Switzerland*[182]
> Dominica filed an Application at the International Court of Justice instituting proceeding against Switzerland concerning alleged violations by the latter of the Vienna Convention on Diplomatic Relations with respect to a diplomatic envoy of Dominica to the UN in Geneva. In its Application, Dominica stated that the diplomat in question, Mr. Roman Lakschin, had been accredited to UN and its Specialized Agencies and to the World Trade Organization (first as Counsellor, later as Chargé d'affaires and Deputy Permanent Representative with the rank of Ambassador). Dominica further emphasized that this accreditation was *"effected to the organizations and not to Switzerland"*, but that, nevertheless, Switzerland had *"claimed the right to withdraw the accreditation"* of the said envoy, *"stating that he is a 'businessman' and that as such he would have no right to be a diplomat."* By letter of 15 May 2006, the Prime Minister of the Commonwealth of Dominica informed the Court that his Government *"did not wish to go on with the proceedings instituted against Switzerland"* and requested the Court to make an Order *"officially recording their unconditional discontinuance"* and *"directing the removal of the case from the General List."* Subsequently, the Swiss Ambassador in The Hague advised the

---

[180] Art. 31 (2)
[181] Art. 31 (4)
[182] ICJ case concerning *Status vis-à-vis the Host State of a Diplomatic Envoy to the United Nations* 2006

> Court that he had informed the competent Swiss authorities of the discontinuance as thus notified. Accordingly, ICJ ordered that the case be removed from the court's registry.

Diplomatic privileges
Subject to its laws and regulations concerning zones entry into which is prohibited or regulated for reasons of national security, the receiving State shall ensure to all members of the mission freedom of movement and travel in its territory.[183] The receiving State shall permit and protect free communication on the part of the mission for all official purposes. In communicating with the Government and the other missions and consulates of the sending State, wherever situated, the mission may employ all appropriate means, including diplomatic couriers and messages in code or cipher.[184] However, the mission may install and use a wireless transmitter only with the consent of the receiving State. The official correspondence of the mission shall be inviolable. Official correspondence means all correspondence relating to the mission and its functions.[185] The diplomatic bag shall not be opened or detained. The packages constituting the diplomatic bag must bear visible external marks of their character and may contain only diplomatic documents or articles intended for official use. The diplomatic courier, who shall be provided with an official document indicating his status and the number of packages constituting the diplomatic bag, shall be protected by the receiving State in the performance of his functions. He shall enjoy personal inviolability and shall not be liable to any form of arrest or detention. The sending State or the mission may designate diplomatic couriers ad hoc. A diplomatic bag may be entrusted to the captain of a commercial aircraft scheduled to land at an authorized port of entry. He shall be provided with an official

---

[183] Art. 26 of the Vienna Convention on Diplomatic Relations 1961
[184] Art. 27
[185] *Ibid*

document indicating the number of packages constituting the bag but he shall not be considered to be a diplomatic courier. The mission may send one of its members to take possession of the diplomatic bag directly and freely from the captain of the aircraft. The fees and charges levied by the mission in the course of its official duties shall be exempt from all dues and taxes.[186] A diplomatic agent shall with respect to services rendered for the sending State be exempt from social security provisions which may be in force in the receiving State.[187]

In respect of taxes the Convention of 1969 states that a diplomatic agent shall be exempt except in such cases as:
"(a) indirect taxes of a kind which are normally incorporated in the price of goods or services;
(b) dues and taxes on private immovable property situated in the territory of the receiving State, unless he holds it on behalf of the sending State for the purposes of the mission;
(c) estate, succession or inheritance duties levied by the receiving State, subject to certain restrictions;
(d) dues and taxes on private income having its source in the receiving State and capital taxes on investments made in commercial undertakings in the receiving State;
(e) charges levied for specific services rendered; and
(f) registration, court or record fees, mortgage dues and stamp duty, with respect to immovable property, subject to certain restrictions."[188]

Subject to local laws, the receiving State shall grant exemption from all customs duties, taxes, and related charges other than charges for storage, cartage and similar services, on articles for the official use of the mission; and articles for the personal use of a diplomatic agent and family members. The personal baggage of a diplomatic

---

[186] Art. 28
[187] Art. 33
[188] Art. 34 *Ibid*

agent shall be exempt from inspection, unless there are serious grounds for presuming that it contains articles which are prohibited or controlled.[189] Family members of a diplomatic agent forming part of his household shall, if they are not nationals of the receiving State, enjoy the privileges and immunities due to the diplomat.[190] Members of the administrative and technical staff of the mission, together with members of their families forming part of their respective households, shall, if they are not nationals of or permanently resident in the receiving State, enjoy the privileges and immunities specified, except that the immunity from civil and administrative jurisdiction of the receiving State *shall not extend to acts performed outside the course of their duties*.[191] Members of the service staff of the mission who are not nationals of or permanently resident in the receiving State shall enjoy immunity in respect of acts performed in the course of their duties, exemption from dues and taxes on the emoluments they receive by reason of their employment.[192] Private servants of members of the mission shall, if they are not nationals of or permanently resident in the receiving State, be exempt from dues and taxes on the emoluments they receive by reason of their employment.[193] In other respects, they may enjoy privileges and immunities only to the extent admitted by the receiving State. However, the receiving State must exercise its jurisdiction over those persons in such a manner as not to interfere unduly with the performance of the functions of the mission. Except insofar as additional privileges and immunities may be granted by the receiving State, a diplomatic agent who is a national of or permanently resident in that State shall enjoy only immunity from jurisdiction, and inviolability, in respect of official

---

[189] Art. 36
[190] Art. 37 (1)
[191] Art. 37 (2)
[192] *Ibid*
[193] Art. 37 (4)

acts performed in the exercise of his functions.[194] Other members of the staff of the mission and private servants who are nationals of or permanently resident in the receiving State shall enjoy privileges and immunities only to the extent admitted by the receiving State. However, the receiving State must exercise its jurisdiction over those persons in such a manner as not to interfere unduly with the performance of the functions of the mission.[195] Every person entitled to privileges and immunities shall enjoy them from the moment he enters the territory of the receiving State on proceeding to take up his post. When the functions of a person enjoying privileges and immunities have come to an end, such privileges and immunities shall normally cease at the moment when he leaves the country, or on expiry of a reasonable period in which to do so, but shall subsist until that time, even in case of armed conflict.[196] However, with respect to acts performed by such a person in the exercise of his functions as a member of the mission, immunity shall continue to subsist. In case of the death of a member of the mission, the members of his family shall continue to enjoy the privileges and immunities to which they are entitled until the expiry of a reasonable period in which to leave the country.

Vienna Convention on Consular Relations

The Vienna Convention on Consular Relations was adopted by the United Nations Conference on Consular Relations held at Vienna (Austria) in the year 1963. The Conference also adopted the Optional Protocol concerning Acquisition of Nationality, the Optional Protocol concerning the Compulsory Settlement of Disputes, the Final Act and three resolutions annexed to that Act. The Convention and the two Protocols were deposited with the Secretary-General of the United Nations. The Final Act, by unanimous decision of the Conference, was deposited in the

---

[194] Art. 38 (1)
[195] Art. 38 (2)
[196] Art. 39

archives of the Federal Ministry for Foreign Affairs of Austria. The Vienna Convention comprises of 79 provisions[197] dealing with operation of consulates, functions of consular agents, privileges and immunities granted to consular officials and consular responsibilities to citizens of their country. Of particular interest for the right of individuals as provided under art. 36 of the Convention of 1963. The said provision outlines certain obligations for competent authorities in the case of an arrest or detention of a foreign national, in order to guarantee the inalienable right to counsel, due process and effective access to consular protection.

Influence of the Instrument on Subsequent Legal Developments
In contemporary times, art. 36 of the Vienna Convention has increasingly been raised at various court proceedings- domestic, regional and the ICJ. In USA, for instance, following the case of *Breard v. Greene*,[198] numerous claims have been filed at various levels such as federal circuit courts, state supreme courts and the US Supreme Court. Interpretations have ranged from the non-recognition of fundamental rights conferred by art. 36[199] to the

---

[197] Test available at https://legal.un.org/avl/ha/vccr/vccr.html; website accessed on 10th April 2020

[198] 523 US 371, 1988

[199] Art. 36 (1) of the Vienna Convention on Consular Relations of 1963 reads;
"With a view to facilitating the exercise of consular functions relating to nationals of the sending State:
(a) consular officers shall be free to communicate with nationals of the sending State and to have access to them. Nationals of the sending State shall have the same freedom with respect to communication with and access to consular officers of the sending State;
(b) if he so requests, the competent authorities of the receiving State shall, without delay, inform the consular post of the sending State if, within its consular district, a national of that State is arrested or committed to prison or to custody pending trial or is detained in any other manner. Any communication addressed to the consular post by the person arrested, in

possibility of individually enforcing those rights. In 1999, the Inter-American Court of Human Rights issued an advisory opinion, recognizing that art. 36 creates individual rights, as a *"notable exception to what are essentially States' rights and obligations accorded elsewhere"* in the Convention.[200] In 2001, the International Court of Justice in *LaGrand case* found that where a violation of art. 36 occurs, a remedy is due consisting of *"review and reconsideration by United States courts of convictions and sentences,"* in light of the breach of the Convention.[201] The *Avena case*[202] marked a turning point regarding art. 36 jurisprudence. The world courts' unprecedented decision of 2004 expressly recognized the interdependence of both individual and State's rights, by asserting that *"violations of the rights of the individual under art. 36 may entail a violation of the rights of the sending State, and that violations of the rights of the latter may entail a violation of the rights of the individual,"*[203] Moreover, the Court stated that the ruling concerned only Mexican nationals cannot be taken to imply that the conclusions reached by it in the *Avena case* do not apply to

---

prison, custody or detention shall be forwarded by the said authorities without delay. The said authorities shall inform the person concerned without delay of his rights under this subparagraph;

(c) *consular officers shall have the right to visit a national of the sending State who is in prison, custody or detention, to converse and correspond with him and to arrange for his legal representation. They shall also have the right to visit any national of the sending State who is in prison, custody or detention in their district in pursuance of a judgement. Nevertheless, consular officers shall refrain from taking action on behalf of a national who is in prison, custody or detention if he expressly opposes such action"*

[200] Advisory Opinion of the Inter-American Court of Human Rights: Due Process of Law is a Fundamental Right (OC-16/99), para. 82

[201] *Germany v. United States of America* Judgment Jurisdiction, Admissibility, Merits, ICJ GL No 104, [2001] ICJ Rep 466, (2001) 40 ILM 1069, ICGJ 51 (ICJ 2001), 27th June 2001

[202] Case Concerning Avena and Other Mexican Nationals (*Mexico v. United States of America*) Judgment, ICJ Reports 2004, 12 General List No. 128

[203] *Ibid*

other foreign nationals finding themselves in similar situations in other countries.

These cases may eventually carry significant consequences for countries legally imposing the death penalty: "*That is, only where the most rigorous standards of fairness and legality of international jurisprudence are scrupulously followed.*"[204] Most recent case is the *Jadhav case*.[205] Here, the proceedings were instituted on 8 May 2017 by the filing in the Registry of an Application by the Republic of India against the Islamic Republic of Pakistan, alleging violations of the Vienna Convention on Consular Relations 1963 with regard to the detention, since March 2016, and trial of an Indian national, Mr. Kulbhushan Sudhir Jadhav. He was accused of performing acts of espionage and terrorism on behalf of India, and sentenced to death by a military court in Pakistan in April 2017. In particular, India contended that Pakistan acted in breach of its obligations under Art. 36 of the Vienna Convention (i) by not informing India, without delay, of the detention of Mr. Jadhav; (ii) by not informing Mr. Jadhav of his rights under Art. 36; and (iii) by denying consular officers of India access to Mr. Jadhav. The Court found in July 2019 that the Islamic Republic of Pakistan, in the matter of the detention and trial of an Indian national, Mr. Kulbhushan Sudhir Jadhav, had acted in breach of the obligations' incumbent on it under Art.36 of the Vienna Convention on Consular Relations.

---

[204] Catherine M. Amirfar, "*The Avena Case in the International Court of Justice,*" **German Law Journal**, No. 4, April, 2004

[205] *India v. Pakistan* ICGJ 515 (ICJ 2017), [2017] ICJ GL No 168

7 The Law of Sea

> **Topics covered**
> - Concept of Open sea
> - Concept of Closed sea
> - Canon Shot rule
> - Truman Proclamation
> - Santiago declaration
> - UNCLOS I
> - UNCLOS II
> - Montevideo Declaration
> - The Lima Declaration
> - The Declaration of Santo Domingo
> - Patrimonial Sea
> - UNCLOS III
> - Dispute Resolution
> - International Seabed Authority
> - Commission on the Limits of the Continental Shelf
> - Order in the Indian Ocean – A case study

Introduction

The UN observes[206] that the oceans had long been subject to the freedom of-the-seas doctrine, a 17th century principle, restricting sovereignty and jurisdiction over the oceans to a narrow sea belt surrounding a nation's coastline. The remainder of the seas was considered free for all and not belonging to anyone country. This position prevailed for about three centuries. During this period, the

---

[206] https://www.un.org/en/sections/issues-depth/oceans-and-law-sea/index.html; website accesses on 11 April 2020

territorial waters of a coastal state extended to the length the coastal artillery could fire. All waters beyond this were considered international waters (free seas, or *mare liberum*).[207] As described by Hugo Grotius, the seas *"were free to all nations but belonged to none of them."* In early 17th century Hugo Grotius, counsel for the Dutch East India Company for Santa Catarina Portuguese carrack issue, propounded the view that the sea was international territory and all nations were free to use it for seafaring trade.[208] The Grotian view was a counter to the Portuguese claim to monopolize East India trade given their prevalent maritime prowess and mercantile aspirations. The logic of the Portuguese was premised on *Mare clausum* policy also known as the closed sea policy.

In terms of their evolution, John Selden's *Mare Clausum* was a direct reply to the *Mare Liberum* of Hugo Grotius. Selden's work by the same name was printed and published towards the end of the year 1635.[209] According to an assessment[210] in 1933, the purpose of the *Mare Clausum* is twofold. The first book argues that by the law of nature or nations the sea is not common to all men, but is as much as the land is susceptible of private dominion and property. In the second book it is maintained that the lordship of the circumfluent and surrounding ocean belongs to the Crown of Great Britain. The Dutch jurist Cornelis van Bijnkershoek, in his treatise titled *De dominio maris*,[211] advocated a compromise principle which sought to accommodate the claims of Grotius as well as Selden.

---

[207] https://sites.tufts.edu/lawofthesea/chapter-one/; website accesses on 11 April 2020

[208] Hugo Grotius, **Mare Liberum, sive de jure quod Batavis competit ad Indicana commercia dissertation** (Lodewijk Elzevir, 1609)

[209] John Selden, **Mare Clausum** (London, John Stansby, 1635)

[210] Eric G. M. Fletcher, *"John Selden and His Contribution to International Law"* 1933 **Transactions of the Grotius Society: Problems of Peace and War**, Vol. 19, pp. 1-12

[211] Cornelis van Bijnkershoek, **De Dominio Maris** (The Hague, 1703)

Bijnkershoek (also called as Bynkershoek) did so by accepting the claim of freedom of navigation, exploitation (of resources) of the high seas as well as the claim of coastal states entitlement to wider range of specific rights in a demarcated territorial sea.[212] This compromise led to widespread acceptance of Bynkershoek's *cannon shot rule*. This rule in practice referred to the effective range of the most powerful coastal artillery cannon (then approximately 3 nautical miles). While this position prevailed up until mid-20th century when the desire to extend national claims over off-shore resources were increasingly articulated by members of the International community.

In 1930, at the Hague Conference on the codification of international law, a report on *territorial sea* stated "*...international law attributes to each Coastal State sovereignty over a belt of sea round its coasts. This must be regarded as essential for the protection of the legitimate interests of the State. The belt of territorial sea forms part of the territory of the State; the sovereignty which the State exercises over this belt does not differ in kind from the authority exercised over its land domain. This sovereignty is however limited by conditions established by international law; indeed, it is precisely because the freedom of navigation is of such great importance to all States that the right of innocent passage through the territorial sea has been generally recognized. There may be said to have been agreement among the delegations on these ideas. With regard, however, to the breadth of the belt over which the sovereignty of the State should be recognized, it soon became evident that opinion was much divided.*"[213] The next important development on the evolution of the law of the sea was the 1945 proclamations by then US

---

[212] https://library.law.yale.edu/news/freedom-seas-part-8;website accessed on 11 April 2020

[213] https://biblio-archive.unog.ch/Dateien/CouncilMSD/C-351-M-145-1930-V_EN.pdf p. 123; website accessed on 11 April 2020

President Harry S. Truman.[214] The operative part of the proclamation reads:

> *Now therefore I, Harry S. Truman, President of the United States of America, do hereby proclaim the following policy of the United States of America with respect to the natural resources of the subsoil and sea bed of the continental shelf. Having concern for the urgency of conserving and prudently utilizing its natural resources, the Government of the United States regards the natural resources of the subsoil and sea bed of the continental shelf beneath the high seas but contiguous to the coasts of the United States as appertaining to the United states, subject to its jurisdiction and control. In cases where the continental shelf extends to the shores of another States, or is shared with an adjacent State, the boundary shall be determined by the United States and the State concerned in accordance with equitable principles. The character as high seas of the waters above the continental shelf and the right to their free and unimpeded navigation are in no way thus affected.*[215]

By another Presidential Proclamation, Truman stated that:

> *"...hereby proclaim the following policy of the USA with respect to coastal fisheries in certain areas of the high seas; In view of the pressing need for conservation and protection of fishery resources, the Government of USA regards it as proper to establish conservation ones in those areas of the high seas contiguous to the coasts of the United states wherein fishing activities have been or in the future may be developed and maintained on a substantial scale. Where such activities have been or shall hereafter be developed by its nationals alone, the United States regards it as proper to establish explicitly bounded conservation zones in which fishing activities shall be subject to the regulation and control of*

---

[214] The Truman Proclamations were opposed by Chile, Argentina and Mexico.

[215] Policy of the United States with Respect to the Natural Resources of the Subsoil and Sea Bed of the Continental Shelf, Presidential Proclamation No. 2667 of 28th September, 1945

> US. Where such activities have been or shall hereafter be legitimately developed and maintained jointly by nationals of US and nationals of other States, explicitly bounded conservation zones may be established under agreements between the United States and such other States, and all fishing activities in such zones shall be subject to regulation and control as provided in such agreements. The right of any State to establish conservation zones off its shores in accordance with the above principle is conceded, provided that corresponding recognition is given to any fishing interests of nationals of the United States which may exist in such areas. The character as high seas of the areas in which such conservation zones are established and the right to their free and unimpeded navigation are in no way thus affected[216]

The first international instrument to proclaim a 200-mile limit came was declared in 1952 in Santiago.[217] The Santiago Declaration titled *Declaration on the Maritime Zone* was signed by three countries that were bordering the South Pacific sea, namely, Chile, Ecuador and Peru. The Declaration reflects the main driving force behind it, namely the desire of those states to develop the resources of their coastal waters. It asserts that *"owing to the geological and biological factors affecting the existence, conservation and development of the marine fauna and flora of the waters adjacent to the coasts of the declarant countries, the former extent of the territorial sea and contiguous zone is insufficient to permit of the conservation, development and use of those resources, to which the coastal countries are entitled."* Therefore, the three governments *"proclaim as a principle of their international*

---

[216] Policy of the United States with Respect to Coastal Fisheries in Certain Areas of the High Seas, Presidential Proclamation No. 2668 of 28th September, 1945

[217] For evolution of legal history of Law of Sea, see generally works of Fijian diplomat Satya Nanda, *"The Exclusive Economic Zone: a historical perspective"* [1987] available at FAO Website http://www.fao.org/docrep/s5280T/s5280t0p.htm; website visited on 11 April 2020

maritime policy that each of them possesses sole sovereignty and jurisdiction over the area of sea adjacent to the coast of its own country and extending not less than 200 nautical miles from the said coast." The Declaration also provided for exclusive sovereignty and jurisdiction over the *sea floor* and *subsoil* and maintained the *principle of innocent passage* through the zone.

Overview of UNCLOS: The UNCLOS is an international treaty which was adopted and signed in 1982. It replaced the then prevailing four Geneva Conventions of 1958 (also known as UNCLOS I) governing territorial sea, contiguous zone, continental shelf, high seas including matters pertaining to fishing and conservation.[218] The 1982 Convention created three new institutions: International Tribunal for the Law of the Sea (ITLOS),[219] International Seabed Authority (ISA)[220] and Commission on the Limits of the Continental Shelf.[221]

Main elements of UNCLOS I: The importance of the Geneva Conventions of 1958 is limited to academic and historical relevance. Widely referred to as the *traditional law of the sea*,[222] its shortcomings and the debates generated thereof, laid the foundations for the transformation in the legal regime governing the seas. The first Conference on the Law of the Sea organized under the auspices of the United Nations was held in Geneva for over a month in 1958.

---

[218] For original text of 1958 Geneva Convention on Law of Seas refer United Nations, Treaty Series, vol. 450, p. 11, p. 82

[219] Art. 287 (1) (a) of the United Nations Convention on the Law of the Sea 1982

[220] Agreement relating to the implementation of Part XI of the United Nations Convention on the Law of the Sea of 10 December 1982 adopted by UNGA Resolution A/RES/48/263

[221] Established pursuant to art. 2 of Annex II to the United Nations Convention on the Law of the Sea 1982

[222] https://legal.un.org/avl/ha/gclos/gclos.html; website accessed on 16 April 2020

On 29 April 1958, the United Nations Conference on the Law of the Sea opened for signature four conventions and an optional protocol: the Convention on the Territorial Sea and the Contiguous Zone (CTS); the Convention on the High Seas (CHS); the Convention on Fishing and Conservation of the Living Resources of the High Seas (CFCLR); the Convention on the Continental Shelf (CCS); and the Optional Protocol of Signature concerning the Compulsory Settlement of Disputes (OPSD).[223]

The Conventions were adopted less than a decade before the famous speech by Arvid Pardo at the UNGA in 1967 triggering off a complete renewal of the law of the sea.[224] By virtue of art. 311 (1) of the rehauled UNCLOS of 1982, the 1982 instrument *"shall prevail, as between States Parties, over the Geneva Conventions on the Law of the Sea of 29 April 1958."* There are currently 168 parties to the UNCLOS of 1982. Furthermore, there are 14 signatories who are yet to ratify. The current membership of 168 States bound by the Geneva Conventions shrinks the relevance of the earlier conventions to be binding only as between, or in the relationships with, the few States that are parties to the relevant Geneva Convention and not parties to the 1982 Convention. Currently member states can be categorized under four heads, states that have ratified, states that have signed the convention but yet to ratify,[225] states that have signed the agreement but are yet to ratify[226] and fourthly observer

---

[223] The CTS sets out in detailed provisions the main rules on the territorial sea and the contiguous zone. Its rules address, in particular, baselines, bays, delimitation between States whose coasts are adjacent or face each other, innocent passage and the contiguous zone

[224] Donald Rothwell, Alex G. Oude Elferink, Karen Nadine Scott, Tim Stephens, **The Oxford Handbook of the Law of the Sea** (Oxford University Press, Oxford, 2015) p.16

[225] As on 16 April 2020 there are 14 states have signed the Convention but have not ratified UNCLOS 1982

[226] USA is the only state that falls within this category. USA signed the Agreement 29 July 1994. Ratification was deferred in 2012 when the

states.[227] The Convention on the High Seas, is predominantly reflected in the 1982 instrument, and whose preamble explicitly specifies that its purpose is *"to codify the rules of international law relating to the high sea."* This has led to widespread belief that parts of UNCLOS 1982 and more specifically those pertaining to CHS have attained the status of customary international law. This is the same as in the case of the Convention on Continental Shelf contributing to the *crystallization* of the customary notion of the continental shelf.

UNCLOS II: Subsequent to the adoption of the 1958 Conventions on the Law of the Sea, at the first United Nations Conference on the Law of the Sea, the General Assembly requested the Secretary-General to convene a Second United Nations Conference on the Law of the Sea to consider the topics of the breadth of the territorial sea and fishery limits,[228] which had not been agreed upon in the said Conventions.[229] The Conference was held over a period of one month leading to the adoption of two resolutions.[230] Substantive decisions on the topics of the breadth of the territorial sea and fishery limits were deferred to a later stage.

Montevideo Declaration 1970: During the first week of May 1970 a meeting on the Law of the Sea was convened at Montevideo at the request of Uruguay attended by delegations of the Republics of Argentina, Brazil, Chile, Ecuador, El Salvador, Nicaragua, Panama, Peru (and Uruguay). This meeting led to the adoption of a

---

US Senate could not reach a 2/3rd consensus required for ratification of an International treaty.

[227] There are currently 15 such observer states that are yet to sign nor acceded either the Convention or the Agreement.

[228] https://wcl.american.libguides.com/c.php?g=563260&p=3877789; website accessed on 16 April 2020

[229] Resolution 1307 (XIII) of 10 December 1958

[230] A/CONF.19/L.15

declaration titled Montevideo Declaration of Principles on the Law of the Sea 1970 which is popularly referred to as the Montevideo Declaration. The Declaration of 8 May 1970 states, *"... the signatory States have, by reason of conditions peculiar to them, extended their sovereignty or exclusive rights of jurisdiction over the maritime area adjacent to their coasts, its soil and its subsoil to a distance of 200 nautical miles from the baseline of the territorial sea."* The Montevideo Declaration contains, *inter alia*, two important propositions:
- ➤ right of coastal states to avail themselves of the national resources of the sea adjacent to their coasts and the sea-bed and subsoil thereof
- ➤ right to establish limits to maritime sovereignty and jurisdiction with the factors governing the rational utilization of existing of marine resources.

Declaration of Latin American States on the Law of the Sea (The Lima Declaration) 1970: During the Montevideo meeting, Peru proposed a second meeting of all Latin American states to be held in Lima in August 1970.[231] Twenty states attended the Lima meeting and the resulting Declaration was approved by fourteen states[232] (the nine signatories of the Montevideo Declaration plus Colombia, the Dominican Republic, Guatemala, Honduras and Mexico). The Lima Declaration reiterates the principles of the Montevideo Declaration with two additional concepts included:
- ➤ the right of the coastal state to prevent contamination
- ➤ the right of the coastal state to authorize, supervise and participate in all maritime scientific research activities[233]

---

[231] James Kraska, **Maritime Power and the Law of the Sea: Expeditionary Operations in World Politics** (Oxford University Press, New York, 2011) p. 137

[232] **Essays in Memory of Jean Carroz: The Law and the Sea** (Food and Agriculture Organization of the United Nations, 1987) p. 177

[233] Committee on the Peaceful Uses of the Sea Bed and the Ocean Floor Beyond the Limits of National Jurisdiction (1970)

The Declaration of Santo Domingo 1972: The Declaration of Santo Domingo of 9 June 1972 is one of the immediate precursors of the exclusive economic zone.[234] It was the Santo Domingo Declaration that brought the concept of the patrimonial sea into focus.[235] The section entitled *Patrimonial Sea* repeated some elements previously stated in the Montevideo and Lima Declarations, but was much more precise about making a distinction between the territorial sea and the patrimonial sea. The patrimonial sea was described as follows:

> ➤ The coastal state has sovereign rights over the renewable and non-renewable natural resources which are found in the waters, in the sea-bed and in the subsoil of an area adjacent to the territorial sea called patrimonial sea.
> ➤ The coastal state has the duty to promote, and the right to regulate, the conduct of scientific research within the patrimonial sea, as well as the right to adopt the necessary measures to prevent marine pollution and to ensure its sovereignty over the resources of the area.
> ➤ The breadth of this zone should be the subject of an international agreement, preferably of a world-wide scope. The whole of the area of both the territorial sea and the patrimonial sea, taking into account geographic circumstances, should not exceed a maximum of 200 nautical miles.
> ➤ The delimitation of this zone between two or more states should be carried out in accordance with the peaceful

---

[234] A sub regional conference, The Special Conference of the Caribbean Countries on Problems of the Sea, was attended by 15 Caribbean states: Barbados, Colombia, Costa Rica, Dominican Republic, Guatemala, Haiti, Honduras, Jamaica, Mexico, Nicaragua, Panama, Trinidad and Tobago and Venezuela. El Salvador and Guyana attended as observers

[235] Shigeru Oda, **Fifty Years of the Law of the Sea** (Kluwar Law International, Hague, 2003) p. 477

procedures stipulated in the Charter of the United Nations.
➢ In this zone, ships and aircraft of all states, whether coastal state or not, should enjoy the right of freedom of navigation and overflight with no restrictions, other than those resulting from the exercise of rights by coastal states within the area. Subject only to these limitations, there will also be freedom for laying of submarine cables and pipelines.[236]

UNCLOS III

On 1 November 1967, Malta's Ambassador to the United Nations, Arvid Pardo in his speech to the UNGA spoke of the super-Power rivalry that was spreading to the oceans, of the pollution of the seas and of the conflicting legal claims. Pardo ended with a call for *"an effective international regime over the seabed and the ocean floor beyond a clearly defined national jurisdiction"*. *"It is the only alternative by which we can hope to avoid the escalating tension that will be inevitable if the present situation is allowed to continue."*[237] The Conference itself was convened in New York in 1973.[238] It ended nine years later with the adoption in 1982 of a constitution for the seas - the United Nations Convention on the Law of the Sea. Representatives of more than 160 sovereign States discussed the issues, bargained and traded national rights and obligations leading to the Convention.[239] Navigational rights,[240] territorial sea limits,[241] economic jurisdiction,[242] legal status of resources on the seabed beyond the

---

[236] Declaration of The Meeting of Ministers on The Territorial Sea, Patrimonial Sea, And Continental Shelf, 1972
[237] Agenda item 92, UNGA 22nd Session, First Committee, 1515th Meeting, 1967
[238] Third United Nations Conference on the Law of the Sea, December 1973
[239] Milenko Milic, Third United Nations Conference on the Law of the Sea, 8 **Case Western Reserve Journal of International Law** 168 (1976)
[240] Art. 90, United Nations Convention on the Law of the Sea, 1982
[241] Art. 3 *Ibid*
[242] Art. 55

limits of national jurisdiction, innocent passage of ships,[243] conservation and management of living marine resources,[244] protection of the marine environment,[245] a marine research regime[246] and, a more unique feature, a binding procedure for settlement of disputes between States[247] - these are among the important features of the treaty. In short, the Convention is an unprecedented attempt by the international community to regulate all aspects of the resources of the sea and uses of the ocean, and thus bring a stable order to mankind's very source of life.[248]

Navigation: Art. 3 of UNCLOS III states, *"Every State has the right to establish the breadth of its territorial sea up to a limit not exceeding 12 nautical miles, measured from baselines determined in accordance with this Convention."*

> In the eighteenth century, the *cannon-shot* rule gained wide acceptance in Europe. Coastal States were to exercise dominion over their territorial seas as far as projectiles could be fired from a cannon based on the shore.[249] According to some scholars, in the eighteenth century the range of land-based cannons was approximately one marine league, or three nautical miles. It is believed that on the basis of this formula developed the traditional

---

[243] Art. 17
[244] Art. 116-120
[245] Art. 145
[246] Art. 143
[247] Art. 186 -190
[248] Aldo Chircop, Norman Letalik, Ted, McDorman, Susan Rolston, **The Regulation of International Shipping: International and Comparative Perspectives** (Martinus Njhoff Publishers, Boston, 2012)
[249] Jessica E. Tauman, *"Rescued at Sea, but Nowhere to Go: The Cloudy Legal Waters of the Tampa Crisis,"* 11 **Pac. Rim L & Pol'y J.** 461 (2002)

> three-mile territorial sea limit.[250] By the late 1960s, a trend to a 12-mile territorial sea had gradually emerged throughout the world, with a great majority of nations claiming sovereignty out to that seaward limit. However, the major maritime and naval Powers clung to a three-mile limit on territorial seas,[251] primarily because a 12-mile limit would effectively close off and place under national sovereignty more than 100 straits used for international navigation.[252]

In the *M/V Norstar case (Panama v. Italy)*, the ITLOS (judgment in April 2019) found that art. 87 (dealing with High Seas) of UNCLOS III *"proclaims that the high seas are open to all States"* and that, *"save in exceptional cases, no State may exercise jurisdiction over a foreign ship on the high seas"* In this context, it observed that the *"freedom of navigation would be illusory if a ship ... could be subject to the jurisdiction of other States on the high seas"*. Recalling its jurisprudence in the *M/V Virginia G Case*, the Tribunal then expressed the view that *"bunkering on the high seas is part of the freedom of navigation to be exercised under the conditions laid down by the Convention and other rules of international law"*. It therefore *"finds that the bunkering of leisure boats carried out by the M/V Norstar on the high seas falls within the freedom of navigation under art. 87."* The Tribunal held that the principle of exclusive flag State jurisdiction *"prohibits not only the*

---

[250] *"The Three-Mile Limit: Its Juridical Status"* 6 **Val. U. L. Rev**. 170 (1972) pp. 170-182

[251] HSK Kent, *"The Historical Origins of the Three-Mile Limit,"* **The American Journal of International Law**, Vol. 48, No. 4 (Oct., 1954), pp. 537-553

[252] A 12-mile territorial sea would place under national jurisdiction of riparian States strategic passages such as the Strait of Gibraltar (8 miles wide) only open access to the Mediterranean, the Strait of Malacca (20 miles wide) main sea route between the Pacific and Indian Oceans, the Strait of Hormuz (21 miles wide) only passage to the oil rich Gulf States) and Bab el Mandeb (14 miles wide) connecting Indian Ocean with Red Sea

exercise of enforcement jurisdiction on the high seas by States other than the flag State but also the extension of their prescriptive jurisdiction to lawful activities conducted by foreign ships on the high seas". In the view of the Tribunal, *"if a State applies its criminal and customs laws to the high seas and criminalizes activities carried out by foreign ships thereon, it would constitute a breach of art. 87 of the Convention, unless justified by the Convention or other international treaties"* and *"this would be so, even if the State refrained from enforcing those laws on the high seas."*

Contiguous zone: Art. 33 deals with contiguous zone which is a zone in which a coastal State may exercise the control necessary to: (a) prevent infringement of its customs, fiscal, immigration or sanitary laws and regulations within its territory or territorial sea; and (b) punish infringement of the above laws and regulations committed within its territory or territorial sea. The contiguous zone may not extend beyond 24 nautical miles from the baselines from which the breadth of the territorial sea is measured.

Transit passage: Art. 37 to 44 deal with the concept of *transit passage*. This applies to straits which are used for international navigation between one part of the high seas or an exclusive economic zone and another part of the high seas or an exclusive economic zone. Art. 38 (2) states, *"Transit passage means the exercise in accordance with this Part of the freedom of navigation and overflight solely for the purpose of continuous and expeditious transit of the strait between one part of the high seas or an exclusive economic zone and another part of the high seas or an exclusive economic zone. However, the requirement of continuous and expeditious transit does not preclude passage through the strait for the purpose of entering, leaving or returning from a State bordering the strait, subject to the conditions of entry to that State."*

> In fact, the issue of passage through straits was one of the early driving forces behind the Third United Nations Conference on the Law of the Sea, when, in early 1967, the United States and the Soviet Union proposed to other Member countries of the United Nations that an international conference be held to deal specifically with the entangled issues of straits, overflight, the width of the territorial sea and fisheries. The compromise that emerged in the Convention is a new concept that combines the legally accepted provisions of innocent passage through territorial waters and freedom of navigation on the high seas. The new concept of *transit passage*, required concessions from both sides.

Exclusive Economic Zone: The exclusive economic zone is one of the most revolutionary features of the Convention, and one which already has had a profound impact on the management and conservation of the resources of the oceans. Simply put, it recognizes the right of coastal States to jurisdiction over the resources of some 38 million square nautical miles of ocean space. To the coastal State falls the right to exploit, develop, manage and conserve all resources - fish or oil, gas or gravel, nodules or Sulphur - to be found in the waters, on the ocean floor and in the subsoil of an area extending 200 miles from its shore.

> Rights, jurisdiction and duties of the coastal State in the exclusive economic zone are covered in Art. 56. Accordingly, the coastal State has sovereign rights for the purpose of exploring and exploiting, conserving and managing the natural resources, whether living or non-living, of the waters superjacent to the seabed and of the seabed and its subsoil, and with regard to other activities for the economic exploitation and exploration of the zone, such as the production of energy from the water, currents and winds. Further the coastal state has jurisdiction with regard to the establishment and use of artificial islands, installations and structures; marine scientific research; the protection and

> preservation of the marine environment; and other rights and duties provided for in UNCLOS III.

It is evident that, it is archipelagic States and large nations with naturally endowed long coastlines that acquire greatest areas under the EEZ regime. But with exclusive rights come responsibilities and obligations for example, the Convention encourages optimum use of fish stocks without risking depletion through overfishing. Each coastal State is to determine the total allowable catch for each fish species within its economic zone and is also to estimate its harvest capacity and what it can and cannot itself catch. Coastal States are obliged to give access to others, particularly neighboring States and land-locked countries, to the surplus of the allowable catch. Such access must be done in accordance with the conservation measures established in the laws and regulations of the coastal State. Coastal States have certain other obligations, including the adoption of measures to prevent and limit pollution and to facilitate marine scientific research in their EEZs.

> *The South China Sea Arbitration*[253]
> On 22 January 2013, the Republic of the Philippine instituted arbitral proceedings against the People's Republic of China under Annex VII to the United Nations Convention on the Law of the Sea. The arbitration concerned the role of historic rights and the source of maritime entitlements in the South China Sea, the status of certain maritime features in the South China Sea, and the lawfulness of certain actions by China in the South China Sea that the Philippines alleged to be in violation of the Convention. China adopted a position of non-acceptance and non-participation in the proceedings. The Permanent Court of Arbitration served as Registry in this arbitration. A unanimous award was issued on 12 July 2016 by the Tribunal in which it concluded that there **was no**

---

[253] *The Republic of Philippines v. The People's Republic of China-The question of historic rights* PCA Case No. 2013-19

Legal basis for China to claim historic rights to resources within the sea areas falling within the 'nine-dash line.' The Tribunal examined the history of the Convention and its provisions concerning maritime zones and concluded that the Convention was intended to comprehensively allocate the rights of States to maritime areas. The Tribunal noted that the question of pre-existing rights to resources (in particular fishing resources) was carefully considered during the negotiations on the creation of the exclusive economic zone and that a number of States wished to preserve historic fishing rights in the new zone.

This position was rejected, however, and the final text of the Convention gives other States only a limited right of access to fisheries in the exclusive economic zone (in the event the coastal State cannot harvest the full allowable catch) and no rights to petroleum or mineral resources. The Tribunal found that China's claim to historic rights to resources was incompatible with the detailed allocation of rights and maritime zones in the Convention and concluded that, to the extent China had historic rights to resources in the waters of the South China Sea, such rights were extinguished by the entry into force of the Convention to the extent they were incompatible with the Convention's system of maritime zones. The Tribunal also found that China had violated the Philippines' sovereign rights in its exclusive economic zone by (a) interfering with Philippine fishing and petroleum exploration, (b) constructing artificial islands and (c) failing to prevent Chinese fishermen from fishing in the zone. The Tribunal also held that fishermen from the Philippines (like those from China) had traditional fishing rights at Scarborough Shoal and that China had interfered with these rights in restricting access. The Tribunal further held that Chinese law enforcement vessels had unlawfully created a serious risk of collision when they physically obstructed Philippine vessels.

Continental Shelf: In 1958, the first United Nations Conference on the Law of the Sea accepted a definition adopted by the International Law Commission, which defined the continental shelf to include:

> "*the seabed and subsoil of the submarine areas adjacent to the coast but outside the area of the territorial sea, to a depth of 200 meters, or, beyond that limit, to where the depth of the superjacent waters admits of the exploitation of the natural resources....*"

Already, as the Third United Nations Conference on the Law of the Sea got under way, there was a strong consensus in favor of extending coastal-State control over ocean resources out to 200 miles from shore so that the outer limit coincides with that of the EEZ.[254] But the Conference had to tackle the demand by States with a geographical shelf extending beyond 200 miles for wider economic jurisdiction. The Convention resolves conflicting claims, interpretations and measuring techniques by setting the 200-mile EEZ limit as the boundary of the continental shelf for seabed and subsoil exploitation, satisfying the geologically disadvantaged. It satisfied those nations with a broader shelf - about 30 States, including Argentina, Australia, Canada, India, Madagascar, Mexico, Sri Lanka and France with respect to its overseas possessions - by giving them the possibility of establishing a boundary going out to 350 miles from their shores or further, depending on certain geological criteria. Thus, the continental shelf of a coastal State comprises the seabed and its subsoil that extend beyond the limits of its territorial sea throughout the natural prolongation of its land territory to the outer edge of the continental margin, or to a distance of 200 miles from the baselines from which the territorial sea is measured, where the outer edge of the continental margin does not extend up to that distance. In cases where the continental margin extends further than 200 miles, nations may claim jurisdiction up to 350 miles from the baseline or

---

[254] See deliberations of Second Committee at the UN Conference on Law of Sea 1973

100 miles from the 2,500-meter depth, depending on certain criteria such as the thickness of sedimentary deposits. These rights would not affect the legal status of the waters or that of the airspace above the continental shelf. To counterbalance the continental shelf extensions, coastal States must also contribute to a system of sharing the revenue derived from the exploitation of mineral resources beyond 200 miles. These payments or contributions - from which developing countries that are net importers of the mineral in question are exempt - are to be equitably distributed among States parties to the Convention through the International Seabed Authority. To control the claims extending beyond 200 miles, the Commission on the Limits of the Continental Shelf was established to consider the data submitted by the coastal States and make recommendations.

> *Case concerning Bangladesh and Myanmar*[255]
> The dispute concerned the delimitation of the maritime boundary between Bangladesh and Myanmar in the Bay of Bengal with respect to the territorial sea, the exclusive economic zone and the continental shelf. It **was the first case of the Tribunal relating to the delimitation of maritime boundaries**. Proceedings in the case were instituted before the Tribunal on 14 December 2009. Further to the filing of written pleadings by the Parties, the hearing took place in September 2011. In its judgment, the Tribunal had to address a number of issues raised by the Parties. Those included: the claim made by Bangladesh that the delimitation of the territorial sea had already been agreed by the Parties in 1974; and the delimitation of the exclusive economic zone and continental shelf within 200 nautical miles from the baselines from which the breadth of the territorial sea is measured. In addition, the Tribunal had to deal with the request

---

[255] *Dispute concerning Delimitation of the Maritime Boundary between Bangladesh and Myanmar in the Bay of Bengal between The People's Republic of Bangladesh* Case No. 16 Judgement dated 14 March 2012

> of Bangladesh that the continental shelf beyond 200 nautical miles limit be delimited, a request which was opposed by Myanmar. The Tribunal then had to decide whether it could and should exercise its jurisdiction in respect of the delimitation of the continental shelf beyond 200 nautical miles. Among other things, the Tribunal noted that the legal regime of the continental shelf has always coexisted with another legal regime in the same area. Initially that other regime was that of the high seas and the other States concerned were those exercising high seas freedoms. Under the Convention, as a result of maritime delimitation, there may also be concurrent exclusive economic zone rights of another coastal State. In such a situation, pursuant to the principle reflected in the provisions of articles 56, 58, 78 and 79 and in other provisions of the Convention, each coastal State must exercise its rights and perform its duties with due regard to the rights and duties of the other. There are many ways in which the Parties may ensure the discharge of their obligations in this respect, including the conclusion of specific agreements or the establishment of appropriate cooperative arrangements. It is for the Parties to determine the measures that they consider appropriate for this purpose.

Deep sea mining: Mining will take place at a depth of more than fifteen thousand feet of open ocean, thousands of miles from land.[256] In the 1950s, the potential of sea bed deposits as sources of minerals such as nickel, copper and cobalt was being acknowledged.[257] Between 1958 and 1968, numerous companies began serious prospecting of the nodule fields to estimate their

---

[256] William Wertenbaker, *"The Law of the Sea"* **The New Yorker**, Vol. 59, Part 4 p. 59
[257] The United Nations Convention on the Law of the Sea: A historical Perspective (Division of Ocean Affairs and the Law of Sea, 1998)

economic potential.²⁵⁸ By 1974, it was well established that a broad belt of sea floor between Mexico and Hawaii and a few degrees north of the equator.²⁵⁹ A factsheet on this zone describes it as spread over 1.7 million square miles. ²⁶⁰ This region is also called as the *Clarion Clipperton zone*. In 1970 the United Nations General Assembly declared the resources of the seabed beyond the limits of national jurisdiction to be *the common heritage of mankind*.²⁶¹

> ISA updates: *No mining operations have commenced. Currently, exploration activities undertaken aimed at gathering the necessary information on the location and quality of the minerals of the seabed as well as to collect all the necessary environmental information. To date, ISA has approved 30 contracts for exploration involving 22 different countries and covering more than 1.3 million km² of the seabed. This represents 0.7% of international deep seabed area and 0.3% of world's oceans. 12 of these contracts are sponsored by developing countries. 13 countries and one intergovernmental consortium currently have contracts for the exploration of polymetallic nodules, 7 countries for the exploration of polymetallic sapphires, and 5 for the exploration of cobalt-rich ferromanganese crusts. Mining code when completed, will provide a holistic regulatory framework for the exploitation of the resources in the Area, reinforcing provisions of the Convention especially for effective protection of the marine environment, biodiversity and life.*²⁶²

---

[258] Baldeo Sahai, **Indian Navy, A perspective: From the Earliest Period to Modern Times** (Ministry of Information and Broadcasting of India Publications Division, New Delhi, 2006) p. 120

[259] Rand McNally, **Atlas of The Oceans** (Rand McNally & Company, Chicago, 1987) p. 165

[260] Pew Trust Factsheet on The Clarion-Clipperton Zone Dec 2017; https://www.pewtrusts.org/en/research-and-analysis/fact-sheets/2017/12/the-clarion-clipperton-zone; website accessed on 17 April 2020

[261] General Assembly resolution 2749 (XXV) of 17 December 1970

[262] https://www.isa.org.jm/frequently-asked-questions-faqs; website accessed on 17 April 2020

Dispute Resolution mechanisms under the UNCLOS III

During the drafting of the Convention, some countries were opposed in principle to binding settlement to be decided by third party judges or arbitrators, insisting that issues could best be resolved by direct negotiations between States without requiring them to bring in outsiders. Others, pointing to a history of failed negotiations and long-standing disputes often leading to a use of force, argued that the only sure chance for peaceful settlement lay in the willingness of States to bind themselves in advance to accept the decisions of judicial bodies.[263] What emerged from the negotiations was a combination of the two approaches, regarded by many as a landmark in international law.[264] If direct talks between the parties fail, the Convention gives them a choice among four procedural options, namely, submission to ITLOS, adjudication by ICJ, submission to international arbitration and lastly submission to special arbitration tribunals. All of these procedures involve binding third-party settlement, in which an agent other than the parties directly involved hands down a decision that the parties are committed in advance to respect.[265] The only exception to these provisions is made for sensitive cases involving national sovereignty. In such circumstances, the parties are obliged to submit their dispute to a conciliation commission, but they will not be bound by any decision or finding of the commission.[266]. The Convention also contains so-called *optional exceptions*, which can be specified at the time a country signs, ratifies or accedes to the

---

[263] Charles Chernor Jalloh, Olufemi Elias, **Shielding Humanity: Essays in International Law in Honour of Judge Abdul G Koroma** (Koninklijke-Brill, Leiden, 2015) p. 143

[264] Clifford E. Griffin, **The Race for Fisheries and Hydrocarbons in the Caribbean Basin** (Ian Randle Publishers, Kingston, 2007) p. 40

[265] See generally, The United Nations Convention on the Law of the Sea: A historical Perspective (Division of Ocean Affairs and the Law of Sea, 1998)

[266] UNCLOS at 30 (United Nations, New York, 2012)

Convention or at any later time.²⁶⁷ In respect of existing disputes pertaining to military activities or matters under deliberations of the UNSC matters, Parties to such dispute may declare not to be bound by one or more of the mandatory procedures. Disputes over seabed activities will be arbitrated by an 11-member Seabed Disputes Chamber, within the International Tribunal for the Law of the Sea.²⁶⁸ The Chamber has compulsory jurisdiction over all such conflicts, whether involving States, the International Seabed Authority or companies or individuals having seabed mining contracts.²⁶⁹

> *Jurisdiction of the ITLOS*
> *"The jurisdiction of the Tribunal comprises all disputes and all applications submitted to it in accordance with this Convention and all matters specifically provided for in any other agreement which confers jurisdiction on the Tribunal."*²⁷⁰
> The Tribunal is vested with contentious and advisory jurisdiction
> *Contentious jurisdiction:* This type of jurisdiction is exercised by ITLOS vis a vis all disputes pertaining to interpretation and application of UNCLOS subject to the provisions of art. 297²⁷¹ and

---

[267] Art. 298 of the United Nations Convention on the Law of the Sea of 1982

[268] Yoshifumi Tanaka, **The International Law of the Sea** (Third Edition, Cambridge University Press, Cambridge, 2019) p. 513

[269] Art. 187 supra note 267

[270] Art. 21 Statute of the International Tribunal for the Law of The Sea

[271] Note: *"When signing, ratifying or acceding to this Convention or at any time thereafter, a State shall be free to choose, by means of a written declaration, one or more of the following means for the settlement of disputes concerning the interpretation or application of this Convention:*
(a) the International Tribunal for the Law of the Sea established in accordance with Annex VI;
(b) the International Court of Justice;
(c) an arbitral tribunal constituted in accordance with Annex VII;
(d) a special arbitral tribunal constituted in accordance with

to the declarations made in accordance with art. 298. However, neither provision precludes parties to a dispute from agreeing to submit to the jurisdiction of ITLOS.[272] The Tribunal also has jurisdiction over all disputes and all applications submitted to it pursuant to the provisions of any other agreement conferring jurisdiction on the Tribunal.

Advisory jurisdiction: The Seabed Disputes Chamber is vested with the power to provide advisory opinion on legal questions falling within the mandate of the ISA's Assembly or Council.[273] The ITLOS is also competent to provide advisory opinion on a legal question pursuant to *"an international agreement related to the purposes of the Convention."*[274]

International Seabed Authority (ISA): Part XI of the UNCLOS is administered by the International Seabed Authority, headquartered in Jamaica.[275] The Authority is divided into three principal organs, an *Assembly*, a *Council* and a *Secretariat* headed by a secretary-general.[276] The *Assembly*, comprises of all members of the Authority with power to set general policy.[277] The *Council* is vested with powers to make executive decisions. It comprises of 36

Annex VIII for one or more of the categories of disputes specified therein" Art. 287 (1) of UNCLOS 1982

[272] Art. 299 of the UNCLOS 1982 *states "A dispute excluded under art. 297 or excepted by a declaration made under art. 298 from the dispute settlement procedures provided for in section 2 may be submitted to such procedures only by agreement of the parties to the dispute"*

[273] Art. 191 of the UNCLOS 1982

[274] Art. 138, Rules of the Tribunal

[275] Art. 156 (4) of the UNCLOS 1982, See also Agreement between The International Seabed Authority and The Government of Jamaica Regarding The Headquarters Of The International Seabed Authority

[276] See generally Rules of Procedure of The Assembly of The International Seabed Authority 1994

[277] Art. 159 of the UNCLOS 1982

members elected from among the members of the Authority.[278] The ISA is comprised of 167 Member States, and the European Union.[279] ISA is mandated as the organization through which Parties to UNCLOS shall organize and control all mineral-related activities in the international seabed area, known also as *the Area*.[280] The international seabed area is the seabed and ocean floor and the subsoil thereof, beyond the limits of national jurisdiction. The international seabed area represents around 54 per cent of the total area of the world's oceans.[281] ISA registered seven Voluntary Commitments at the 2017 UN Conference on Oceans aimed at achieving concretely one or more goals and targets of the 2030 Agenda.[282] Five are directly oriented to reinforce ISA's efforts towards developing countries and in particular, Small Island Developing States (SIDS), Least Developed Countries (LDCs), and Land Locked Developing Countries (LLDCs). These include promoting marine scientific research, enhancing the role of women in research, increasing the socio-economic benefits for SIDS, and supporting Africa's Blue Economy. ISA takes all necessary measures in accordance with UNCLOS to ensure the effective protection of the marine environment, including marine biodiversity from harmful effects which may arise from activities in the Area. This is a core part of ISA's mandate. The draft regulations for deep seabed mining will incorporate specific provisions to ensure the effective protection of the marine environment and conservation of marine biodiversity, human

---

[278] For composition of council from 1996-2020 see https://ran-s3.s3.amazonaws.com/isa.org.jm/s3fs-public/files/documents/council1996-2020-i.pdf website accessed on 12 April 2020

[279] https://www.isa.org.jm/member-states; website accessed on May 2020

[280] Art. 157 of the UNCLOS 1982

[281] ISA Secretary-General Michael W Lodge, *Strengthening the participation of women and girls in ocean science to achieve the Sustainable Development Goals,*" **ISA Opinion Pieces,** 10 February 2020

[282] Voluntary Commitments Registered at the 2017 Ocean Conference

health and safety and equitable sharing of financial and other economic benefits. ISA also established a Regional Environmental Management Plan (REMP) in the Clarion-Clapperton-Zone in 2012.[283] The REMP is an area-based management tool and the 2012 document comprising of nine Areas of Particular Environmental Interests (APEIs), where mining is prohibited. The ISA is in the process of developing REMPs in other areas where exploration contracts have been granted.

Commission on the Limits of the Continental Shelf (CLCS): The purpose of CLCS is to facilitate the implementation of the UNCLOS III in respect of the establishment of the outer limits of the continental shelf beyond 200 nautical miles from the baselines from which the breadth of the territorial sea is measured.[284] Under the Convention, the coastal State shall establish the outer limits of its continental shelf where it extends beyond 200 nautical miles.[285] The Commission shall make recommendations to coastal States on matters related to the establishment of those limits;[286] its recommendations and actions shall not prejudice matters relating to the delimitation of boundaries between States with opposite or adjacent coasts.[287] The Commission, in practice meets twice a year, but is expected to meet at least once a year,[288] ordinarily at the UN Headquarters in New York.[289] The convening of these sessions and services to be provided are subject to approval by the General

---

[283] Decision of the Council relating to an environmental management plan for the Clarion-Clipperton Zone 2012, ISBA/18/C/22

[284] Art. 1 Annex II, Commission on The Limits of The Continental Shelf, UNCLOS III 1982

[285] Art. 76 of the United Nations Convention on the Law of the Sea of 1982

[286] See art. 3,4 and 7 Annex II, Commission on The Limits Of The Continental Shelf, UNCLOS III 1982

[287] Art. 9 *Ibid*

[288] Rule 2, Rules of Procedure of the Commission on the Limits of the Continental Shelf of 2008

[289] Rule 4 *Ibid*

Assembly of the United Nations in its annual resolutions on oceans and the law of the sea.[290]

Order in the Indian Ocean – A case study
The Indian Ocean Region has increased in strategic value in recent times. Home to 36 countries,[291] housing six regional seas,[292] she measures about 70 million square kilometers,[293] connecting three continents--Africa towards her west, Asia to her North and Australia to her east. In terms of the earths' ocean basins, one has to cross the Indian ocean to reach the Atlantic to her west and the Pacific, eastwards. Historically, intertwined with the Mediterranean and Persian civilizations by culture, trade and commerce, the Indian Ocean has witnessed the rise and fall of empires and nation-states during its 4000-year-old documented maritime connectivity.[294] Since the turn of 20th Century, the Indian Ocean had a checkered period with extra regional powers exercising influence. It was named *British lake*,[295] challenged by

---

[290] Rule 3, 5, 16 *Ibid*
[291] South Africa, Mozambique, Madagascar, Mauritius, Comoros, Tanzania, Seychelles, Kenya, Somalia, Somaliland, Djibouti, Eritrea, Sudan, Egypt, Israel, Jordan, Saudi Arabia, Yemen, Oman, United Arab Emirates, Qatar, Bahrain, Kuwait, India, Iran, Iraq, Pakistan, Maldives, Sri Lanka, Bangladesh, Myanmar, Thailand, Malaysia, Singapore, Indonesia, Timor-Leste, Australia
[292] Andaman Sea, Arabian Sea, Bay of Bengal, Laccadive Sea, Red Sea, Timor Sea
[293] https://www.ngdc.noaa.gov/mgg/global/etopo1_ocean_volumes.pdf; website accessed on 21 April 2020
[294] EA Alpers, **The Indian Ocean in World History** (Oxford University Press, 2013)
[295] A. Johnson, **The British empire in the Indian Ocean, Geopolitical Orientations, Regionalism and Security in the Indian Ocean** (South Asian Publishers, New Delhi, 2004) pp.34–55 for contra view of description of Indian Ocean as the British Lake see H. V. Bowen,

Japanese raids,[296] shadowed by nuclearization,[297] dominated by US[298] and attracted considerable attention from China.[299] During the last two decades a fragile peace has taken over the Indian Ocean region. By one account maritime traffic has increased by 300 per cent over a short span of 20 years (1992-2012)[300] and with approximately 1,20,000 ships crisscrossing the Indian Ocean on a yearly basis.[301] About a third of the global population live in the littoral countries of the Indian Ocean region.[302] These shipping lanes provide access to about two-thirds of global oil, one-half of container traffic and one-third of global cargo.[303] It has become an increasingly crowded space. Interestingly a significant portion of this traffic serves the demand of non-littoral states and states which are located beyond the IOR region. This in particular has increased the stakes of the Indian Ocean contributing to its strategic value.

Britain's Oceanic Empire: Atlantic and Indian Ocean Worlds (Cambridge University Press, New York, 2012) p. 52

[296] David H. Lippman, *"The Indian Ocean Raid: Disaster for the Royal Navy"* War History Network; https://warfarehistorynetwork.com/2016/11/30/the-indian-ocean-raid-disaster-for-the-royal-navy/; website accessed on 22 April 2020

[297] TT Poulose, **Indian Ocean Power Rivalry** (Young Asia Publications, New Delhi, 1974) p. 201

[298] US Military interest and presence in the Indian Ocean region is largely attributed to the reactivation of the US 5th Fleet in 1995. See Akhilesh Pillalamarri, *"A Brief History of the US Navy in the Indian Ocean,"* **The Diplomat** dated 14 October 2015

[299] Bertil Lintner, **The Costliest Pearl: China's Struggle for India's Ocean** (Hurst Publishers, London, 2019)

[300] Jean Tournadre, *"Anthropogenic pressure on the open ocean: The growth of ship traffic revealed by altimeter data analysis"* 2014 **Geophysical Research Letters** Vol. 41 No. 22 pp. 7924-7932

[301] Statement by Indian Navy Chief Admiral R K Dhowan at a Press Conference in New Delhi dated 12 July 2018

[302] Vijay Sakhuja and Kapil Narula, **Maritime Safety and Security in the Indian Ocean** (National Maritime Foundation, Gandhinagar, 2016)

[303] *Ibid*

Simultaneously, the land mass in particular of Asia, has undergone significant political and economic transformation. 33 of 36 Indian Ocean Littoral countries attained independence during the 20th Century from colonial powers.[304] 35 of the 36 countries share a colonial history[305] and 31 attained independence after world war II.[306] Moving on to the economic transition, some important trends are to be noted. In a background paper prepared by the Lakshman Kadirgamar Institute of International Relations and Strategic Studies for an International Conference on Indian Ocean Region the following estimates were flagged: 28 states of the IOR in the global economy[307] accounted for 15.7% of world trade and 18.5% of global GDP.[308] Speaking at the occasion, former Sri Lankan Prime Minister

---

[304] South Africa, Mozambique, Madagascar, Mauritius, Comoros, Tanganyika and Zanzibar merged into Tanzania, Seychelles, Kenya, Somalia, Somaliland, Djibouti, Eritrea, Sudan, Egypt, Israel, Jordan, Yemen, Oman, United Arab Emirates, Qatar, Bahrain, Kuwait, India, Iraq, Pakistan, Maldives, Sri Lanka, Bangladesh, Myanmar, Malaysia, Singapore, Indonesia, Timor-Leste, Australia

[305] Iran and Thailand did manage to retain their independence but had been significantly under the influence of Colonial Powers; for Colonialism in Iran see H. Lyman Stebbins, **British Imperialism in Qajar Iran: Consuls, Agents and Influence in the Middle East** (Bloomsbury Academic, London, 2017), for Colonialism in Thailand see Thanet Aphornsuvan, **Rebellion in Southern Thailand: Contending Histories** (East West Center, Washington DC, 2007)

[306] South Africa (1910) and Egypt (1922) became independent prior to World War II

[307] This includes Australia, Bangladesh, Brunei Darussalam, Cambodia, Comoros, India, Indonesia, Iran or Islamic Republic of Iran, Kenya, Madagascar, Malaysia, the Maldives, Mauritius, Mozambique, Myanmar, Oman, Pakistan, Seychelles, Singapore, Somalia, South Africa, Sri Lanka, Timor-Leste, Thailand, the United Arab Emirates, United Republic of Tanzania, Viet Nam, and Yemen.

[308] https://www.lki.lk/wp-content/uploads/2019/05/Navigating-Challenges-and-Prospects-in-the-Indian-Ocean-Towards-a-shared-understanding.pdf; website accessed on 22 April 2020

Ranil Wickremesinghe recalled the commitment and contribution of Sri Lanka towards a rules based order in the maritime domain when Sri Lanka chaired the momentous UN Conference on the Law of the Sea in 1973, which led to the adoption of the UNCLOS. He also highlighted the leadership of the late Mrs. Sirimavo Bandaranaike in declaring the Indian Ocean as a Zone of Peace at the UN General Assembly as early as 1971. Explaining the importance of Sri Lanka taking leadership in the dialogue process, Ranil Wickremesinghe stated, *"we see the imperative for strengthening the regional rules-based order, which treats small and large countries alike. Smaller states have a long history of advocating for a rules-based order. In the multipolar world of the Indian Ocean, where there is no overarching security architecture or unilateral security guarantor, it is imperative that only a shared understanding based on rules-based order will ensure the security of both larger and smaller states."*

Shivshankar Menon, on the future for a stable order in Asia has identified three scenarios as possible choices (a) an order centered around a single power (b) an order based on G2 and (c) an issue-based coalition, indicating the third choice as a potentially more viable option.[309] History does provide invaluable lessons and perhaps the most important among them is to not draw inapplicable analogies to contemporary scenarios. Global power distribution is unprecedented. Drawing inspiration from past models such as *Pax Romana, Pax Britannica* or *Pax Americana* would be unwise given the diverse accumulation of power. Sri Lankas' Vision 2030 Document in the context of International Relations states *"Sri Lanka continues to conduct its foreign relations in an independent and non-aligned manner, and pursues its foreign policy with the aim to make Sri Lanka safer and more prosperous through beneficial bilateral and multi-stakeholder partnerships... The Global power is transitioning from the west to the east and a maritime super region is*

---

[309] Speech by Shivshankar Menon titled *The New Asian Geopolitics* at Institute for Human Sciences (IWM), Vienna 29 Sep 2019

envisaged with the Asian Oceans at its center."[310] This statement augers well for non-aligned countries as well as multi-regional and extra-regional powers.

Challenges in the Indian Ocean Region

There are a number of challenges in the Indian Ocean Region. First, is the phenomenon of *trade* and controllable *choke points*. The intensity of trade over the Indian Oceans has been highlighted above. In the Indian Ocean these choke points include the Strait of Hormuz, the Suez Canal, the Straits of Bab-el Mandeb, Malacca Straits, Lombok Straits, Sunda Strait, Six Degree Channel, Nine Degree Channel and the Cape of Good Hope. Amongst these, Hormuz and Malacca are particularly significant in terms of oil transportation (during 2011-2016).[311] States are cognizant of the existence of narrow straights that drastically reduce the time and cost for maritime transportation. One may recall former Chinese President Hu Jintao's *Malaccan dilemma* in light of dependence on imported oil through straits. The salience of chokepoints is expected to continue until a cheaper and quicker alternative is available. One fall-out of this geographical reality is the desire to maintain control towards free flow and movement of cargo. In this context there has been tensions with the emergence of new ports. Part of the tensions arise from the dual-use capacity of civilian sea ports.

Secondly, sea-based transportation scores over land and air on the basis of time taken and cost incurred in mass transportation. The latest addition is the undersea – pipeline transportation. This option has its limitations and is linked to average depth/height of

---

[310] Sustainable Sri Lanka 2030 Vision and Strategic Path (Presidential Expert Committee) 2019; http://www.presidentsoffice.gov.lk/wp-content/uploads/2019/05/Final-v2.4-Typeset-MM-v12F-Cov3.pdf p. 25

[311] Report of US Energy Information Administration titled, *World Oil Transit Chokepoints*, July, 2017

the seabed. By one estimate, complete operationalization of Indian Ocean pipelines is expected to support around 25 per cent of existing transported material.[312] In this context, innovation in expeditious and cost-effective transportation over the sea is an avenue for multilateral cooperation.

Thirdly the existence of *outside powers* and *inside powers* in the context of Indian Ocean region. The UNCLOS of 1982 provides an agreed legal regime for peaceful and legitimate use of the ocean but stops short of providing a Code of Conduct on the High Seas. It is a realty that the Indian peninsula extends into the ocean with a vast expanse of the Lakshadweep and Andamans Islands. In light of this reality it is natural that India and the littoral states are the *de facto* first responders for a variety of reasons. The military presence of outside powers is a matter of concern.

Fourthly, the problem of *piracy* and *floating armories*. There have been times in history when escort vehicles have guarded merchant ships and pirates have served as navies. The latter has been outlawed under the UNCLOS,[313] whereas floating armories operate in a gray zone. Instances such as *USS Seaman Guard Ohio* entering territorial waters have been addressed through judicial processes,[314] the problem of floating armories is a continuing one in the Indian Ocean Region.[315] This is supposedly linked to address

---

[312] Key note address by Vice Chief of Indian Navy, Ashok Kumar at International Conference on India and the Indian Ocean Region: Dynamics of Geopolitics, Security, and Global Commons (The Peninsula Foundation), 12 July 2019

[313] Articles 100-107 and 110 of the United Nations Convention on the Law of the Sea (UNCLOS), 1982

[314] https://www.maritime-executive.com/editorials/seaman-guard-ohio-crew-acquitted; website accessed on 22 April 2020

[315] Chapsos, Ioannis & Holtom, Paul, *"Stockpiles at Sea: Floating Armories in the Indian Ocean"* Weapons and the World - Small Arms Survey Yearbook 2015

the problem of piracy. However, such unregulated travel could be a source of potential tension between states.

Fifthly, the problem of terrorism, gun running, illegal arms and human trafficking and drug smuggling over the Indian Ocean. The disarray in the oil rich Persian-gulf is reflected eastward into the sea. Piracy has also shifted beyond the Somalian coast. These problems have heightened post 9/11. The spread of violent extremism in some parts of South Asia is a matter of concern. The *Easter attacks* in Colombo are a case in point. Violent extremism has also manifested in attacks by the sea e.g. the *Mumbai attacks*.

Multilateralism over the Waters
A number of multilateral initiatives have emerged in the last two decades. The composition has been varied, comprising of *inside powers*, some comprise of a combination of *inside* and *outside powers*, given the geographical construct of the region. Their efficiency has been varied. As such, trends indicate that the older, post-world war II multilateral institutions are gradually losing relevance.[316] Newer coalitions appear to hold promise, some to deal with the foregoing challenges and other to facilitate economic aspirations.

Indo-Pacific: The global/regional security dimension is enmeshed into the global energy dimension in multiple ways in the Indo-Pacific region. While there is no one agreed upon definition of Indo-Pacific, there is consensus that the Indo-Pacific region has all the qualifications to become the new center of gravity in global politics. The United States has had and maintained considerable strategic advantages in this region since the period of World War Two. The ANZUS Treaty parties had to agree to undo their alliance on account of the changed position of one of allies, namely New Zealand in respect of both energy and security-nuclear energy and

---

[316] Sunod Jacob, "*Withering away of World War II era Multilateralism,*" **Modern Diplomacy** dated 14 December 2019

nuclear-powered submarines.³¹⁷ In the case of the ASEAN, the Treaty of Amity and Cooperation (TAC) provided the comfort and advantage of joint action among the ten countries³¹⁸ which got a boost in 1986 with the Agreement on Energy Cooperation and the ASEAN Petroleum Security Agreement. The TAC also influenced the ASEAN-sponsored Declaration on the Conduct of Parties in the South China Sea in November 2002 under which China also agreed to shelve disputes and undertake joint development of energy resources in the South China Sea. Japanese Prime Minister Shinzo Abe's Free and Open Indo-Pacific has three pillars.³¹⁹ Pillar One, promotion and establishment of rule of law, freedom of navigation and free trade. Pillar Two, pursuit of economic prosperity. Pillar three, commitment for peace and stability (capacity building on maritime law enforcement, HA/DR cooperation). In Sri Lanka, the main mechanism is the India-Japan Cooperation, such as the development of LNG-related infrastructure. For the United States policy, it would be useful to refer to the US Department of state document of November 2019 titled, *A Free and Open Indo-Pacific: A shared vision*.³²⁰ The highlights of the energy dimension in this document are as follows:

---

[317] Amy L. Catalinac, "Why New Zealand Took Itself out of ANZUS: Observing Opposition for Autonomy' in Asymmetric Alliances," **Foreign Policy Analysis** (2010) 6, pp. 317–338

[318] The 1986 Agreement was supported by the ASEAN vision of **economic resilience** enshrined in Art. 11 of the TAC Agreement in the following manner;
The high Contracting Parties shall endeavor to strengthen their respective national resilience in their political, economic, sociocultural as well as security fields in conformity with their respective ideals and aspirations, free from external interference as well as internal subversive activities in order to preserve their respective national identities"

[319] https://www.mofa.go.jp/files/000430632.pdf; website accessed on 28 March 2020

[320] **A Free and Open Indo-Pacific Advancing A Shared Vision**, US Department of State, 4 Nov 2019

> The International Energy Agency projects that the Indo-Pacific region will account for approximately 60 percent of global growth in energy demand by 2040, requiring more than USD 1 trillion in annual energy infrastructure investment. To meet this, countries will need access to safe trade routes.
> USAID's 2019 partnership with the ADB to mobilize USD 7 billion of energy investments for projects in Asia and the Pacific seeks to boost the capacity of clean energy systems by six gigawatts and increase regional energy trade by 10 percent over the next five years.
> India is also a growing energy partner, with purchases of U.S. mineral fuel products jumping 119 percent in 2018 alone to USD 6.2 billion. Under the U.S.-India Strategic Energy Partnership, cooperation in power, renewable, efficiency, and oil/gas segments are being pursued.

Under PM Narendra Modi, India has been actively fleshing out the Indo-Pacific concept. His Government's Act East policy plays a central role in it. He outlined India's own vision of the Indo-Pacific in Singapore in June 2018.[321] Then along with Indonesian President Widodo he set out a Shared Vision on Maritime Cooperation in the Indo-Pacific.[322] At the East Asia Summit in Bangkok in November 2019, Prime Minister Modi suggested an Indo-Pacific Oceans' Initiative.[323] In point four, Prime Minister Modi notes, "*We should all have equal access as a right under international law to the use of common spaces on sea..we all agree to live by that code, our sea lanes will be pathways to prosperity and corridors of peace.*"

---

[321] Prime Minister of India's Keynote Address, Shangri La Dialogue, 1 June 2018

[322] Shared Vision of India-Indonesia Maritime Cooperation in the Indo-Pacific, **India-Indonesia Bilateral Joint Statement**, 30 May 2018

[323] Prime Minister of India's Statement at the East Asia Summit, 4 November 2019

The starting point for Australia's acknowledgment of the Indo-Pacific concept traces back to its 2009 Defense White Paper.[324] While the Indian Ocean was initially considered less a strategic priority, its future importance was flagged: *"The Indian Ocean will have an increasingly strategic role to play... Australian defence planning will have to contemplate operational concepts for operating in the Indian Ocean region, including with regional partners with whom we share similar strategic interests."* This setting paved the way for the 2012 White Paper, Australia in the Asian Century, in which Indo-Pacific was referred to as a *"regional construct... linking the Indian and Pacific oceans as one strategic arc that includes Southeast Asia..."* This Indo-Pacific construct was Australia's prime consideration in its 2013 Defence White Paper, and was reiterated in the 2016 Defence White Paper and the 2017 Foreign Policy White Paper. Chapter three of the 2017 Foreign Policy White Paper of the Australian Government is devoted to *A stable and prosperous Indo–Pacific*.[325] The policies to support a stable and prosperous Indo–Pacific and which in their description *"complement our trade, investment and economic engagement with the region"* were fleshed out in chapter four. Specifically, on energy it states,

> *"Global developments in energy technology and consumption will influence demand for major Australian exports like iron ore, coal and LNG. The increasing use of high efficiency, low-emission coal technologies, cleaner gas plants and advances in renewable energy and carbon capture and storage technologies will create export and investment opportunities for Australia. Even so, global energy markets are becoming more competitive, including because of the exploitation of unconventional energy reserves in the United States, and more responsive to changing demand."*

---

[324] Lloyd Alexander M. Adducul, "The Indo-Pacific Construct in Australia's White Papers: Reflections for ASEAN-Australia Future Strategic Partnership" **Center for International Relations and Strategic Studies Commentary, Foreign Service Institute,** Vol. V, No. 6, March 2018

[325] Australian Government Foreign Policy White Paper, 2017

QUAD: The meeting of the Quad group of countries, namely India, Japan, Australia and USA have been in place for a while (since 2007). In the first decade of the 21st century the momentum petered out in view of the divergent position with regards to China.[326] In recent years, there has been minor progress with meetings being incrementally scaled up. In one assessment, it was argued that following the first meeting in November 2017 of the resurrected Quadrilateral Security Dialogue, the US has been consistent in discussing the security objectives it seeks to promote through the consultations.[327] However, US interactions with other QUAD partners appears to have convinced Washington to repackage public presentation of the dialogues and manage its expectations of what QUAD can realistically achieve.[328] The absence of a joint statement by the four countries after their meetings has been commented upon.[329]

Belt and Road Initiative: The National Development and Reform Commission (NDRC) and the National Energy Administration (NEA) of China jointly drafted and published a white paper in May 2017.[330] The white paper identified that the cooperation must adhere to the following principles: open and inclusive; seeks mutual benefit; is market-oriented; safe and secure; green and efficient; and the cooperation will be harmonious. The cooperation

---

[326] Cary Huang, *"US, Japan, India, Australia ... is Quad the first step to an Asian NATO?"* **South China Morning Post**, 25 Nov, 2017

[327] Derek Grossman, *"How the U.S. Is Thinking About the Quad"*, **Australian Strategic Policy Institute Commentary** 7 February 20

[328] Sunod Jacob, **Post Millennium Trends in the Global Energy Security Architecture** (BV, 2020)

[329] A Gnanasagaran, *"Is the Quad still relevant?"* **The Asean Post**, 5 December 2018; See also: Mark J. Valencia, *"The Quad: Whistling by Its Grave – Analysis,"* **Eurasia Review**, 20 March 2019

[330] Vision and Actions on Energy Cooperation in Jointly Building Silk Road Economic Belt and 21st-Century Maritime Silk Road, (BRI Official Document) 2017

priorities were: Policy coordination; Unimpeded trade; Energy investment cooperation; Energy production capacity cooperation; Energy infrastructure connectivity; Sustainable energy for all; & Better global energy governance structure. According to a May 2017 report[331] by the Office of the Leading Group for the Belt and Road Initiative titled, *Building the Belt and Road: Concept, Practice and China's Contribution,* China is active in cooperating with relevant countries to promote their energy connectivity, build oil, gas and power infrastructure, maintain the safe operation of cross-border oil and gas pipelines, and optimize the distribution of energy resources among countries and regions.

In recent years, some of the BRI projects have become controversial as they were causing excessive debt obligations for the recipient countries and there were also socio-economic problems being created in the wake. Others have cited environmental concerns, as Chinese companies build coal power projects around the world.[332] China's approach towards the arbitration that was instituted at the Permanent Court of Arbitration at The Hague by The Philippines in respect of entitlements in the South China Sea is also instructive. While it did not join the arbitration, China made its position clear in a White Paper in July 2013.[333] Regarding energy, the Middle Kingdom drew a connect between freedom and safety of navigation in the South China Sea and energy access. The White Paper also stressed the public goods argument by mentioning that it had *"made every effort to provide services, such as navigation and navigational aids, search and rescue, as well as sea conditions and*

---

[331] Office of the Leading Group for the Belt and Road Initiative, **Building the Belt and Road: Concept, Practice and China's Contribution,** (Foreign Languages Press, Beijing, 2017)

[332] *"Belt and Road forum: China's 'project of the century' hits tough times,"* **The Guardian,** 25th April 2019

[333] https://www.fmprc.gov.cn/nanhai/eng/snhwtlcwj_1/t1380615.htm; website accessed on 28 March 2020

meteorological forecast, through capacity building in various areas."

Eventually, the unanimous award issued on 12 July 2016 found that China had violated the Philippines' sovereign rights in its exclusive economic zone amongst other things by interfering with Philippine fishing and petroleum exploration. The award found that China's claim to historic rights to resources was incompatible with the detailed allocation of rights and maritime zones in the UNCLOS. While the stated aim of China and the ASEAN side is to hammer out a Code of Conduct by 2021, the fact is that the earlier document, namely the 2002 Declaration of Conduct of Parties in the South China Sea has proved inept in the circumstances.

Blue Economy: Unlike the above-mentioned approaches which have been fairly successful with the exception of the QUAD, the blue economy initiatives in the Indian Ocean Region have been slow in evolution. Take the case of the Indian Ocean Rim Association [IORA] which had blue economy as the special focus at the 14th IORA Ministerial Meeting in Perth in October 2014 and the First IORA Ministerial Blue Economy Conference (BEC) which was held in Mauritius on 2-3 September 2015 where the Blue Economy Declaration was adopted. As on date, the six priority pillars of IORA Secretariat areas-of-work are: Fisheries and Aquaculture; Renewable Ocean Energy; Seaports and Shipping; Offshore Hydrocarbons and Seabed Minerals; Marine Biotechnology, Research and Development; and Tourism. The IORA comprises of 22 member states[334] and six dialogue partners[335] cooperating of six priority areas (Maritime Safety and Security, Trade and Investment

---

[334] Australia, Bangladesh, Comoros, India, Indonesia, Iran, Kenya, Madagascar, Malaysia, Maldives, Mauritius, Mozambique, Oman, Seychelles, Singapore, Somalia, South Africa, Sri Lanka, Tanzania, Thailand, United Arab Emirates and Yemen

[335] Italy, Japan, Germany, China, UK, USA, France Republic, Egypt, Turkey and Korea

Facilitation, Fisheries Management, Disaster Risk Management, Academic, Science and Technology Cooperation, Tourism and Cultural Exchanges and two cross-cutting areas (Blue Economy and Women's Economic Empowerment).[336] More recently, Sri Lanka led Meeting of IORA Maritime Safety and Security (MSS) Working Group in August 2019, the Work Plan for Action was finalized.[337]

Bay of Bengal Initiative for Multi-Sectoral Technical and Economic Cooperation: The situation in the case of the BIMSTEC is almost identical. At the 4th Summit of the Bay of Bengal Initiative for Multi-Sectoral Technical and Economic Cooperation held in Kathmandu, Nepal in 2018, the leaders recognized the high potential of energy resources in the region, particularly renewable and clean energy sources and decided to constitute an intergovernmental group of experts to enhance energy cooperation, including in hydro-power and other sources of renewable energy. This is small consolation for a body which has been in existence for a while (since 1997) and which has been holding summits since 2004. Specifically, on energy, an Energy Sector Committee of Experts/ Officials and Energy Ministers Conferences have been held since the turn of the century. An MoU for establishment of the BIMSTEC grid interconnection was signed in Kathmandu in August 2018 with the purpose of providing a broad framework for the Parties to cooperate towards the implementation of grid interconnections for the trade in electricity.

Indian Ocean Naval Symposium: While Blue Economy provides a conceptual vision and IORA provides a political framework for dialogue and cooperation, IONS provides a field level operational naval cooperation over the Indian ocean region. Launched in 2008,

---

[336] Annex 1 to the Charter of The Indian Ocean Rim Association (as Amended in November 2018)

[337] https://www.mfa.gov.lk/iora_wg-_eng/; accessed on 28 March 2020

it comprises of 24 littoral Navies as members[338] and 8 observers.[339] This forum is intended to facilitate peaceful relations between nations, which is a pre-requisite towards building an effective maritime security architecture in the Indian Ocean Region.[340] It comprises of Working Groups focused on issues specific to Indian Ocean region on Maritime Security, Humanitarian Assistance and Disaster Relief, Information Sharing & Interoperability. These working groups also called as IWG are smaller groupings in terms of participation. IONS is unique in relation to other multilateral institutions in the Indian Ocean region. It is voluntary, non-binding and a hence a relatively loose coalition.

Conclusion

Actors operating within the Indian Ocean region are of two varieties, those that believe in inclusive rule-based order and those who distance themselves from such notions. Some countries has envisioned has expressed an interest in crafting an Indian Ocean Order with accepted rules and agreements that would guide interactions between states. This position is particularly important in the absence of a security architecture. With US emerging as energy independent, the economic interests of the US in the Persian-gulf region are declining. Meanwhile the Chinese economic growth has fueled its appetite for oil from the very same zone and through the very same ocean. Militarily, the build-up of US naval power has reached unprecedented levels. By one account US naval power is equal to 16 of the next powerful naval countries put together (in contrast to the earlier naval powers at their peak). US

---

[338] Bangladesh, India, Maldives, Pakistan, Seychelles, Sri Lanka, United Kingdom, Iran, Oman, Saudi Arabia, United Arab Emirates, France, Kenya, Mauritius, Mozambique, South Africa, Tanzania, Australia, Indonesia, Malaysia, Myanmar, Singapore, Thailand and Timor-Leste

[339] China, Germany, Italy, Japan, Madagascar, Netherlands, Russia and Spain

[340] https://www.navy.gov.au/ions; website accessed on 22 April 2020

naval presence is continuing in both the Asia and the pacific region. Chinese Navy flirting in the Indian Ocean region has caused much discomfort to the US. How the US-China rivalry at sea plays out is a matter of concern for the littorals. The littorals have their own concerns of military presence of outside powers. With significant economic growth in Asia, the center of gravity has indeed shifted. It has shifted from Europe to Asia and from Pacific-ocean into the Indian Ocean. Indian Ocean which is described on a lighter note as the ocean where fishes live and die out of old age, is now contributing to 28% of global fishing. With this combination of factors, it appears difficult to de-hyphenate security and growth in the Indian Ocean Region. An interesting set of coalitions is reflected by the emergence of new multilateral institutions in this region. There is no one multilateral institution inclusive of all littorals and outside powers. Despite a shared colonial history, there is no singular multilateral institution inclusive of all 36 littorals. What has evolved is an interesting myriad of regional and supra-regional institutions operating within the same region. While it appears disjointed, this mix has provided a sense of order in the region. In the absence of an alternative order, it remains to be seen whether these institutions can maintain the peace in the IOR for long and whether these institutions can get countries to agree to an inclusive rule-based order.

8 Space Law

> **Topics covered**
> - The Outer Space Treaty
> - The Rescue Agreement
> - The Liability Convention
> - The Registration Convention
> - The Moon Agreement
> - Important Space Law Resolutions
> - Committee on the Peaceful Uses of Outer Space
> - International Space Station
> - ASAT
> - Space weaponization

Introduction

Space law can be described as the body of law governing space-related activities. Space law, much like general international law, comprises a variety of international agreements, treaties, conventions, and United Nations General Assembly resolutions as well as rules and regulations of international organizations. The term *space law* is most often associated with the rules, principles and standards of international law appearing in the five international treaties and five sets of principles governing outer space which have been developed under the auspices of the United Nations. In addition to these international instruments, many states have national legislation governing space-related activities. Space law addresses a variety of matters, such as, for example, the preservation of the space and Earth environment, liability for damages caused by space objects, the settlement of disputes, the rescue of astronauts, the sharing of information about potential dangers in outer space, the use of space-related technologies, and international cooperation. A number of fundamental principles guide the conduct of space activities, including the notion of space as the province of all humankind, the freedom of exploration and use of outer space by all states without discrimination, and the principle of non-appropriation of outer space.

The Committee on the Peaceful Uses of Outer Space [COPUOS] is the forum for the development of international space law. The Committee has concluded five international treaties and five sets of principles on space-related activities. These five treaties deal with issues such as the non-appropriation of outer space by any one country, arms control, the freedom of exploration, liability for damage caused by space objects, the safety and rescue of spacecraft and astronauts, the prevention of harmful interference with space activities and the environment, the notification and registration of space activities, scientific investigation and the exploitation of natural resources in outer space and the settlement of disputes. Each of the treaties stresses the notion that outer space, the activities carried out in outer space and whatever benefits might be accrued from outer space should be devoted to enhancing the well-being of all countries and humankind, with an emphasis on promoting international cooperation.

The treaties commonly referred to as the five United Nations treaties on outer space are:
> The Outer Space Treaty 1967[341]

---

[341] Treaty on Principles Governing the Activities of States in the Exploration and Use of Outer Space, including the Moon and Other

- The Rescue Agreement 1968[342]
- The Liability Convention 1972[343]
- The Registration Convention 1976[344]
- The Moon Agreement 1984[345]

The five declarations and legal principles are:
- The Declaration of Legal Principles (Declaration of Legal Principles Governing the Activities of States in the Exploration and Uses of Outer Space)[346]
- The Broadcasting Principles (The Principles Governing the Use by States of Artificial Earth Satellites for International Direct Television Broadcasting)[347]
- The Remote Sensing Principles (The Principles Relating to Remote Sensing of the Earth from Outer Space)[348]
- The Nuclear Power Sources Principles (The Principles Relevant to the Use of Nuclear Power Sources in Outer Space)[349]
- The Benefits Declaration (The Declaration on International Cooperation in the Exploration and Use of Outer Space for the Benefit and in the Interest of All States)[350]

Celestial Bodies; Adopted by the General Assembly in its resolution 2222 (XXI)

[342] Agreement on the Rescue of Astronauts, the Return of Astronauts and the Return of Objects Launched into Outer Space; Adopted by the General Assembly Resolution 2345 (XXII)

[343] Convention on International Liability for Damage Caused by Space Objects; Adopted by the General Assembly Resolution 2777 (XXVI)

[344] Convention on Registration of Objects Launched into Outer Space; Adopted by General Assembly Resolution 3235 (XXIX)

[345] Agreement Governing the Activities of States on the Moon and Other Celestial Bodies; Adopted by General Assembly Resolution 34/68

[346] General Assembly resolution 1962 (XVIII) of 13 December 1963

[347] General Assembly resolution 37/92 of 10 December 1982

[348] General Assembly resolution 41/65 of 3 December 1986

[349] General Assembly resolution 47/68 of 14 December 1992

[350] General Assembly resolution 51/122 of 13 December 1996

The Outer Space Treaty 1967: **The Outer Space Treaty, as it is known, was the second of the so-called** *no armament* **treaties; its concepts and some of its provisions were modeled on its predecessor, the Antarctic Treaty. Like that Treaty it sought to prevent** *a new form of colonial competition* **and the possible damage that self-seeking exploitation might cause.**[351] In early 1957, even before the launching of Sputnik in October, developments in rocketry led the United States to propose international verification of the testing of space objects. The development of an inspection system for outer space was part of a Western proposal for partial disarmament put forward in August 1957. The Soviet Union, however, which was in the midst of testing its first ICBM and was about to orbit its first Earth satellite, did not accept these proposals.

Between 1959 and 1962 the Western powers made a series of proposals to bar the use of outer space for military purposes. Their successive plans for general and complete disarmament included provisions to ban the orbiting and stationing in outer space of weapons of mass destruction. Addressing the General Assembly on September 22, 1960, President Eisenhower proposed that the principles of the Antarctic Treaty be applied to outer space and celestial bodies. Soviet plans for general and complete disarmament between 1960 and 1962 included provisions for ensuring the peaceful use of outer space. The Soviet Union, however, would not separate outer space from other disarmament issues, nor would it agree to restrict outer space to peaceful uses unless U.S. foreign bases at which short-range and medium-range missiles were stationed were eliminated also. The Western powers declined to accept the Soviet approach; the linkage, they held, would upset the military balance and weaken the security of the West. After the signing of the Limited Test Ban Treaty, the Soviet

---

[351] https://fas.org/nuke/control/ost/intro.htm website accessed on 7 May 2020

Union's position changed. It ceased to link an agreement on outer space with the question of foreign bases. On September 19, 1963, Foreign Minister Gromyko told the General Assembly that the Soviet Union wished to conclude an agreement banning the orbiting of objects carrying nuclear weapons. Ambassador Stevenson stated that the United States had no intention of orbiting weapons of mass destruction, installing them on celestial bodies or stationing them in outer space. The General Assembly unanimously adopted a resolution on October 17, 1963, welcoming the Soviet and U.S. statements and calling upon all states to refrain from introducing weapons of mass destruction into outer space.

The United States supported the resolution, despite the absence of any provisions for verification; the capabilities of its space-tracking systems, it was estimated, were adequate for detecting launchings and devices in orbit. Seeking to sustain the momentum for arms control agreements, the United States in 1965 and 1966 pressed for a Treaty that would give further substance to the U.N. resolution. On June 16, 1966, both the United States and the Soviet Union submitted draft treaties. The U.S. draft dealt only with celestial bodies; the Soviet draft covered the whole outer space environment. The United States accepted the Soviet position on the scope of the Treaty, and by September agreement had been reached in discussions at Geneva on most Treaty provisions. Differences on the few remaining issues -- chiefly involving access to facilities on celestial bodies, reporting on space activities, and the use of military equipment and personnel in space exploration -- were satisfactorily resolved in private consultations during the General Assembly session by December. On the 19th of that month the General Assembly approved by acclamation a resolution commending the Treaty. It was opened for signature at Washington, London, and Moscow on January 27, 1967. On April 25 the Senate gave unanimous consent to its ratification, and the Treaty entered into force on October 10, 1967.

Highlights: The Outer Space Treaty (also called the Treaty on Principles Governing the Activities of States in the Exploration and Use of Outer Space, including the Moon and Other Celestial Bodies) was considered by the Legal Subcommittee in 1966 and agreement was reached in the General Assembly in the same year.[352] The Treaty was largely based on the Declaration of Legal Principles Governing the Activities of States in the Exploration and Use of Outer Space, which had been adopted by the General Assembly in its resolution 1962 (XVIII) in 1963, but added a few new provisions. The Treaty was opened for signature by the three depository Governments (the Russian Federation, the United Kingdom and the United States of America) in January 1967, and it entered into force in October 1967. The Outer Space Treaty provides the basic framework on international space law, including the following principles:

- the exploration and use of outer space shall be carried out for the benefit and in the interests of all countries and shall be the province of all mankind;
- outer space shall be free for exploration and use by all States;
- outer space is not subject to national appropriation by claim of sovereignty, by means of use or occupation, or by any other means;
- States shall not place nuclear weapons or other weapons of mass destruction in orbit or on celestial bodies or station them in outer space in any other manner;
- the Moon and other celestial bodies shall be used exclusively for peaceful purposes;
- astronauts shall be regarded as the envoys of mankind;
- States shall be responsible for national space activities whether carried out by governmental or non-governmental entities;
- States shall be liable for damage caused by their space

---

[352] Resolution 2222 (XXI)

objects; and
- States shall avoid harmful contamination of space and celestial bodies.

Art. II of the Outer Space Treaty states that *"Outer space, including the moon and other celestial bodies, is not subject to national appropriation by claim of sovereignty, by means of use or occupation, or by any other means."* The substance of the arms control provisions[353] is in Art. IV. This article restricts activities in two ways:
- First, it contains an undertaking not to place in orbit around the Earth, install on the moon or any other celestial body, or otherwise station in outer space, nuclear or any other weapons of mass destruction.
- Second, it limits the use of the moon and other celestial bodies exclusively to peaceful purposes and expressly prohibits their use for establishing military bases, installation, or fortifications; testing weapons of any kind; or conducting military maneuvers.

Other treaty provisions underscore that space is no single country's domain and that all countries have a right to explore it.[354] These provisions state that: (a) Space should be accessible to all countries and can be freely and scientifically investigated; (b) Space and celestial bodies are exempt from national claims of ownership; (c) Countries are to avoid contaminating and harming space or celestial bodies; (d) Countries exploring space are responsible and liable for any damage their activities may cause; and (e) Space exploration is to be guided by *"principles of cooperation and mutual assistance,"* such as obliging astronauts to provide aid to one another if needed. Like other treaties, the Outer Space Treaty allows for

---

[353] https://fas.org/nuke/control/ost/intro.htm; website accessed on 7 May 2020

[354] https://www.armscontrol.org/factsheets/outerspace; website accessed on 7 May 2020

amendments or member withdrawal. Art. XV permits countries to propose amendments. An amendment can only enter into force if accepted by a majority of states-parties, and it will only be binding on those countries that approve the amendment. Art. XVI states a country's withdrawal from the treaty will take effect a year after it has submitted a written notification of its intentions to the depositary states-the United States, Russia, and the United Kingdom.

The Rescue Agreement

The Rescue Agreement was considered and negotiated by the Legal Subcommittee from 1962 to 1967. Consensus on the agreement was reached in the General Assembly in 1967,[355] and the Agreement entered into force in December 1968. The Agreement, elaborating on elements of articles 5 and 8 of the Outer Space Treaty[356] provides that States shall take all possible steps to rescue and assist astronauts in distress and promptly return them to the launching State, and that States shall, upon request, provide assistance to launching States in recovering space objects that return to Earth outside the territory of the Launching State.

---

[355] Resolution 2345 (XXII)

[356] Art. V of the OST states, "*States Parties to the Treaty shall regard astronauts as envoys of mankind in outer space and shall render to them all possible assistance in the event of accident, distress, or emergency landing on the territory of another State Party or on the high seas. When astronauts make such a landing, they shall be safely and promptly returned to the State of registry of their space vehicle. In carrying on activities in outer space and on celestial bodies, the astronauts of one State Party shall render all possible assistance to the astronauts of other States Parties. States Parties to the Treaty shall immediately inform the other States Parties to the Treaty or the Secretary-General of the United Nations of any phenomena they discover in outer space, including the moon and other celestial bodies, which could constitute a danger to the life or health of astronauts.*"

The Liability Convention

The Liability Convention was considered and negotiated by the Legal subcommittee from 1963 to 1972.[357] Agreement was reached in the General Assembly in 1971,[358] and the Convention entered into force in September 1972. Elaborating on Art. 7 of the Outer Space Treaty,[359] the Liability Convention provides that a launching State shall be absolutely liable to pay compensation for damage caused by its space objects on the surface of the Earth or to aircraft, and liable for damage due to its faults in space. The Convention also provides for procedures for the settlement of claims for damages.

The Registration Convention

The Registration Convention was considered and negotiated by the Legal Subcommittee from 1962. It was adopted by the General Assembly in 1974,[360] opened for signature on 14 January 1975 and entered into force on 15 September 1976. Building upon the desire expressed by States in the Outer Space Treaty, the Rescue Agreement and the Liability Convention to make provision for a mechanism that provided States with a means to assist in the identification of space objects, the Registration Convention expanded the scope of the United Nations Register of Objects Launched into Outer Space that had been established in 1961[361] and

---

[357] The Outer Space Treaty and the Liability Convention have their roots in a prior international covenant: the 1944 Convention on International Civil Aviation, more commonly known as the Chicago Convention.

[358] Resolution 2777 (XXVI)

[359] Art. VII of the OST states, "Each State Party to the Treaty that launches or procures the launching of an object into outer space, including the moon and other celestial bodies, and each State Party from whose territory or facility an object is launched, is internationally liable for damage to another State Party to the Treaty or to its natural or juridical persons by such object or its component parts on the Earth, in air or in outer space, including the moon and other celestial bodies."

[360] General Assembly Resolution 3235 (XXIX)

[361] By Resolution 1721B (XVI) of December 1961

addressed issues relating to States Parties responsibilities concerning their space objects. The Secretary-General was, once again, requested to maintain the Register and ensure full and open access to the information provided by States and international intergovernmental organizations.

The Moon Agreement

The Moon Agreement was considered and elaborated by the Legal Subcommittee from 1972 to 1979. The Agreement was adopted by the General Assembly in 1979 in resolution 34/68. It was not until June 1984, however, that the fifth country, Austria, ratified the Agreement, allowing it to enter into force in July 1984. The Agreement reaffirms and elaborates on many of the provisions of the Outer Space Treaty as applied to the Moon and other celestial bodies, providing that those bodies should be used exclusively for peaceful purposes, that their environments should not be disrupted, that the United Nations should be informed of the location and purpose of any station established on those bodies. In addition, the Agreement provides that the Moon and its natural resources are the common heritage of mankind and that an international regime should be established to govern the exploitation of such resources when such exploitation is about to become feasible.

Important Space Law Resolutions

Resolutions adopted by the United Nations General Assembly and documents produced by Committee on the Peaceful Uses of Outer Space have been a constant driver for the development of space law and international cooperation of Member States in their space activities. While resolutions adopted by the United Nations General Assembly are not legally binding, many resolutions dealing with issues related to outer space offer valuable guidance to States on the conduct of space activities. Many provisions of the General Assembly resolutions related to outer space have become widely accepted by the international space community. Similarly, considerable authority is to be attributed to certain documents produced by the Committee on the Peaceful Uses of Outer Space. Some of the important resolutions include the following:

a) Declaration on the fiftieth anniversary of the Treaty on Principles Governing the Activities of States in the Exploration and Use of Outer Space, including the Moon and Other Celestial Bodies, 2017[362]
b) Recommendations on national legislation relevant to the peaceful exploration and use of outer space, 2013[363]
c) Recommendations on enhancing the practice of States and international intergovernmental organizations in registering space objects, 2007[364]
d) Application of the concept of the *launching State*, 2004[365]
e) International Cooperation in the Peaceful Uses of Outer Space, 2000[366]
f) International Co-operation in the Peaceful Uses of Outer Space, 1961[367]
g) Space Debris Mitigations Guidelines of the Committee on the Peaceful Uses of Outer Space, 2010[368]
h) Safety Framework for Nuclear Power Source Applications in Outer Space, 2009[369]

The United Nations has also held four **UNISPACE Conferences** since 1968. Highlights of the conferences were as follows:

> UNISPACE I (1968): Progress in space exploration, international cooperation and creating an "*expert on space applications*" within UNOOSA. The United Nations body

---

[362] A/RES/72/78
[363] A/RES/68/74
[364] A/RES/62/101
[365] A/RES/59/115
[366] A/RES/55/122
[367] RES 1721 (XVI)
[368] ST/SPACE/49
[369] A/AC.105/934

then had several workshops in the 1970s on space applications such as remote sensing, telecommunications and cartography.
- ➤ UNISPACE II/UNISPACE 82 (1982): Peaceful exploration of space (specifically, how to avoid an arms race). Following the conference, UNOOSA worked more closely with developing countries to develop their space technology capabilities.
- ➤ UNISPACE III (July 1999): Protecting the space environment, giving developing countries more access to space and protecting Earth's environment. This led to the Vienna Declaration on Space and Human Development, with 33 recommendations for space-faring countries to follow. A follow-up report to the declaration was issued in 2004, five years after the conference.
- ➤ The UNISPACE+50 High-level Segment, held on 20 - 21 June 2018, was an opportunity for United Nations Member States and Permanent Observers to reflect on the outcomes of the three UNISPACE conferences and consider the future of international cooperation in the peaceful uses of outer space, as well as the work and mandates of COPUOS and UNOOSA. Member States endorsed a UNISPACE+50 resolution on 20 June 2018.

Committee on the Peaceful Uses of Outer Space

The Committee on the Peaceful Uses of Outer Space (COPUOS) was set up by the General Assembly in 1959 to govern the exploration and use of space for the benefit of all humanity: for peace, security and development. The Committee was tasked with reviewing international cooperation in peaceful uses of outer space, studying space-related activities that could be undertaken by the United Nations, encouraging space research programmers, and studying legal problems arising from the exploration of outer space. The Committee was instrumental in the creation of the five treaties and five principles of outer space. International cooperation in space exploration and the use of space technology applications to meet global development goals are discussed in the Committee every year. Owing to rapid advances in space technology, the space agenda is constantly evolving. The Committee therefore provides a unique platform at the global level to monitor and discuss these developments. The Committee has two subsidiary bodies: The Scientific and Technical Subcommittee, and the Legal Subcommittee, both established in 1961. The Committee reports to the Fourth Committee of the General Assembly, which adopts an annual resolution on international cooperation in the peaceful uses of outer space.

International Space Station

The International Space Station (ISS) is a spacecraft built by a partnership of 16 nations, namely the United States, Canada, Japan, Russia, Brazil, Belgium, Denmark, France, Germany, Italy, the Netherlands, Norway, Spain, Sweden, Switzerland and the United Kingdom. The ISS[370] includes three main modules connected by nodes: the US Laboratory Module Destiny, the European Research Laboratory Columbus, and the Japanese Experiment Module Kebo (Hope). Each was launched separately and connected in space by astronauts. Its total mass is 925,335 pounds (419,725 kilograms); has a habitable volume of 13,696 cubic feet (388 cubic meters); and a solar array length of 239.4 feet (73 meters). As of August 2019, there have been 218 spacewalks conducted for station assembly and maintenance, a total of more than 56 days. In May 2016, the space station marked its 100,000th orbit of the Earth. It orbits Earth 16 times a day. The operation of the ISS is governed by the Intergovernmental Agreement on the International Space Station (IGA) which addresses a number of legal topics, such as civil and criminal jurisdiction, intellectual property, and the operational

---

[370] https://edition.cnn.com/2013/10/22/world/international-space-station-fast-facts/index.html website accessed on 6 May 2020

responsibilities of the partner states.[371]

ASAT

An anti-satellite (ASAT) weapon destroys or interferes with satellites, impeding a nation's ability to collect intelligence or direct attacks. Such a weapon can be air, land, or sea-based.[372] Research into anti-satellite systems began after the Soviet Union launched the world's first satellite, Sputnik, in October 1957. By the 1980s, both the United States and the Soviet Union had performed anti-satellite missile tests—all of them arguably in technical violation of a 1967 UN treaty banning such activities.[373] In March 2019, India tested an anti-satellite weapon, saying the indigenously produced interceptor was used to destroy an object in orbit.

Such a weapon allows for attacks on enemy satellites - blinding them or disrupting communications - as well as providing a technology base for intercepting ballistic missiles. In 1985, the United States tested the ASM-135, launched from an F-15 fighter jet, destroying an American satellite called Sol wind P78-1. There were no tests for more than 20 years. Then in 2007, China entered the anti-satellite arena by destroying an old weather satellite in a high, polar orbit. The test created the largest orbital debris cloud in history, with more than 3,000 objects, according to the Secure World Foundation, a group that advocates sustainable and peaceful uses of outer space. The next year, the United States

---

[371] https://aerospace.org/sites/default/files/policy_archives/Space%20Station%20Intergovernmental%20Agreement%20Jan98.pdf website accessed on 6 May 2020

[372] https://www.reuters.com/article/us-india-satellite-tests-factbox/factbox-anti-satellite-weapons-rare-high-tech-and-risky-to-test-idUSKCN1R80UW website accessed on 6 May 2020

[373] https://www.cfr.org/backgrounder/chinas-anti-satellite-test; website accessed on 7 May 2020

carried out Operation Burnt Frost, using a ship-launched SM-3 missile to destroy a defunct spy satellite.

Space weaponization
There are a number of international agreements which ban the use of weapons of mass destruction in space but not anti-satellite tests or the use of ground-based lasers to harm satellites.[374] Agreements dealing with space security include:

> *Outer Space Treaty:* Signed into effect in 1967, the agreement prohibits stationing or using weapons of mass destruction in space. The treaty also bans contamination of space and holds nations liable for damage caused by space devices. Ninety-eight states—including Russia, China, and the United States—have ratified the treaty and twenty-seven have signed it.

> *Limited Test Ban Treaty*: This 1963 agreement bans nuclear weapons testing in space, as well as in the atmosphere and underwater, with the goal of preventing radioactive contamination.[375] The United States, Russia, and the United Kingdom originally ratified the agreement, and 105 other countries, including China, have done so.

> *Missile Technology Control Regime:* This export-control protocol was established in 1987 has thirty-four member states, including most of the world's missile manufacturers. The regime seeks to limit proliferation, including of space

---

[374] https://www.cfr.org/backgrounder/chinas-anti-satellite-test; website accessed on 11 May 2020

[375] The largest concern associated with the LTBT was its verification and inspections systems. Erstwhile USSR had proposed an international control system. On the other hand, USA was wary of uncontrolled and clandestine efforts. In 1988, it was proposed that the LTBT be extended to all environments, making it a comprehensive test ban, but the United States stood in strong opposition to any amendment that made the Treaty comprehensive.

rockets, by restricting sales of missiles and related equipment capable of launching weapons of mass destruction. The United States and Russia are members, but not China.

9 International Environmental Law

> **Topics covered**
> ➤ Climate change
> ➤ UNFCC
> ➤ Kyoto Protocol
> ➤ Sustainable Development
> ➤ Biodiversity
> ➤ Trans frontier pollution
> ➤ Marine pollution
> ➤ Endangered species
> ➤ Hazardous materials and activities
> ➤ Cultural and Natural Heritage preservation
> ➤ Desertification
> ➤ Recent ICJ Cases

Environmental law is a foundation for environmental sustainability[376] and the full realization of its objectives is ever more urgent vis a vis growing environmental pressures.[377] Violations of environmental law undermine the achievement of all dimensions of sustainable development and environmental sustainability.[378]

---

[376] Lee Paddock, Du Qun, Louis J. Kotzé, David L. Markell, Kenneth J. Markowitz, Durwood Zaelk **Compliance and Enforcement in Environmental Law: Toward More Effective Implementation** (Edward Elgar Publishing, Northampton, 2011)

[377] https://www.un.org/ruleoflaw/thematic-areas/land-property-environment/environmental-law/ website accessed on 11 May 2020

[378] 27th Session of UNEP Governing Council/Global Ministerial Environment Forum 2013

Historically, the timeline of treaties that are often identified as monumental in the formation of international environmental law include: the Stockholm Conference (1972),[379] UN Convention on the Law of the Sea (UNCLOS) (1982), World Conference on Environment and Development (1987),[380] Rio Conference (1992),[381] and the Johannesburg Earth Summit (2002).[382] Growth of international environmental law as a separate area of public international law began in the 1970s with the Stockholm Conference on the Environment in 1972.[383] According to a compilation carried in the American Society of International Law (ASIL)[384], international environmental law encompasses a diverse group of topics, including:

- climate change (United Nations Framework Convention on Climate Change and the Kyoto Protocol on Global Warming)
- sustainable development (The Rio Declaration on Environment and Development)
- biodiversity (Convention on Biological Diversity)
- trans frontier pollution (Convention on Long-Range Transboundary Air Pollution)
- marine pollution (Convention on the Prevention of Marine Pollution by Dumping of Wastes and Other Matter)
- endangered species (Convention on International Trade in Endangered Species (CITES)

---

[379] The United Nations Conference on the Human Environment 1972 A/CONF.48/14/REV.1

[380] Report of the World Commission on Environment and Development: Our Common Future Transmitted to the General Assembly as an Annex to document A/42/427

[381] United Nations Conference on Environment & Development 1992 A/CONF.151/26

[382] World Summit on Sustainable Development 2002

[383] https://guides.ll.georgetown.edu/InternationalEnvironmentalLaw; website accessed on 11 May 2020

[384] Anne Burnett, **International Environmental Law** (ASIL, 2015) p. 4

> hazardous materials and activities (Basel Convention on the Control of Transboundary Movements of Hazardous Wastes and Their Disposal)
> cultural preservation (Convention Concerning the Protection of the World Cultural & Natural Heritage)
> desertification (United Nations Convention to Combat Desertification) and
> uses of the seas (United Nations Convention on Law of the Sea (UNCLOS)

Environmental law is also cutting across other areas of international law, such as commercial/business law, trade, and human rights.[385]

Climate change
UNFCCC: The UNFCCC entered into force on 21 March 1994.[386] Today, it has near-universal membership. The 197 countries that have ratified the Convention are called Parties to the Convention. The UNFCCC is a '**Rio Convention'**, one of two opened for signature at the '**Rio Earth Summit'** in 1992. Its sister Rio Conventions are the UN Convention on Biological Diversity and the Convention to Combat Desertification. The three are intrinsically linked. In short, the UNFCC:
> **Recognized that there was a problem** (This was remarkable for its time. Remember, in 1994, when the UNFCCC took effect, there was less scientific evidence than there is now. The UNFCCC borrowed a very important line from one of the most successful multilateral environmental treaties in

---

[385] https://guides.ll.georgetown.edu/InternationalEnvironmentalLaw website accessed on 29 April 2020
[386] https://unfccc.int/process-and-meetings/the-convention/what-is-the-united-nations-framework-convention-on-climate-change website accessed on 29 April 2020

history (the Montreal Protocol, in 1987): it bound member states to act in the interests of human safety even in the face of scientific uncertainty)

➢ **Sets a lofty but specific goal** (The ultimate objective of the Convention is to stabilize greenhouse gas concentrations *"at a level that would prevent dangerous anthropogenic (human induced) interference with the climate system."* It states that *"such a level should be achieved within a time-frame sufficient to allow ecosystems to adapt naturally to climate change, to ensure that food production is not threatened, and to enable economic development to proceed in a sustainable manner."*

➢ **Puts the onus on developed countries to lead the way** (The idea is that, as they are the source of most past and current greenhouse gas emissions, industrialized countries are expected to do the most to cut emissions on home ground. They are called Annex I countries and belong to the Organization for Economic Cooperation and Development (OECD). They include 12 countries with *economies in transition* from Central and Eastern Europe. Annex I countries were expected by the year 2000 to reduce emissions to 1990 levels. Many of them have taken strong action to do so, and some have already succeeded)

➢ **Directs new funds to climate change activities in developing countries** (Industrialized nations agree under the Convention to support climate change activities in developing countries by providing financial support for action on climate change- above and beyond any financial assistance they already provide to these countries. A system of grants and loans has been set up through the Convention and is managed by the Global Environment Facility. Industrialized countries also agree to share technology with less-advanced nations.)

➢ **Keeps tabs on the problem and what's being done about it** (Industrialized countries (Annex I) have to report regularly on their climate change policies and measures, including issues governed by the Kyoto Protocol (for countries which have ratified it). They must also submit an annual inventory of their greenhouse gas emissions, including data for their base year (1990) and all the years since. Developing countries (Non-Annex I Parties) report in more general terms on their actions both to address climate change and to adapt to its impacts - but less regularly than Annex I Parties do, and their reporting is contingent on their getting funding for the preparation of the reports, particularly in the case of the Least Developed Countries)

➢ **Charts the beginnings of a path to strike a delicate balance** (Economic development is particularly vital to the world's poorer countries. Such progress is difficult to achieve even without the complications added by climate change. The Convention takes this into consideration by accepting that the share of greenhouse gas emissions produced by developing nations will grow in the coming years. Nonetheless, in the interests of fulfilling its ultimate goal, it seeks to help such countries limit emissions in ways that will not hinder their economic progress. One such win-win solution was to emerge later, when the Kyoto Protocol to the Convention was conceived)

➢ **Kicks off formal consideration of adaptation to climate change** (The Convention acknowledges the vulnerability of all countries to the effects of climate change and calls for special efforts to ease the consequences, especially in developing countries which lack the resources to do so on their own. In the early years of the Convention, adaptation received less attention than mitigation, as Parties wanted more certainty on impacts of and vulnerability to climate change. When IPCC's Third Assessment Report was released, adaptation gained traction, and Parties agreed on a process to address adverse effects and to establish funding arrangements for adaptation. Currently, work on adaptation takes place under different Convention bodies.

The Adaptation Committee, which Parties agreed to set up under the Cancun Adaptation Framework as part of the Cancun Agreements, is a major step towards a cohesive, Convention-based approach to adaptation.)

Kyoto Protocol: The Kyoto Protocol was adopted on 11 December 1997. Owing to a complex ratification process, it entered into force on 16 February 2005.[387] Currently, there are 192 Parties to the Kyoto Protocol. Kyoto Protocol operationalizes the United Nations Framework Convention on Climate Change by committing industrialized countries to limit and reduce greenhouse gases (GHG) emissions in accordance with agreed individual targets. The Convention itself only asks those countries to adopt policies and measures on mitigation and to report periodically.

The Kyoto Protocol is based on the principles and provisions of the Convention and follows its annex-based structure. It only binds developed countries, and places a heavier burden on them under the principle of *common but differentiated responsibility and respective capabilities*, because it recognizes that they are largely responsible for the current high levels of GHG emissions in the atmosphere. In its Annex B, the Kyoto Protocol sets binding emission reduction targets for 36 industrialized countries and the European Union.

Overall, these targets add up to an average 5 per cent emission reduction compared to 1990 levels over the five-year period 2008–2012 (the first commitment period). In Doha, Qatar, on 8 December 2012, the Doha Amendment to the Kyoto Protocol was adopted for a second commitment period, starting in 2013 and lasting until 2020. However, the Doha Amendment has not yet entered into force; a total of 144 instruments of acceptance are required for entry into force of the amendment. The amendment includes:

---

[387] https://unfccc.int/kyoto_protocol website accessed on 29 April 2020

- New commitments for Annex I Parties to the Kyoto Protocol who agreed to take on commitments in a second commitment period from 1 January 2013 to 31 December 2020;
- A revised list of GHG to be reported on by Parties in the second commitment period; and
- Amendments to several articles of the Kyoto Protocol which specifically referenced issues pertaining to the first commitment period and which needed to be updated for the second commitment period.

On 21 December 2012, the amendment was circulated by the Secretary-General of the United Nations, acting in his capacity as Depositary, to all Parties to the Kyoto Protocol in accordance with Art. 20 and 21 of the Protocol. During the first commitment period, 37 industrialized countries and the European Community committed to reduce GHG emissions to an average of five percent against 1990 levels. During the second commitment period, Parties committed to reduce GHG emissions by at least 18 percent below 1990 levels in the eight-year period from 2013 to 2020; however, the composition of Parties in the second commitment period is different from the first. One important element of the Kyoto Protocol was the establishment of flexible market mechanisms, which are based on the trade of emissions permits. Under the Protocol, countries must meet their targets primarily through national measures. However, the Protocol also offers them an additional means to meet their targets by way of three market-based mechanisms: (I) International Emissions Trading; (II) Clean Development Mechanism (CDM); and (III) Joint implementation

Sustainable development
The United Nations Conference on Environment and Development met in Rio de Janeiro from 3 to 14 June 1992 and adopted a Declaration *"with the goal of establishing a new and equitable global partnership through the creation of new levels of cooperation among*

States, key sectors of societies and people, working towards international agreements which respect the interests of all and protect the integrity of the global environmental and developmental system, recognizing the integral and interdependent nature of the Earth, our home." The Rio Declaration identified 27 principles.

> *Principle 1: Human beings are at the centre of concerns for sustainable development. They are entitled to a healthy and productive life in harmony with nature.*
> *Principle 2: States have, in accordance with the Charter of the United Nations and the principles of international law, the sovereign right to exploit their own resources pursuant to their own environmental and developmental policies, and the responsibility to ensure that activities within their jurisdiction or control do not cause damage to the environment of other States or of areas beyond the limits of national jurisdiction.*
> *Principle 3: The right to development must be fulfilled so as to equitably meet developmental and environmental needs of present and future generations.*
> *Principle 4: In order to achieve sustainable development, environmental protection shall constitute an integral part of the development process and cannot be considered in isolation from it.*
> *Principle 5: All States and all people shall cooperate in the essential task of eradicating poverty as an indispensable requirement for sustainable development, in order to decrease the disparities in standards of living and better meet the needs of the majority of the people of the world.*
> *Principle 6: The special situation and needs of developing countries, particularly the least developed and those most environmentally vulnerable, shall be given special priority. International actions in the field of environment and development should also address the interests and needs of all countries.*
> *Principle 7: States shall cooperate in a spirit of global partnership to conserve, protect and restore the health and integrity of the Earth's ecosystem. In view of the different contributions to global environmental*

degradation, States have common but differentiated responsibilities. The developed countries acknowledge the responsibility that they bear in the international pursuit of sustainable development in view of the pressures their societies place on the global environment and of the technologies and financial resources they command.

Principle 8: To achieve sustainable development and a higher quality of life for all people, States should reduce and eliminate unsustainable patterns of production and consumption and promote appropriate demographic policies.

Principle 9: States should cooperate to strengthen endogenous capacity-building for sustainable development by improving scientific understanding through exchanges of scientific and technological knowledge, and by enhancing the development, adaptation, diffusion and transfer of technologies, including new and innovative technologies.

Principle 10: Environmental issues are best handled with the participation of all concerned citizens, at the relevant level. At the national level, each individual shall have appropriate access to information concerning the environment that is held by public authorities, including information on hazardous materials and activities in their communities, and the opportunity to participate in decision-making processes. States shall facilitate and encourage public awareness and participation by making information widely available. Effective access to judicial and administrative proceedings, including redress and remedy, shall be provided.

Principle 11: States shall enact effective environmental legislation. Environmental standards, management objectives and priorities should reflect the environmental and developmental context to which they apply. Standards applied by some countries may be inappropriate and of unwarranted economic and social cost to other countries, in particular developing countries.

Principle 12: States should cooperate to promote a supportive and open international economic system that would lead to economic growth and sustainable development in all countries, to better address the problems of environmental degradation. Trade policy measures for environmental purposes should not constitute a means of arbitrary or unjustifiable discrimination or a disguised restriction on international trade. Unilateral actions to deal with environmental challenges outside the jurisdiction of the importing country should be avoided. Environmental measures addressing transboundary or global environmental problems should, as far as possible, be based on an international consensus.

Principle 13: States shall develop national law regarding liability and compensation for the victims of pollution and other environmental damage. States shall also cooperate in an expeditious and more determined manner to develop further international law regarding liability and compensation for adverse effects of environmental damage caused by activities within their jurisdiction or control to areas beyond their jurisdiction.

Principle 14: States should effectively cooperate to discourage or prevent the relocation and transfer to other States of any activities and substances that cause severe environmental degradation or are found to be harmful to human health.

Principle 15: In order to protect the environment, the precautionary approach shall be widely applied by States according to their capabilities. Where there are threats of serious or irreversible damage, lack of full scientific certainty shall not be used as a reason for postponing cost-effective measures to prevent environmental degradation.

Principle 16: National authorities should endeavour to promote the internalization of environmental costs and the use of economic instruments, taking into account the approach that the polluter should, in principle, bear the cost of pollution, with due regard to the public interest and without distorting international trade and investment.

Principle 17: Environmental impact assessment, as a national instrument, shall be undertaken for proposed activities that are likely to have a significant adverse impact on the environment and are subject to a decision of a competent national authority.

Principle 18: States shall immediately notify other States of any natural disasters or other emergencies that are likely to produce sudden harmful effects on the environment of those States. Every effort shall be made by

> the international community to help States so afflicted.
> Principle 19: States shall provide prior and timely notification and relevant information to potentially affected States on activities that may have a significant adverse transboundary environmental effect and shall consult with those States at an early stage and in good faith.
> Principle 20: Women have a vital role in environmental management and development. Their full participation is therefore essential to achieve sustainable development.
> Principle 21: The creativity, ideals and courage of the youth of the world should be mobilized to forge a global partnership in order to achieve sustainable development and ensure a better future for all.
> Principle 22: Indigenous people and their communities and other local communities have a vital role in environmental management and development because of their knowledge and traditional practices. States should recognize and duly support their identity, culture and interests and enable their effective participation in the achievement of sustainable development.
> Principle 23: The environment and natural resources of people under oppression, domination and occupation shall be protected.
> Principle 24: Warfare is inherently destructive of sustainable development. States shall therefore respect international law providing protection for the environment in times of armed conflict and cooperate in its further development, as necessary.
> Principle 25: Peace, development and environmental protection are interdependent and indivisible.
> Principle 26: States shall resolve all their environmental disputes peacefully and by appropriate means in accordance with the Charter of the United Nations.
> Principle 27: States and people shall cooperate in good faith and in a spirit of partnership in the fulfilment of the principles embodied in this Declaration and in the further development of international law in the field of sustainable development.

The 2030 Agenda for Sustainable Development, adopted by all

United Nations Member States in 2015, provides a shared blueprint for peace and prosperity for people and the planet, now and into the future. At its heart are the 17 Sustainable Development Goals (SDGs), which are an urgent call for action by all countries - developed and developing - in a global partnership. They recognize that ending poverty and other deprivations must go hand-in-hand with strategies that improve health and education, reduce inequality, and spur economic growth – all while tackling climate change and working to preserve our oceans and forests.

Biodiversity

United Nations Environment Program (UNEP) convened the Ad Hoc Working Group of Experts on Biological Diversity in November 1988 to explore the need for an international convention on biological diversity. Soon after, in May 1989, it established the Ad Hoc Working Group of Technical and Legal Experts to prepare an international legal instrument for the conservation and sustainable use of biological diversity. The experts were to take into account *"the need to share costs and benefits between developed and developing countries"* as well as *"ways and means to support innovation by local people."* By February 1991, the Ad Hoc Working Group had become known as the Intergovernmental Negotiating Committee. Its work culminated on 22 May 1992 with the Nairobi Conference for the Adoption of the Agreed Text of the Convention on Biological Diversity. The Convention was opened for signature on 5 June 1992 at the United Nations Conference on Environment and Development (the *Rio Earth Summit*). It remained open for signature until 4 June 1993, by which time it had received 168 signatures. The Convention entered into force on 29 December 1993, which was 90 days after the 30th ratification. The first session of the Conference of the Parties was scheduled for 28 November – 9 December 1994 in the Bahamas.

The Convention on Biological Diversity (CBD) has 3 main objectives:

- The conservation of biological diversity
- The sustainable use of the components of biological diversity
- The fair and equitable sharing of the benefits arising out of the utilization of genetic resources.

Art. 3 of the CBD states, *"States have, in accordance with the Charter of the United Nations and the principles of international law, the sovereign right to exploit their own resources pursuant to their own environmental policies, and the responsibility to ensure that activities within their jurisdiction or control do not cause damage to the environment of other States or of areas beyond the limits of national jurisdiction."*

Trans frontier pollution
Since 1979 the Convention on Long-range Transboundary Air Pollution has addressed some of the major environmental problems of the UNECE [UN Economic Commission for Europe] region through scientific collaboration and policy negotiation.[388] The Convention has been extended by eight protocols that identify specific measures to be taken by Parties to cut their emissions of air pollutants. The Convention, which now has 51 Parties identifies the Executive Secretary of UNECE as its secretariat. The aim of the Convention is that Parties shall endeavour to limit and, as far as possible, gradually reduce and prevent air pollution including long-range transboundary air pollution. Parties develop policies and strategies to combat the discharge of air pollutants through exchanges of information, consultation, research and monitoring. The Parties meet annually at sessions of the Executive Body to review ongoing work and plan future activities including a workplan for the coming year. The three main subsidiary bodies - the Working Group on Effects, the Steering Body to EMEP and the Working Group on Strategies and Review - as well as the

---

[388] http://www.unece.org/fileadmin//DAM/env/lrtap/welcome.html; website accessed on 29 April 2020

Convention's Implementation Committee, report to the Executive Body each year. Currently, the Convention's priority activities include review and possible revision of its most recent protocols, implementation of the Convention and its protocols across the entire UNECE region (with special focus on Eastern Europe, the Caucasus and Central Asia and South-East Europe) and sharing its knowledge and information with other regions of the world.

Marine pollution
The Convention on the Prevention of Marine Pollution by Dumping of Wastes and Other Matter 1972, the *London Convention* for short, is one of the first global conventions to protect the marine environment from human activities and has been in force since 1975. Its objective is to promote the effective control of all sources of marine pollution and to take all practicable steps to prevent pollution of the sea by dumping of wastes and other matter. Currently, 87 States are Parties to this Convention. In 1996, the *London Protocol* was agreed to further modernize the Convention and, eventually, replace it. Under the Protocol all dumping is prohibited, except for possibly acceptable wastes on the so-called *reverse list*. The Protocol entered into force on 24 March 2006 and there are currently 51 Parties to the Protocol.

Endangered species
CITES [Convention on International Trade in Endangered Species of Wild Fauna and Flora] was drafted as a result of a resolution adopted in 1963 at a meeting of members of IUCN (The World Conservation Union).[389] The text of the Convention was finally agreed at a meeting of representatives of 80 countries in Washington, D.C., the United States of America, on 3 March 1973, and on 1 July 1975 CITES entered in force. The original of the Convention was deposited with the Depositary Government in the

---

[389] https://www.cites.org/eng/disc/what.php; website accessed on 29 April 2020

English, French and Spanish languages, each version being equally authentic. The Convention is also available in Chinese and Russian. CITES is an international agreement to which States and regional economic integration organizations adhere voluntarily. States that have agreed to be bound by the Convention (joined CITES) are known as Parties. Although CITES is legally binding on the Parties – in other words they have to implement the Convention – it does not take the place of national laws. Rather it provides a framework to be respected by each Party, which has to adopt its own domestic legislation to ensure that CITES is implemented at the national level. For many years CITES has been among the conservation agreements with the largest membership, with now 183 Parties.

Hazardous materials and activities

The Basel Convention on the Control of Transboundary Movements of Hazardous Wastes and their Disposal was adopted on 22 March 1989 by the Conference of Plenipotentiaries in Basel, Switzerland, in response to a public outcry following the discovery, in the 1980s, in Africa and other parts of the developing world of deposits of toxic wastes imported from abroad. The overarching objective of the Basel Convention is to protect human health and the environment against the adverse effects of hazardous wastes.[390] Its scope of application covers a wide range of wastes defined as *hazardous wastes* based on their origin and/or composition and their characteristics, as well as two types of wastes defined as *other wastes*, namely, household waste and incinerator ash. The provisions of the Convention center around the following principal aims:

> ➢ the reduction of hazardous waste generation and the promotion of environmentally sound management of hazardous wastes, wherever the place of disposal;
> ➢ the restriction of transboundary movements of hazardous

---

[390] http://www.basel.int/TheConvention/Overview/tabid/1271/Default.aspx; website visited on 6 May 2020

wastes except where it is perceived to be in accordance with the principles of environmentally sound management; and
➢ a regulatory system applying to cases where transboundary movements are permissible.

Cultural preservation

The Convention concerning the Protection of the World Cultural and Natural Heritage entered into force on 17 December 1975, three months after the date of the deposit of the twentieth instrument of ratification, acceptance or accession.[391] Efforts aimed at the preservation of artistic and historic heritage can be traced to the efforts under the auspices of the League of Nations.[392] The establishment of the United Nations Educational, Scientific and Cultural Organization (UNESCO), on 16 November 1945, was a short in the arm towards this end.[393] In 1966 during the 15th General Conference, the UNESCO's instructed the Director-General to coordinate and secure the international adoption of appropriate principles and scientific, technical and legal criteria for the protection of cultural property, monuments and sites.[394] In 1970, the General Conference entrusted the Acting Director-General with drafting an international convention and invited him to convene a Special Committee tasked with examining and finalizing the drafts.[395] The Committee completed its work with the adoption of the draft Convention for the Protection of the Cultural and Natural World Heritage and the draft Recommendation Concerning the

---

[391] Pursuant to Art. 33 of The Convention concerning the Protection of the World Cultural and Natural Heritage of 1975

[392] For historic evolution see generally https://legal.un.org/avl/ha/ccpwcnh/ccpwcnh.html; website accessed on 16 April 2020

[393] Conference for the Establishment of the United Nations Educational, Scientific and Cultural Organization, held at the Institute of Civil Engineers, London, November, 1945 ECO/CONF/29

[394] By Res. 3.342

[395] By Res 3.412

Protection, at National Level, of the Cultural and Natural Heritage in April 1972.[396] The said Convention comprised of 38 provisions spread over eight parts namely, Definition, National and International, Intergovernmental Committee, Fund for Protection, International Assistance, Educational Programs, Reporting mechanism and Final Clauses. By far the most important aspect of the 1972 World Heritage Convention is that it stitches together in a single instrument the protection of nature conservation and the preservation of cultural properties. The Convention recognizes the way in which people interact with nature, and the fundamental need to preserve the balance between the two.[397]

Desertification

Established in 1994, the United Nations Convention to Combat Desertification (UNCCD) is the sole legally binding international agreement linking environment and development to sustainable land management.[398] The Convention addresses specifically the arid, semi-arid and dry sub-humid areas,[399] where some of the most vulnerable ecosystems and peoples can be found. The new UNCCD 2018-2030 Strategic Framework is the most comprehensive global commitment to achieve Land Degradation Neutrality (LDN).[400] The parties to the Convention on Desertification work together to improve the living conditions for people in drylands, to maintain and restore land and soil productivity, and to mitigate the effects of drought. The UNCCD is particularly committed to a bottom-up

---

[396] Authentic texts submitted to the 17th session of the General Conference on 15 November 1972 and adopted immediately

[397] https://whc.unesco.org/en/convention/; website visited on 16 April 2020

[398] United Nations Convention to Combat Desertification in Those Countries Experiencing Serious Drought and/or Desertification, Particularly in Africa 1994

[399] Art. 1 Annex I Regional Implementation Annex for Africa of 1994

[400] The Future Strategic Framework Of The Convention Decision 7/COP.13 ICCD/COP(13)/21/Add.1

approach, encouraging the participation of local people in combating desertification and land degradation. The UNCCD secretariat facilitates cooperation between developed and developing countries, particularly around knowledge and technology transfer for sustainable land management.[401] As the dynamics of land, climate and biodiversity are intimately connected, the UNCCD collaborates closely with the other two Rio Conventions; the Convention on Biological Diversity (CBD)[402] and the United Nations Framework Convention on Climate Change (UNFCCC),[403] to meet these complex challenges with an integrated approach and the best possible use of natural resources.

Uses of the seas (Covered in chapter on law of sea.)

Recent ICJ cases
Application of bilateral environment related treaties: In Pulp Mills on the River Uruguay (*Argentina v. Uruguay*), on 4 May 2006, Argentina filed an Application instituting proceeding against Uruguay concerning alleged breaches.[404] The breaches were pertaining to obligations incumbent upon it under the Statute of the River Uruguay, a treaty signed by the two States[405] for the purpose of establishing the joint machinery necessary for the optimum and rational utilization of that part of the river which constitutes their joint boundary. The ICJ noted that Uruguay had not informed the Administrative Commission of the River Uruguay of the projects as

---

[401] Art. 23 *Supra* Note 283

[402] Art. 4 (j) *Ibid*

[403] Art. 8

[404] ICJ Application instituting proceedings filed in the registry of the Court on 4 May 2006 Pulp Mills on the River Uruguay (*Argentina v. Uruguay*) 2006 General List No. 135

[405] Treaty between the Argentine Republic and the Eastern Republic of Uruguay of 7 April 1961 concerning the Boundary Constituted by the River Uruguay United Nations, Treaty Series, Vol. 635, No. 9074

prescribed in the Statute.[406] The Administrative Commission of the River Uruguay — commonly referred to by its Spanish acronym CARU — is a body established under the Statute for the purpose of monitoring the river, including assessing the impact of proposed projects on the river.[407] The Court concluded that, by not informing CARU of the planned works before the issuing of the initial environmental authorizations for each of the mills and for the port terminal adjacent to the Orion mill, and by failing to notify the plans to Argentina through CARU, Uruguay had violated the 1975 Statute.[408]

Importance of Environment Impact Assessment & Compensation for environmental harm: In the case concerning Construction of a Road in Costa Rica along the San Juan River the ICJ in its Judgment delivered on 16 December 2015 found that the construction of the road by Costa Rica carried a risk of significant transboundary harm and, therefore, it found that Costa Rica had not complied with its obligation under general international law to carry out an environmental impact assessment (EIA).[409] Turning to the reparation requested by Nicaragua, the Court concluded that a declaration of wrongful conduct in respect of Costa Rica's violation of the obligation to conduct an EIA was the appropriate measure of satisfaction. This constituted the first judgement where the ICJ, in

---

[406] Pulp Mills on the River Uruguay (*Argentina v. Uruguay*), Judgment, ICJ Reports 2010, p. 14

[407] See Part III on Functions of CARU, The River Uruguay Executive Commission Comisión Administradora Del Rio Uruguay; http://www.caru.org.uy/web/pdfs_publicaciones/The-River-Uruguay-executive-commission-Uruguay-Paysandu.pdf website accessed on 14 April 2020

[408] *Supra* Note 406

[409] Certain Activities Carried Out by Nicaragua in the Border Area (*Costa Rica v. Nicaragua*) and Construction of a Road in Costa Rica along the San Juan River (*Nicaragua v. Costa Rica*), Judgment, I.C.J. Reports 2015, p. 665

contemporary legal history that a world court has addressed the question of compensation for environmental harm.[410] Drawing from the jurisprudence created in the Chorzow Factory Case the court explained that *"damage to the environment, and the consequent impairment or loss of the ability of the environment to provide goods and services, is compensable under international law and such compensation may include indemnification for the impairment or loss of environmental goods and services in the period prior to recovery and payment for the restoration of the damaged environment."*[411]

The Whaling Case: At the ICJ, proceedings were instituted on 31 May 2010 by Australia, which accused Japan of pursuing *"a large-scale program of whaling under the Second Phase of its Japanese Whale Research Program under Special Permit in the Antarctic ('JARPA II')"*, in breach of obligations assumed by Japan under the 1946 International Convention for the Regulation of Whaling and of other international obligations for the preservation of marine mammals and the marine environment.[412] Court indicated that JARPA II could broadly be described as a *scientific research* programme. It concluded that the special permits issued by Japan for the killing, taking and treating of whales in connection with JARPA II were not granted *"for purposes of scientific research"* pursuant to Art. VIII, paragraph 1, of the 1946 Convention.[413]

---

[410] James Harrison, *"Significant International Environmental Law Cases: 2017–18"* **Journal of Environmental Law**, 2018 Vol. 30, pp. 527–541

[411] *Supra* note 283

[412] Application instituting proceedings filed in The Registry of the Court on 31 May 2010 Whaling in The Antarctic (*Australia V. Japan*) 2010 General List No. 148

[413] Whaling in the Antarctic (*Australia v. Japan: New Zealand intervening*), Judgment, ICJ Reports 2014, p. 226

10 International Humanitarian Law

Topics covered
➢ Relevance and scope of the term 'armed conflict'
➢ Non-International Armed Conflict
➢ International Armed Conflict
➢ Relevance of International Humanitarian Law during absence of hostilities
➢ When International Humanitarian Law ceases to apply
➢ Protection under International Humanitarian Law
➢ Belligerent Occupation and effective control
➢ Legal Consequences of Belligerent Occupation
➢ Definition of 'combatants'
➢ Combatant's privilege
➢ Definition of civilians and civilian population
➢ Fundamental Principles of Humanitarian Law
➢ Prohibited means of warfare
➢ Emblems
➢ Prisoners of War
➢ Humanitarian issues in South Asia: An area study

Introduction
The UN, which succeeded the League of Nations, was created with a determination, as articulated in the preambular provision of the UN Charter of 1945, to save the *"succeeding generations from the scourge of war."*[414] The year 2019 marked the 70th Anniversary of the Geneva Conventions of 1949 (also described as the law of war) which updated after WWII the previous instruments on the subject

---

[414] UN Charter 1945

to regulate and mitigate the effects of war. Both documents, the UN Charter 1945 as well as the Geneva Conventions of 1949 were creations of the post-World War II era and even to this day remain among the very few (near) universally accepted instruments in the world. These developments took place in three phases:
(a) the cold war era up until the fall of the Berlin wall, succeeded by
(b) the short but tumultuous unipolar moment and
(c) the contemporary era witnessing the rise of China and revival of Russia.

These phases witnessed certain movements, running concurrently such as emergence and formation of newly independent states, transition in the international political economy, waves of violence such as those used by some national liberation movements and the increasing resort to unconventional warfare. At the same time, rapid and momentous developments were taking place on two fronts, namely (a) defence and weapons and (b) urbanization.

The advancements in weapons technology and the diffusion thereof as well as the transformation of villages to towns to cities and dense population in urban settings are closely interlinked from a humanitarian perspective. The development of weapons of mass destruction has blurred the distinction between what is strategically offensive and what is strategically defensive. The influential German jurist Oppenheim, a person whose life and work very much coincided with the anarchist revolutionary wave of political violence, in perhaps his most influential work on International law chose to write 2 volumes, one dedicated to Law of '*Peace*'[415] and the other dedicated to Law of '*War and Neutrality*'.[416] Arriving at a consensus as to what denotes war and what denotes

---

[415] http://www.gutenberg.org/ebooks/41046 website accessed on 23 March 2020

[416] https://gallica.bnf.fr/ark:/12148/bpt6k93563t/f3.image website accessed on 23 March 2020

peace continues to be elusive and the latter has rather become more complicated in these 7 decades. Perhaps the least contentious description of peace would be *the absence of hostilities*. The period also witnessed a slippage into irrelevance of the historic concept of *long peace* and increasing relevance of *regional peace*. Needless to mention that the words *law of war* has during this period, gradually subsumed by the words *law of armed conflict* and later *International Humanitarian Law*. Considering civilians as part of the Public International Law has not been without tensions. Some of this can be traced back to the feeble effort in the intermediate period between the two great wars when a *Tokyo Draft* was proposed in the 1930s.[417]

The draft never saw the light of the day. Fissures emerged in post-World War II period, in the negotiations leading to the adoption of the Geneva Conventions of 1949, in including internal armed conflicts (in particular common art. 3[418]). Some prefer to call this

---

[417] https://ihldatabases.icrc.org/applic/ihl/ihl.nsf/Treaty.xsp?action=openDocument&documentId=85EE9A58C871B072C12563CD002D6A15 website accessed on 23 March 2020

[418] *"In the case of armed conflict not of an international character occurring in the territory of one of the High Contracting Parties, each Party to the conflict shall be bound to apply, as a minimum, the following provisions:*
(1) Persons taking no active part in the hostilities, including members of armed forces who have laid down their arms and those placed ' hors de combat ' by sickness, wounds, detention, or any other cause, shall in all circumstances be treated humanely, without any adverse distinction founded on race, colour, religion or faith, sex, birth or wealth, or any other similar criteria.
To this end, the following acts are and shall remain prohibited at any time and in any place whatsoever with respect to the above-mentioned persons:
(a) violence to life and person, in particular murder of all kinds, mutilation, cruel treatment and torture;
(b) taking of hostages;
(c) outrages upon personal dignity, in particular humiliating and degrading

mellowed down provision, a *convention within a convention*. The evolution of International law during this period of seven decades has been remarkable in many senses, but in terms of establishing international rule of law, there is a lot more to be done. The interface between law of peace and law of war on matters of occupation, International human rights, refugee law, IDPs, Outer space, Cyberspace, civilians and combatants, use of force and pre-emptive use of force are illustrative of some of the stresses within the international community. Hence, the following analysis would not be compartmentalized into law of peace and law of war, as had been done a few centuries ago. In a state driven system of international order and law, it would be rather appropriate to commence the analysis from the standpoint of two postulates which states may assume to opt as policy. First, as Kautilya in his advices to the Mauryan King Chandragupta, *The Arthashasthra*[419] and Sun Tzu in his treatise *The Art of War*,[420] conveyed a few thousand years ago, the ultimate victory lies in winning without fighting, which also means war is the last resort to settling disputes. Niccolo Machiavalli also gave similar advice to *The Prince*.[421] The other postulate is that War is an extension of policy by other means as conveyed by Von Clauswitz in his seminal book *On War*.[422] A

---

treatment;

(d) the passing of sentences and the carrying out of executions without previous judgment pronounced by a regularly constituted court, affording all the judicial guarantees which are recognized as indispensable by civilized peoples.

(2) The wounded and sick shall be collected and cared for...."

[419] https://archive.org/details/Arthasastra_English_Translation; website accessed on 23 March 2020

[420] https://sites.ualberta.ca/~enoch/Readings/The_Art_Of_War.pdf website accessed on 23 March 2020

[421] https://ebooks.adelaide.edu.au/m/machiavelli/niccolo/m149p/complete.html website accessed on 23 March 2020

[422] http://www.clausewitz.com/readings/OnWar1873/TOC.htm website accessed on 23 March 2020

discourse of war and peace needs to consider these postulates, considering that as on date there are in excess of 40 conflicts taking place around the world. Not to forget that several other conflicts (and concluded) have taken place post 1945[423] and the enormous suffering and damages that were caused since the operationalization of the UN Charter and Geneva Conventions.[424]

Timeline of evolution of modern IHL (in three phases)
1864 -1914
1864: First Geneva Convention (Wounded on battlefield
1868: St Petersburg Declaration - outlawing of certain projectiles
1899/1907: Hague Conferences
1906: Second Geneva Convention (Wounded at sea)
1914-1945
1925: Geneva Gas Protocol
1929: Third Geneva Convention (Prisoners of War)
1949 onwards
1949: Four Geneva Conventions
1954: Hague Convention on Protection of Cultural Property
1972: Biological Weapons Convention
1977: Addition Protocols to Geneva Convention of 1949 I, II
1980: Chemical Weapons Convention
1997: Anti-Personnel Land Mines Convention
2000: Optional Protocol Child Soldiers
2005: Addition Protocols to Geneva Convention of 1949 III

Relevance and scope of the term 'armed conflict'
International humanitarian law is designed principally for governing extraordinary circumstances i.e *'armed conflict'* and to that end regulating the conduct of hostilities and mitigating the effects thereof. Once an armed conflict exists, all conduct pertaining to the conflict must conform with the norms of International humanitarian Law. In other words, the application of this body of

---

[423] http://www.systemicpeace.org/warlist/warlist.htm website accessed on 23 March 2020

[424] See Annual Reports and International Review of Red Cross for Humanitarian efforts https://international-review.icrc.org/

law is triggered-off with the onset of a situation of armed conflict. So what is an armed conflict? There is no universally accepted legal definition. There are numerous laudable scholarly works by individuals and non-governmental organizations attempting to define the term. Nevertheless, for a practical lawyer such definitions and descriptions are of little use. Law does recognize two categories of violent situations as amounting to armed conflict namely:

a) *International armed conflict* and
b) *Conflicts not of international nature* also known as Non-International Armed Conflict (NIAC), also known as Internal Armed Conflict

International Armed conflict is described by the four Geneva Conventions of 1949 in the following manner:

> *"the present Convention shall apply to all cases of declared war or of any other armed conflict which may arise between two or more of the High Contracting Parties, even if the state of war is not recognized by one of them."*[425]

The applicability of IHL governing international armed conflicts begins with a declaration of war or, in the absence of such declaration, with the actual use of armed force expressing belligerent intent. It is also triggered by the mere fact of one State invading another with a view to occupying all or part of its territory, even when such invasion meets with no armed resistance. Since, the Geneva Conventions are open to accession only to nation states, humanitarian law is made applicable to hostile situations between two or more high contracting parties. There is no express reference to the pre-requisite of a threshold of violence between the concerned states. With the UN Charter laying down a general prohibition on resort of unilateral use of force,[426] stopping short of

---

[425] Art.2 common to all four Geneva Conventions of 1949
[426] Art. 2 (4) of the UN Charter 1945 reads:

outlawing war (and supplementary albeit limited applicable formal literature suggesting no reference to the scale or magnitude of violence)[427] the following inferences can be drawn. There are two essential ingredients to this description of International armed conflicts i.e. legal status of parties i.e. states and nature (not scale) of military confrontation.[428] International Humanitarian Law also applies *"to all cases of partial or total occupation of the territory of a High Contracting Party, even if the said occupation meets with no armed resistance."* In essence, belligerent occupation occurs when one State invades another State and establishes military control over part or all of its territory. Accordingly, Art. 42 of the Hague Regulations states;

> *"Territory is considered occupied when it is actually placed under the authority of the hostile army. The occupation extends only to the territory where such authority has been established and can be exercised."*

Applicability of humanitarian law to the other category i.e. Internal armed conflict is denoted in the following manner;

> *"In the case of armed conflict not of an international character occurring in the territory of one of the High Contracting Parties, each Party to the conflict shall be bound to apply, as a minimum, the following provisions..."*[429]

"All members shall refrain in their international relations from the threat or use of force against the territorial integrity or political independence of any state, or in any other manner inconsistent with the purposes of the United Nations"

[427] *"an armed conflict exists whenever there is a resort to armed force between States"* ICTY, *The Prosecutor v. Dusko Tadic*, Decision on the Defence Motion for Interlocutory Appeal on Jurisdiction, IT-94-1-A, 2 October 1995, para. 70

[428] Art. 1 (4) of the Protocol Additional to the Geneva Conventions of 12 August 1949, and relating to the Protection of Victims of International Armed Conflicts (Protocol I), 8 June 1977 identifies armed resistance against *'colonial domination'*, *'alien occupation'* or *'racist regimes'* with international armed conflicts

[429] Art. 3 common to the four Geneva Conventions 1949

On the ingredients of NIACs, two inferences can be deduced from the existing construct of the said provision i.e. the extraordinary situation exists within a nation state and that there are at the minimum two adversaries engaged in hostilities. The use of the word *party* indicates that the entity engaged in hostilities may range from a nation-state to a non-state actor. Supplementary literature from judgements of ICTY suggests that *hostilities must reach a minimum level of intensity* and the *parties to the conflict possess organized armed forces*.[430] This dichotomy between international and non-international armed conflicts is generally a result of political history and in particular, the political influence of the legal notion of sovereignty.[431]

> Note: IHL is not relevant in closely resembling violent circumstances such as internal disturbances and tensions, riots, organized crimes. In such circumstance the relevant local legislation of the respective state concerned shall apply.

Relevance of International Humanitarian Law during absence of hostilities

The factual existence of an armed conflict constitutes an absolute prerequisite for the invocation and applicability of international humanitarian law. However, some of the duties it stipulates may apply during ordinary circumstances on a continuing basis. Some of the obligations in this category are benign functions. These include efforts towards expeditious execution and observance,[432] sharing of official translations and relevant local legislation

---

[430] ICTY, *The Prosecutor v. Fatmir Limaj*, Judgment, IT-03- 66-T, 30 November 2005, para. 135-170

[431] See Rogier Bartels, "*The Relationship between International Humanitarian Law and the Notion of State Sovereignty,*" **Journal of Conflict and Security Law**, Volume 23, Issue 3, Winter 2018, pp. 461–486

[432] Art. 80 of the Additional Protocol I, 1977

between states,[433] dissemination of humanitarian law;

> "The High Contracting Parties undertake, in time of peace as in time of war, to disseminate the text of the present Convention as widely as possible in their respective countries, and, in particular, to include the study thereof in their programmes of military and, if possible, civil instruction, so that the principles thereof may become known to all their armed forces and to the entire population."[434]

The other category of obligations in the inter-war context were intended to be more proactive in nature and functions. These include certain protections in the post-conflict setting and weapons related obligations. For instance, the Additional Protocol I of 1977 prescribes a review of weapons prior to deployment and operationalizing in the field;

> "In the study, development, acquisition or adoption of a new weapon, means or method of warfare, a High Contracting Party is under an obligation to determine whether its employment would, in some or all circumstances, be prohibited by this Protocol or by any other rule of international law applicable to the High Contracting Party"[435]

Weapons related conventions under International humanitarian law can be broadly categorized on the lines of weapons which are absolutely prohibited and weapons that are regulated. For instance, weapons that are indiscriminatory and/or whose physical impact is

---

[433] Geneva Conventions of 1949; First Convention, Art. 48; Second Convention, Art. 49; Third Convention, Art. 128; Fourth Convention, Art. 145

[434] First Convention, Art. 47; Second Convention, Art. 48; Third Convention, Art. 127; Fourth Convention, Art. 144

[435] Art. 36 (1) of the Additional Protocol I, 1977

irreversible such as exploding bullets,[436] chemical weapons,[437] blinding lasers[438] are outlawed *per se*. Illustrative in this context is the obligation on states undertaken under the auspices of the Biological Weapons Convention;

> *"Party to this Convention undertakes never in any circumstances to develop, produce, stockpile or otherwise acquire or retain:*
> *(1) Microbial or other biological agents, or toxins whatever their origin or method of production, of types and in quantities that have no justification for .. peaceful purposes;*
> *(2) Weapons, equipment or means of delivery designed to use such agents or toxins for hostile purposes or in armed conflict."*[439]

In the case of most weapons, the prohibition was agreed after development and consequently, in addition to prohibition on development, states are obliged to prevent sale, transfer or alternatively destroy existing stockpiles. It is to be noted that in the case of nuclear weapons, the international community has yet to arrive at a universal consensus on its legality, be it possession or threat of use or actual use. The ICJ in its advisory opinion stated that,

> *"...the Court cannot conclude definitively whether the threat or use of nuclear weapons would be lawful or unlawful in an extreme circumstance of self-defence, in which the very survival of a State*

---

[436] St Petersburg Declaration of 1868

[437] Convention on the Prohibition of the Development, Production, Stockpiling and Use of Chemical Weapons and on their Destruction 1992; note the OPCW is vested with the responsibility of overseeing the implementation and observance of the CWC which including monitoring facilities; in the case of India, the Ministry of Chemicals and Fertilizers is the nodal contact point for the OPCW given the dual use i.e. civilian use of certain chemicals

[438] Protocol IV of the 1980 Convention on Certain Conventional Weapons

[439] Art. 1 of the Convention on the Prohibition of the Development, Production and Stockpiling of Bacteriological (Biological) and Toxin Weapons and on their Destruction 1972

would be at stake"

> *When International Humanitarian Law ceases to apply*
> An international armed conflict ends with a peace treaty,[440] or with a unilateral declaration, such as a capitulation, declaration of surrender,[441] or unconditional, permanent and complete withdrawal from previously contested territory.[442] Today, international armed conflicts witness a greater tendency towards a slow and progressive decrease in intensity of hostilities.

Protection under International Humanitarian Law
One of the important obligations undertaken by the international community is to 'respect' and 'ensure respect' for the treaty provisions. This expression can be found in Art. 1 common to the four Geneva Conventions of 1949 and Art. 1 (1) of the Additional Protocol (I) 1977;

> *"The High Contracting Parties undertake to respect and to ensure respect for the present Convention in all circumstances"*

An aspect to be noted here is that, the provision follows the principle of *pacta sunt servanda* i.e. practice your obligations in good faith. This is a customary principle of public international law and reiterated in Art. 26 of the Vienna Conventions on the Law of Treaties 1969. This was further reaffirmed by the ICJ in the Nicaragua case (Merits) case 1986, when it observed that this obligation is derived not only from the Geneva Conventions, but

---

[440] E.g. **Agreement on Ending the War and Restoring Peace in Vietnam 27 Jan 1973**

[441] E.g. **Instrument of Surrender of Pakistan forces in Dacca,** 16 December 1971

[442] See generally Jann Kleffner, *"Scope of Application of International Humanitarian Law"*, in Dieter Fleck (ed.), **The Handbook of International Humanitarian Law** (3rd edition, Oxford University Press, Oxford, 2013) 4

"from the general principles of humanitarian law to which the Conventions merely give specific expression."[443]

Consequently, *pact sunt servanda* applies in equal measure to *jus in bello* i.e. conduct during war as well as to *jus ad bellum* i.e. conduct leading to war. This could beget the question, what conduct is permitted in war. Considering that humanitarian law seeks to humanize warfare but stops well short of being a tool kit for conducting warfare. A better question to be addressed is how does humanitarian law humanize warfare? It identifies whom and what is to be protected and how to mitigate the suffering. As far as protection is concerned, IHL provides protection to the animate, inanimate and tangible property. To that extent, protection can be broadly categorized under three heads; namely, *general protection* which is pertaining to civilians and civilian objects who/that have no involvement in hostilities, *special protection* which is premised on special status due to vulnerability and/or hazardous nature *and enhanced protection,* specifically applicable to tangible cultural heritage. Persons protected under IHL include combatants as well as non-combatants and can be listed as follows;

- Civilians;
- Wounded, sick and shipwrecked;
- Persons hors de combat;
- Prisoners of war;
- Religious personnel;
- Medical personnel;
- Humanitarian personnel;
- Peacekeeping forces

Property or objects protected under IHL can be listed as follows;
- Civilian objects: undefended, or open, towns or non-defended localities[444]

---

[443] *The Republic of Nicaragua v. The United States of America* 1986 I.C.J. 14
[444] Arts. 48 and 59 of the Additional Protocol (I) 1977

> Hospital and safety zones, demilitarized zones[445]
> Neutralized zones[446]
> Cultural property[447]
> Objects indispensable for the survival of the civilian population such as water, energy etc[448]
> Works and installations containing dangerous forces (dams, dykes, nuclear power plants[449]
> The natural environment[450]

Belligerent Occupation and effective control
"*Territory is considered occupied when it is actually placed under the authority of the hostile army. The occupation applies only to the territory where such authority is established, and in a position to assert itself.*"[451]

In effect, territorial limits of law of military occupation extends to the degree to which effective control has actually been established and can be exercised by the occupying party. Consequently, occupation may be described as total or partial according to the circumstances. Resistance, armed or otherwise, is not a pre-requisite for application of rights and duties in times of occupation. Temporal application of law of occupation ceases when the occupying forces are driven out of or evacuate the territory.[452] The inhabitants of occupied territory are collectively considered as having fallen *into the hands* of the occupying power and are

---

[445] GC I, art. 24; GC IV, art. 14; AP I, art. 60
[446] GC IV, art. 15; AP I, art. 60
[447] AP I, art. 53; and, specific conventions
[448] AP I, art. 54
[449] AP I, art. 56
[450] AP I, art. 55
[451] Art. 42 of the Convention (II) with Respect to the Laws and Customs of War on Land and its annex: Regulations concerning the Laws and Customs of War on Land. The Hague, 29 July 1899
[452] Art. 6 of the Geneva Convention IV

therefore entitled to the full protection of the Fourth Geneva Convention immediately upon establishment of effective control;

> "Persons protected by the Convention are those who, at a given moment and in any manner whatsoever, find themselves, **in case of a conflict or occupation**, in the hands of a Party to the conflict or Occupying Power of which they are not nationals....."[453]

Legal Consequences of Belligerent Occupation

As in the case of all armed conflicts, the right of the belligerent parties to choose methods or means of warfare is not unlimited. In addition to this and other general prohibitions, the 'occupier' as well as the 'occupied' are vested with certain protections and responsibilities.

Civilians inhabiting occupied territory
- Individual civilians enjoy protection against attack unless and for such time as they directly participate in hostilities.
- civilian population of an occupied territory owes no allegiance to the occupying power. Resisting civilians lose civilian status[454] and are expected to carry their weapons openly[455]
- civilians cannot be forced to fight its own country, cannot be involved in any way with the armed forces
- taking civilians as hostages is not permitted[456]
- civilians cannot be made to provide military assistance to the occupying power
- civilians are at all times entitled to respect for their persons and dignity
- Entitled to family rights, religious convictions, and manners

---

[453] Art. 4 of the Geneva Conventions (IV) of 1949
[454] Art. 44 *Ibid*
[455] Art. 43
[456] Art.34

and customs[457]
- rights over private property stays protected[458]
- no discrimination (race, nationality, language, religious convictions and practices, political opinion, social origin etc.) is permitted[459]
- must be humanely treated in all circumstances and protected from any acts of violence, including by third parties
- Collective punishments, reprisals, pillage are not permitted[460]
- legal rights of the inhabitants of occupied territory cannot be curtailed by any agreement or other arrangement between the occupying power and the authorities of the occupied territory[461]
- inhabitants of the occupied territory cannot renounce their rights[462]
- Individual or mass forcible transfers and deportations of the civilian population from occupied territory are prohibited, so also civilians of occupiers cannot be transferred to occupied territory[463]

In addition to the corresponding obligations of the occupying authority vis a vis civilians and the territory, the role of such authorities can be broadly categorized under three heads, namely; *Law making*: The occupying power may well decide to repeal penal

---

[457] Art. 46 of the Convention (IV) respecting the Laws and Customs of War on Land and its annex: Regulations concerning the Laws and Customs of War on Land. The Hague, 18 October 1907

[458] *Ibid*

[460] Art. 33 of the Geneva Conventions (IV) of 1949

[461] Art. 47 *Ibid*

[462] See Art. 13

[463] Art. 49

laws of occupied territory or to enact penal provisions of its own. However, these powers do not extend to imposing disproportionate penal sanctions.[464]

Administrative functions: This includes restoration and ensuring, *as far as possible*, law & order, public safety, respect laws in force before occupation (unless absolutely prevented from doing so), and ensure that there is no change in status of judges and public officials[465]

Law enforcement: For e.g. criminal offences in occupied territory should continue to be prosecuted by local courts. However, such jurisdiction could pass, to military courts of occupying power if local courts are not able to function properly.[466] Military courts so established must comply with rule of law, ensure fair trial in compliance with fundamental tenets of criminal justice system[467]

Definition of combatants

In a generic sense, combatants are members of the fighting forces of the belligerent parties. The legal definition of this term is derived from Art. 3 of the Hague Regulations of 1907 and has been endorsed in the Geneva Conventions in the following manner:

> *"The armed forces of a Party to a conflict consist of all organized armed forces, groups and units which are under a command responsible to that Party for the conduct of its subordinates......Members of the armed forces of a Party to a conflict are combatants, that is to say, they have the right to participate directly in hostilities"*[468]

---

[464] See Art. 68, 75 - 77
[465] Art. 43 of the Hague Regulations 1907
[466] Art. 66, 73 of the Geneva Conventions (IV) 1949
[467] Art. 65, 67, 69, 71-73 *Ibid*
[468] Art. 43

However, mercenaries, spies or civilians (with the exception of levee en masse) taking a direct part in hostilities are not entitled to combatant status.

Combatant's privilege
For the purposes of the principle of distinction, the most important consequence associated with combatant status is the loss of civilian status and of protection against direct attack. Moreover, combatant status entails the *combatant's privilege*, namely *the right to participate directly in hostilities* on behalf of a party to an international armed conflict. The combatant's privilege as such has no immediate consequences in terms of the principle of distinction but is of greater relevance for the status and rights afforded to an individual after capture by the enemy. Combatant status and combatant's privilege are exclusive to situations of international armed conflict and are not provided for in IHL governing internal armed conflicts

Definition of civilians and civilian population
In IHL, the civilian population is negatively defined as comprising all persons who are neither members of the armed forces of a party to the conflict nor participants in a *levee en masse*. Thus, the definition also includes civilians accompanying the armed forces without being incorporated therein, such as war correspondents and, as a general rule, private contractors and civilian intelligence or law enforcement personnel, even if some of them may be entitled to prisoner-of-war status upon capture.

Fundamental Principles of Humanitarian Law
Distinction
"*In order to ensure respect for and protection of the civilian population and civilian objects, the Parties to the conflict shall at all times distinguish between the civilian population and combatants and between civilian objects and military objectives and accordingly shall direct their operations only against military objectives.*"[469]

---

[469] Art. 48 of the Additional Protocol 1, 1977

Proportionality
The principle of proportionality prohibits attacks
> "*which may be expected to cause incidental loss of civilian life, injury to civilians, damage to civilian objects, or a combination thereof, which would be excessive in relation to the concrete and direct military advantage anticipated.*"[470]

Given that direct attacks against civilians and civilian objects are already prohibited, the proportionality evaluation is relevant only when attacks are directed against lawful targets.

Precaution in attack and presumptions in case of doubt
It has to be stressed that, during all phases of an attack, the principle of precautions in attack must be applied in conjunction with, but also independently of, the principle of proportionality. In other words, even if the expected incidental loss of civilian life, injury to civilians and damage to civilian objects is not excessive in relation to the concrete and direct military advantage anticipated in the attack, the attacking party must still take all feasible precautions to choose means and methods of warfare that will avoid as much incidental harm to civilians as possible.

Conduct of Warfare
Modern IHL has developed an extensive body of rules prohibiting or regulating the development, possession and use of certain weapons (means of warfare) and prohibiting or restricting the ways in which such weapons can be used or hostilities can be conducted (methods of warfare). The distinction between *means* and *methods* of warfare is important because any weapon (means) can be used in an unlawful manner (method), whereas the use of weapons that have been prohibited because of their inherent characteristics is unlawful regardless of the manner in which they are employed.

---

[470] Art. 51 (5) (b) Protocol Additional to the Geneva Conventions of 12 August 1949, and relating to the Protection of Victims of International Armed Conflicts (Protocol I), 8 June 1977

Prohibited methods of warfare (some examples)
a) Protection of persons hors de combat
According to a longstanding rule of customary and treaty IHL, it is prohibited to attack persons who are recognized or who, in the circumstances, should be recognized as being hors de combat. A person is hors de combat if he or she is in the power of an adverse Party, clearly expresses an intention to surrender or is incapable of defending himself or herself because of unconsciousness, shipwreck, wounds or sickness, and, in all those cases, abstains from any hostile act and does not attempt to escape

b) *Denial of quarter*
> "it is prohibited to order that there shall be no survivors, to threaten an adversary therewith or to conduct hostilities on this basis."[471]

The prohibition of denial of quarter makes it illegal to deliberately refuse or render impossible an enemy's surrender or to put to death those who are *hors de combat*. Where adversaries have been captured "*under unusual conditions of combat which prevent their evacuation,*" they may be disarmed, but treaties expressly require that "*they shall be released and all feasible precautions shall be taken to ensure their safety.*"

c) *Perfidy or treachery:* Perfidy or treachery denotes
> "acts inviting the confidence of an adversary to lead him to believe that he is entitled to, or is obliged to accord, protection under the rules of international law applicable in armed conflict, with intent to betray that confidence."[472]

Protocol I outlaws perfidy. In essence, the prohibition against perfidy or treachery upholds the good faith of the belligerents in the protections afforded by IHL. Note: It does not prohibit ruses of war, that is to say, acts that are intended to mislead an adversary or

---

[471] Art. 40 of the 1977 Additional Protocol I
[472] Art. 37(1) of the 1977 Additional Protocol I

to induce him to act recklessly, but which do not mislead him with respect to IHL protection and do not otherwise violate IHL.

d) Misuse of emblems, signs and uniforms (see Annexure to this chapter)
It is prohibited to make improper use of emblems, signs or signals provided for in IHL, such as the red cross, red crescent or red crystal,[473] protective emblems, signs or signals, including PoW or IC camps,[474] flag of truce,[475] protective emblem of cultural property,[476] distinctive signs of civil defense[477] and of installations containing dangerous forces,[478] and the distinctive emblem UN.[479]

Detention and Prisoners of War: Persons who have fallen into the power of an adverse party to a conflict are entitled to prisoner-of-war status if they qualify as:
(a) combatants (members of the armed forces or participants in a *levee en masse*)
(b) civilians formally authorized to accompany the armed forces
(c) demobilized military personnel in occupied territory
(d) military personnel interned in neutral territory

Benefit of doubt is provided to the person if the PoW status is under doubt. In such circumstances the status shall be determined by a

---

[473] Protocol additional to the Geneva Conventions of 12 August 1949, and relating to the Adoption of an Additional Distinctive Emblem (Protocol III), 8 December 2005

[474] Art. 66 of the Protocol Additional to the Geneva Conventions of 12 August 1949, and relating to the Protection of Victims of International Armed Conflicts; June 8, 1977

[475] Art. 38(1) of the 1977 Additional Protocol I

[476] Hague Convention for the Protection of Cultural Property in the Event of Armed Conflict 1954

[477] Supra note 474

[478] Art. 56

[479] Art. 3 of the Convention on the Safety of United Nations and Associated Personnel; December 9, 1994

competent tribunal.[480] Prisoners of war benefit from the protection of their status from the time they fall into the power of the enemy and until their final release and repatriation. Privileged treatment is justified only by rank, sex, age, medical condition or professional qualifications. After capture, prisoners of war must be evacuated to camps situated at a safe distance from the combat zone. They must be provided with the necessary food, water, clothing and medical care, and suitable precautions must be taken to ensure their safety during evacuation.[481] Similar conditions apply to transfers of prisoners of war after their arrival in a camp.

Early termination of captivity
After their evacuation, prisoners of war will usually be interned until the end of active hostilities. There are three circumstances in which captivity may end earlier: a) repatriation, or accommodation in a neutral country, of wounded or sick prisoners of war for medical reasons; b) successful escape (recaptured PoWs may be subjected only to disciplinary punishment); c) death.

A PoWs escape is considered successful when he:
(1) has rejoined his own or co-belligerent armed forces;
(2) has left the territory controlled by the detaining power or its allies; or
(3) has reached a friendly or allied ship in the territorial waters, but not under the control, of the detaining power

---

[480] IHL Treaty does not specify which bodies can be regarded as *"competent tribunals"* for the determination of individual entitlement to prisoner-of-war status

[481] The duty to evacuate prisoners is subject to two exceptions. First, wounded or sick prisoners of war may be temporarily kept back if their medical condition is such that being evacuated would expose them to greater risks than remaining in a danger zone. Second, when prisoners of war are captured during unusual conditions of combat that prevent their evacuation, such as during commando operations behind enemy lines, they may be disarmed, but must be released and all feasible precautions must be taken to ensure their safety.

IHL and its relevance to South Asia: An area study

The South Asian region has had its share of recent historical experiences with large scale violations as well as allegations of large scale violations of international humanitarian law (IHL).[482] This applies as much to instances of international and non-international armed conflict as it does to the situations created by new threats to peace and security such as terrorism. Memories of some of these unfortunate events have not faded over the years. For the sake of convenience, the paper is divided into two parts. The first part elaborates specific examples of IHL related issues in South Asia and also deals with some of the major thematic issues in the context of the region. The second part highlights the challenges to IHL application and implementation in this region. The conclusion summarizes the main strands in IHL's relevance to the South Asian context. The most interesting aspect of our enquiry that stares us in the face is the fact that IHL related issues apply to almost all South Asian countries. The degree of intensity may differ but the fact remains that acts that attract universally applicable IHL provisions are found aplenty in the region.

Part I: IHL Related Issues in South Asia

IHL does not define the term *'human dignity'* in any of the four Geneva Conventions or the Additional Protocol. However, scholarly work strongly suggests that through various provisions of the Geneva Conventions, respect of human dignity does constitute an inviolable obligation of states.[483] Likewise one of the most fundamental obligations of IHL is humane treatment of

---

[482] Framework of reference used at: http://www.icrc.org/eng/assets/files/other/what_is_ihl.pdf; website visited on 1/05/2020

[483] See Christopher Harland's views on *'Human Dignity'*, **Basic Documents on International Humanitarian Law- South Asia Collection** (Second Edition, ICRC, New Delhi, 2011) p. 1361

PoWs.[484] It is definitely not possible to capture the entire history of the IHL relevant experiences and questions of South Asia within a few pages.[485] The effort of the author therefore is limited, namely to capture the major running and current trends and draw broad conclusions about the relevance of IHL to the South Asian context.

Accountability for war crimes in Sri Lanka: It is a widely alleged and equally debated that war crimes were committed by both sides – the LTTE and the Sri Lankan Armed Forces - during the internal armed conflict in Sri Lanka that ended in 2009. The 2011 Report of the Secretary-General's Panel of Experts on Accountability in Sri Lanka has enumerated many instances of such violations. The Human Rights Council in Geneva has also taken cognizance of the atrocities during that period and called on Sri Lanka to take all necessary steps to ensure justice and accountability including through its own mechanism of Lessons Learnt and Reconciliation Commission (LLRC). The country report by Human Rights Watch testifies, very little follow-up has taken place and meaningful measures have been hard to come by.[486] The situation has been compounded by subsequent reported assaults on freedom of journalists, restriction of the space for civil society to debate these issues as well as a general trend of constricting of the democratic space.[487] There is a substantial body of scholarly work and expert opinion that makes a strong argument that Sri Lanka has also been a clear instance of R2P failure. Equally, there are influential voices

---

[484] For detailed analysis see Michael Schmitt, *"Wound, Capture, or Kill"*, **E.J.I.L.** 2013, 24(3), pp. 855-861

[485] For detailed historical perspective of IHL in South Asia see V.S. Mani, **Handbook of International Humanitarian Law in South Asia** (Oxford University Press, New Delhi, 2007)

[486] World Report 2013, Human Rights Watch, pp. 368-373

[487] *Ibid*

that stress that Libya and Sri Lanka cannot be put in the same basket.[488]

IHL and use of drones in South Asia: A few years ago, a United Nations investigation had then identified 33 drone strikes around the world that have resulted in civilian casualties and may have violated international humanitarian law, including in Pakistan[489] and Afghanistan. Besides, Pakistan, the report enumerates the instances of use of drones in Afghanistan. For instance, it states, "*In Afghanistan, the US and the UK have relied increasingly on remotely piloted aircraft...According to UNAMA, there was a steady recorded rise in the number of weapons released by remotely piloted aircraft from 2009 to 2012. Figures released by the United States Air Force in November 2012 confirm this...*"

The seminal report[490] by Ben Emmerson, UN Special Rapporteur on Human Rights and Counterterrorism argued that "*While the fact that civilians have been killed or injured does not necessarily point to a violation of international humanitarian law, it undoubtedly raises issues of accountability and transparency.*" Further, the report alleged there is "*strong evidence*" to suggest that between June 2004 and June 2008

---

[488] For instance, in September 2008, Gareth Evans, former Australian Foreign Minister and now a leading advocate of the Responsibility to Protect principle said that there was no reason then for Sri Lanka to be a R2P case. See: Gareth Evans, *Remembering Sri Lanka's Killing Fields*, **Project Syndicate** (Worldwide Distribution), 26 October 2012

[489] http://www.theguardian.com/world/2013/oct/18/drone-strikes-us-violate-law-un; website visited on 1/05/2020

[490] The Report of the Special Rapporteur on the Promotion and Protection of Human Rights and Fundamental Freedoms while Countering Terrorism was the third annual report submitted to the UN General Assembly by the current Special Rapporteur, Ben Emerson. The report which carries a document No. A/68/389 was submitted in accordance with General Assembly Resolution 66/171 and Human Rights Council Resolution 15/15

drone strikes in Pakistan were conducted *"with the active consent and approval of senior members of the Pakistani military and intelligence service, and with at least the acquiescence and, in some instances, the active approval of senior government figures."* The Permanent Representative of Pakistan to the United Nations rejected the notion that the strikes were carried out with consent while debating the Emmerson report at the General Assembly's Third (Social, Humanitarian and Cultural) Committee.[491] The drone strikes have also become a bilateral issue in Pakistan-US relations with Pakistan Prime Minister Nawaz Sharif telling US President Barack Obama on 23 October 2013 to end drone strikes in Pakistan.[492] Later, the National Assembly of Pakistan unanimously approved a resolution that said that drone attacks were against the sovereignty of the country and should be stopped at once.[493] The resolution further said that drone strikes were not only against solidarity of the country, but it was also in brazen violation of the United Nations Charter and human rights.

Child soldiers in Nepal and Sri Lanka: The use of child soldiers during the conflict in Sri Lanka is well-documented. For instance, the 2011 Report of the Secretary-General's Panel of Experts on Accountability in Sri Lanka states that the LTTE *"implemented a policy of forced recruitment throughout the war, but in the final stages, greatly intensified its recruitment of people of all ages, including children as young as fourteen."*[494] The report also documents the sufferings of

---

[491] See Statement by Ambassador Masood Khan, Permanent Representative of Pakistan to UN [Doc: A/C.3/68/L.61/Rev.I]

[492] http://www.reuters.com/article/2013/10/23/us-usa-pakistan-drones-idUSBRE99M19D20131023; website visited on 1/05/2020

[493] National Assembly of Pakistan Resolution dated 10/12/2013

[494] The Report of the SG's Panel of Experts also records: *"The LTTE was known for its forced recruitment and use of child soldiers, including boys and girls. Its tactics led to the organization's proscription in numerous countries, including Canada, the European Union, India, the United Kingdom and the United States; its proscription intensified after 11 September 2011."*

displaced children, including their inability to continue their schooling. On the other hand, the Report noted that during the war the Sri Lankan Ministry of Defense opposed the provision of a high nutrition biscuit for children, which the UNICEF wanted to send in, arguing that it would be used by the LTTE. After the war, the Sri Lankan Government expelled the spokesperson for UNICEF who had been vocal about violations against children.[495]

The situation in the case of Nepal is equally well-documented, though marginally better. Consequent to an agreement with the UN,[496] the final batch of the nearly 3,000 child soldiers who served in the Maoist army during Nepal's decade-long civil war were discharged and re-entered civilian life in February 2010.[497] Accountability and rehabilitation issues remain. It may also be noted that despite acceding to the framework of international humanitarian law, i.e. the four Geneva Conventions, Nepal in particular evidenced a general lack of will to amend its domestic laws and harmonize them to its international obligations.[498]

Bangladesh-The Lingering Wounds of 1971: The recent execution of Abdul Majed for his role in the assassination of Bangabandhu,[499] brings back memories of the birth of Bangladesh, an important landmark in the historical experience of IHL in South Asia. The society in Bangladesh continues to grapple with the crimes perpetrated in 1971. In fact, as lately as December 2013, the

---

[495] https://www.theguardian.com/world/2009/sep/06/sri-lanka-expels-unicef-official; website visited on 1/05/2020
[496] Nepal-UCPN-M, Action Plan, December 2009
[497] http://www.un.org/apps/news/story.asp?NewsID=33696&Cr=Nepal&Cr1#.UqqKreQjL9k; website visited on 1st May 2020
[498] As opined in *Advocate Raja Ram Dhakal v. Prime Minister of Nepal*; Writ No 2942, 2059 of year 2004
[499] https://www.dhakatribune.com/bangladesh/2020/04/12/bangabandhu-killer-majed-hanged; website visited on 1/05/2020

Bangladesh Supreme Court upheld a death sentence for Abdul Quader Mollah[500] for 1971 crimes and executed him.[501] There are credible allegations of genocide committed during 1971. The ICRC's role in Bangladesh has been widely applauded. The 1971 war had left 120,000 Bengalis stranded in Pakistan and thousands of Pakistani civilian internees and prisoners of war remained in Bangladesh. On 28 August 1973, the governments of India, Pakistan and Bangladesh concluded an agreement in New Delhi for arranging the repatriation of Bengalis in Pakistan and Pakistanis interned in Bangladesh. In this humanitarian operation which lasted from 1971 to 1975, ICRC facilitated the return home of 118,070 Bengalis to Bangladesh and 117,727 people to Pakistan, an operation taking several years.[502]

Violence against Women: The use of violence against women in situations of armed conflict and inter-state armed conflict is well-recorded in South Asia. For instance, the Report of the UNSG's Panel on Experts on Sri Lanka observed, *"Gender-based violence, including rape, sexual harassment and sexual exploitation, has also occurred despite legal protection."* This has also been witnessed in other countries and for a continuous and substantial period of time. However, there are credible videos that have emerged evidencing the violence against women in the Sri Lankan crises allegedly perpetrated by the armed forces of the state[503] (which it continues to deny). Interestingly, as early as 2000, the UN Security Council

---

[500] Criminal Appeal Nos.24-25 of 2013 (Appeal against ICT-BD No.2, judgment dated 5.2.2013)

[501] http://www.thehindu.com/news/international/south-asia/bangladesh-sc-upholds-jamaat-leaders-death-penalty/article5451053.ece; website visited on 1/05/2020

[502] *"Bangladesh: ICRC honored for helping victims of 1971 conflict"*; http://www.icrc.org/eng/resources/documents/feature/2012/bangladesh-feature-2012-04-19.htm; website visited on 1/05/2020

[503] See Sri Lanka's Killing Fields; documentary aired by Channel 4 on14 June 2011

passed a resolution recognizing the role of women in peace process.[504]

Terrorism in South Asia: The fight against terrorism in some countries of South Asia predates the West's war on terrorism at least by two and half decades. To this day, there remain allegations and counter allegations of the use of terrorism to handle geopolitical rivalry. There is an entire body of strong and highly persuasive arguments about the corrosive effect of high-handed government responses to the activities of terrorist groups. Elimination of the terror network leaders in foreign soil, though a contentious issue under International law is being actively pursued as a strategy.[505] Neither side comes out unscathed from such scrutiny. The concept of *zero tolerance* for terrorism which was adopted by the UN Security Council's Counter-Terrorism Committee [CTC] seeks to find a fine balance between respect for human rights and humanitarian norms on the one hand and the sovereign right of each nation-state to protect itself and its nationals from the scourge of terrorism.

It may be recalled that at a special meeting of the CTC held on 28 September 2011 to mark the tenth anniversary of the adoption of UN Security Council Resolution 1373, member-states were urged to *"ensure zero tolerance towards terrorism and take urgent action to prevent and combat terrorism in all its forms and manifestations."* However, it is to be noted that the relationship between terrorism and IHL is subject to scrutiny and needs to pass the defining tests of International or Non-International Armed Conflicts.

The Curious Case of Peacekeeping Histories: Many commentators wonder in amazement at the idiosyncrasies that dominate the

---

[504] Women, Peace and Security", UNSC Resolution 1325 (2000)
[505] Dominic McGoldrick, A.P.V. Rogers, "*Assassination and Targeted Killing - The Killing of Osama Bin Laden*", **I.C.L.Q.** 2011, 60(3), pp. 778-788

interface between the South Asian Governments and Armed Forces on one hand and IHL actors on the other. This is particularly stark given the fact that most of these countries are strong votaries and advocates of the UN's peacekeeping role and in fact are among the largest contributors to most major peacekeeping missions. India, Pakistan and Bangladesh are the top three in the world both in terms of number of personnel (with roughly 10,000 troops each) and in terms of the ultimate sacrifice of death in the service of world peace (runs into the hundreds). For instance, in 2010, out of Congo's 17,000 peacekeepers, about 4,300 were from India, 3,500 from Pakistan and 1,300 from Bangladesh.[506] Off late Bhutan has also commenced contributing troops to the UN.[507] Further, it is worthwhile mentioning that Indian women peacekeepers have done the country proud in places such as Liberia. Yet, when it comes to respect for IHL norms including crimes against women and children in armed conflict and inter-state conflict situations, South Asian countries are lagging behind. This represents a major feature of the IHL regime in the sub-continent.

Part II: Challenges to IHL in the South Asian Region

It is fair to state that major IHL related challenges in the South Asian region are extremely diverse in nature with some concerning its interpretation and applicability and others concerning its compliance and implementation. While it is admitted that not all of these challenges may not be unique to South Asia nevertheless their relevance is undeniable. Furthermore, considering space constraints some of the more significant challenges have been highlighted and some have been left out. Hence, this should not in any manner be concluded as an exhaustive list.

---

[506] For a more nuanced understanding see: David Axe, "*Why South Asia loves Peacekeeping,*" **The Diplomat**, dated 20 December 2010

[507] https://peacekeeping.un.org/sites/default/files/02_countryranking_21.pdf; website visited on 2/05/2020

Lack of State Cooperation vis-a-vis Non-International Armed Conflicts: State cooperation is central to successful humanitarian operations. However, lack of desired cooperation is common in South Asia and the same has manifested in more ways than one. One of the challenges to IHL that needs to be addressed is with respect to the exercise of state's prerogative to recognize the existence of a Non-International Armed Conflict within its territorial jurisdiction. Consequently, IHL which constitutes *lex specialis* cannot be invoked and hence treaty rules of protection are not applied. While, there is no doubt that human rights as provided under international law such as UDHR, ICCPR etc. does apply at all times, the standards of protection vary. International Humanitarian Law which is more suited to deal with conflict situations provides appropriate standards of protection as it is closer to ground realities. While, IHL principles apply automatically, in case of NIACs, states' formal acknowledgement of the existence of armed conflict becomes a prerequisite for practical application. Also closely associated with this issue is the lacuna surrounding legal determination of Non-International Armed Conflicts. Precise classification of conflicts is integral to invoking the application of International Humanitarian Law.[508] Newer varieties of NIAC are emerging[509] and standards of protection vary from IAC to NIAC.[510] Yet another form of non-cooperation by the state is the lack of consistent consent to external humanitarian support and refusal to acknowledge a status of NIAC. In the case of India, Kashmir conflict and the Naxal

---

[508] Marco Sassoli, *The Implementation of International Humanitarian Law: Current and Inherent Challenges*, **Yearbook of International Humanitarian Law**, 10, 2007, pp. 45-73

[509] "International Humanitarian Law and the Challenges of Contemporary Armed Conflicts", Report by the International Committee of the Red Cross, October 2011

[510] Sandesh Sivakumaran, *"Re-envisaging the International Law of Internal Armed Conflict"*, **E.J.I.L.** 2011, 22(1), pp. 219-264

movement are characterized by such positions. Parts of eastern and southern India which is commonly described as the *red corridor* is a region deeply disturbed by the *naxal* movement. The recent experience in Chhattisgarh stands testimony to this view. The government's decision to shut down humanitarian operations after merely 2 years was surprising to humanitarians, given the reeling crises for several decades.

Destruction of Cultural Property and Environment: Destruction of Cultural Property is quite common in times of war[511] and any such conduct by perpetrators shall be deemed as violative of law.[512] Deliberate targeting of cultural property intended to decimate cultural identities, is particularly true in case of Taliban's demolition of 1500 years old Buddhas of Bamiyan in Afghanistan. As a result of the same conflict, constant exposure to polluted environment in Asthana led to serious destruction of the land and water resources.[513] Considering the strong religious and ideological factors that drive armed groups in South Asia, annihilation of cultural objects is likely to be a means to demean cultural identity particularly cultural property that symbolizes diversity in a homogenous or heterogeneous community.

Disproportionate Use of Force: Proportionality of responses to an attack is a recognized norm governing conduct in furtherance of private defense in all South Asian nations and beyond. However, in an era where *preemptive strikes* and *collateral damage* is common, significant advances in weapons technology is a challenge to

---

[511] Micaela Frulli, *"The Criminalization of Offences against Cultural Heritage in times of Armed Conflict: The Quest for Consistency"*, **E.J.I.L.** 2011, 22(1), pp. 203-217

[512] Additional Protocol II to Hague Convention on Protection of Cultural Property in Times of Armed Conflict;1954

[513] UNEP, Ground Contamination Assessment Report: Military Waste Storage Site, Astana, Afghanistan, December 2006

effective prevention and mitigation of suffering. While precision strikes is the order of the day, application of *double tapping* techniques while deploying drones affords no scope for giving effect to the *no-quarter* norm.[514] While *military necessity* is usually cited as justification for widespread damage,[515] in a region where *asymmetrical confrontation* is common, protection of civilians as well as *hors de combat* indeed confronts and constrains implementation of IHL principles.

High Proportion of Civilian Casualty: IHL draws clear lines of distinction as to the standards of treatment vis a vis combatants and non-combatants and the inviolability of the latter group is in fact a customary principle of international law. Unfortunately, it is the civilian population which constitutes the overwhelming majority of victims in any given conflict zone generally. South Asia has been no exception to this phenomenon. However, the reason that may be attributed to this unfortunate consequence is multiple. For instance, the Sri Lankan crisis, particularly in its final phases witnessed civilians being used as human shields by the LTTE. The Sri Lankan forces have also been alleged to have bombarded hospitals (as a military strategy) which are to be treated as safe zones as per both conventional and customary norms. Conflicts have also taken place in densely populated locations mainly due to the mingling of fighters within civilian population (particularly in case of NIAC). Also, NIAC involves armed groups that are likely to be ignorant of IHL norms and hence disregard even fundamental norms.

Due Process during NIAC: Preventive detention i.e. internment of persons perceived as potential threats at times or places of conflict is an inevitable global reality. While the law can be categorically

---

[514] See ICRC Commentary on Art. 40 of Additional Protocol I; see also Art. 8(b)(xii) &Art. 8(e)(x) of Rome Statute, 1998

[515] David Luban, "*Military Necessity and the Cultures of Military Law*", **L.J.I.L.** 2013, 26(2), pp. 315-349

described as clear in this regard vis-a-vis non-combatants in case of International Armed Conflicts,[516] the same cannot be said to be true in case of Non-International Armed Conflicts. IHL is silent, hence leaving due process either as a mandate of the state as per domestic laws or as per rules of International law on Human Rights. Any attempt to convince states to accede to either new interpretations of existing IHL or new rules of IHL is likely to be perceived by states with suspicion and as a threat to state sovereignty. In light of the complex myriad of NIAC prevailing in India, subverting such suspicions and perceptions are likely to be an upcoming challenge to the evolution of IHL. At this point, I would like to draw an analogy with procedures for preventive detention in case of Non-International Armed Conflict in India. As mentioned earlier, India has its own share of NIAC's. The due process to be followed in these places is guided by special legislation.[517] However, the standards prescribed under IHL in case of Internment of non-combatants are of much order when compared to the standards envisaged under the special laws.

Conclusion

The foremost conclusion of our enquiry that stares us in the face is the fact that IHL related issues apply to almost all South Asian countries. The degree of intensity may differ but the fact remains that acts that attract universally applicable IHL provisions are found aplenty in the region.

Secondly, it is difficult to separate the political and ethnic dimensions of the IHL related issues in the region from the legal dimension. This is critical since without a doubt there is a strong legalistic tradition and knowledge of the intricacies of the legalities

---

[516] Geneva Convention relative to the Protection of Civilian Persons in Time of War, 1949

[517] E.g. Armed Forces Special Powers Act 1958; Armed Forces Special Powers Act (Assam & Manipur) 1958; Armed Forces Special Powers Act (Punjab & Chandigarh) 1983

of armed conflict situations amongst South Asian governing elites that have to be adequately factored in each and every case.

Thirdly, the cross-boundary influences amongst and within countries of the region make the task of enforcing IHL norms all the more complicated. Not that this is unique to South Asia. Merely, that the salience of such influences becomes magnified many times over and can begin to confuse the protectors and supporters of an appropriate IHL regime in the region.

Fourthly, terrorism poses an extremely significant threat to regional peace and stability as far as the South Asian region is concerned. The impact of terror groups and the efforts to abate terrorism on local population is disturbing. Yet, given the legal issues, provision for humanitarian support continues to be constrained.

Fifthly, focused efforts to harmonize municipal due process standards for preventive detention with IHL prescribed standards regulating internment are desirable. This is particularly true considering the fact that the existence and control exercised by *foreign elements* in NIAC's in India virtually blurs the traditional distinction of armed conflicts.

Finally, nowhere else in the world have the new and non-conventional threats to peace and security compounded the security situation as they have done in South Asia. By all indications the complexities introduced by such challenges are only likely to become more pronounced over the near future. The most pressing example is the drawdown of the International stabilization Force in Afghanistan (ISAF), where its departure may have important security implications.[518] Consequently innovative and robust methods of enforcing IHL norms have to be found out.

---

[518] See "UN Peacekeeping: The Next 5 Years," Report by NYU Centre on International Cooperation, 2012

A Handbook on Contemporary Public International Law

Protected Emblems

Annexure I

Annexure II

 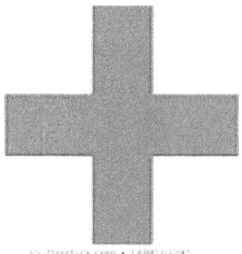 

Annexure III

A Handbook on Contemporary Public International Law

Annexure IV   **Annexure V**

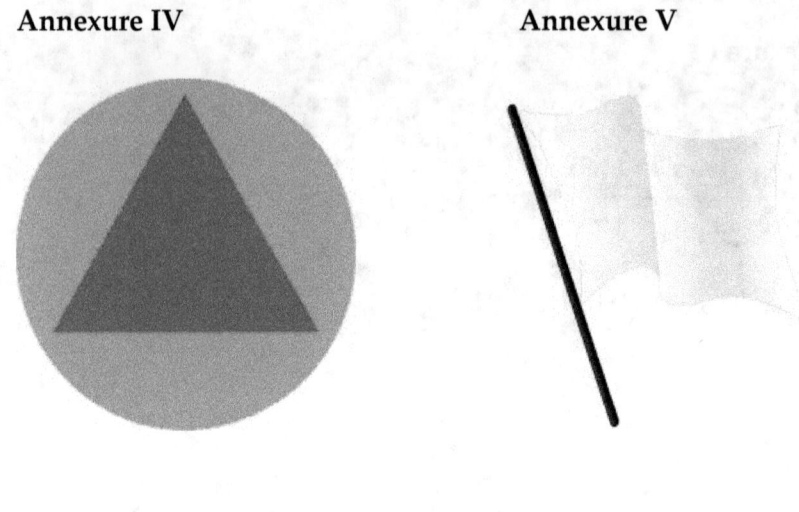

Annexure VI

11 International Human Rights Law

Topics covered
➤ Universal Declaration of Human Rights
➤ International Covenant on Economic, Social and Cultural Rights
➤ International Covenant on Civil and Political Rights
➤ International Convention on the Elimination of all Forms of Racial Discrimination
➤ Convention on the Elimination of all Forms of Discrimination against Women
➤ Convention against Torture and other Cruel, Inhuman or Degrading Treatment or Punishment
➤ Convention on the Rights of the Child
➤ International Convention on the Protection of the Rights of all Migrant Workers and Members of their Families
➤ Overlap of IHL and IHRL in Situations of Armed Conflict
➤ International Refugee Law

International Human Rights Law (IHRL) did not exist prior to World War 2. During that period, it was diffused and disaggregated. A series of international human rights treaties and other instruments have emerged since 1945, conferring legal form to inherent human rights. The creation of the United Nations provided an ideal forum for the development and adoption of international human rights instruments. Other instruments have been adopted at a regional level reflecting the particular human rights concerns of the region. Most States have also adopted constitutions and other laws which formally protect basic human rights. Art. 1(3) UN Charter deals with human rights and Fundamental Freedoms, but not concrete obligations on member states. The UN Charter also provides enabling tools for the UN to develop human rights instruments.[519] At its first meeting in 1946, the UN General Assembly transmitted a draft Declaration of Fundamental Human Rights and Freedoms to the Commission on Human Rights, through the Economic and Social Council, relative to the preparation of an international bill of human rights. In 1948, the draft declaration was revised and submitted through the Economic and Social Council to the General Assembly. On 10 December 1948, the Universal Declaration of Human Rights was adopted and by 1950, the General Assembly passed a resolution declaring that the *"enjoyment of civil and political freedoms and of economic, social and cultural rights are interconnected and interdependent."* In 1966, two International Covenants on Human Rights were completed (instead of the one originally envisaged): the International Covenant on Economic, Social and Cultural Rights (ICESCR) and the International Covenant on Civil and Political Rights (ICCPR), which effectively translated the principles of the Universal Declaration into treaty law. In conjunction with the Universal Declaration of Human Rights, the two Covenants are referred to as the *International Bill of Human Rights*.

Universal Declaration of Human Rights
The UDHR consists of a Preamble and 30 articles, setting out the human rights and fundamental freedoms to which everyone is entitled, without distinction of any kind.[520] The Universal

---

[519] Art 55 (3), Art. 56 of the UN Charter, 1945
[520] Art. 2 of the UDHR, 1948

Declaration recognizes that, the inherent dignity of all members of the human family is the foundation of freedom, justice and peace in the world.[521] It recognizes fundamental rights as inherent to every human being[522] including, inter alia, the right to life, liberty and security of person,[523] the right to an adequate standard of living,[524] the right to seek and enjoy asylum from persecution in other countries,[525] the right to freedom of opinion and expression,[526] the right to education,[527] freedom of thought, conscience and religion,[528] right to freedom from torture and degrading treatment[529] and property rights.[530] These inherent rights are to be enjoyed by every man, woman and child throughout the world, as well as by all groups in society.

International Covenant on Economic, Social and Cultural Rights (ICESCR)

After 20 years of drafting debates, the ICESCR was adopted by the General Assembly in 1966 and entered into force in 1976.[531] Historically, greater international attention has been paid to civil and political rights when compared to social, economic and cultural rights. In contemporary legal history, the latter stands fully recognized by the international community and is progressively gaining attention. These rights are designed to ensure the protection of people, based on the expectation that people can enjoy rights, freedoms and social justice simultaneously. The Covenant

---

[521] Preambular provision of the UDHR, 1948
[522] *Ibid*
[523] Art. 3
[524] Art. 25
[525] Art. 14
[526] Art. 19
[527] Art. 26
[528] Art. 18
[529] Art. 5
[530] Art. 17
[531] General Assembly resolution 2200A (XXI) of 16 December 1966

embodies some of the most significant international legal provisions including, inter alia, rights relating to work in just and favourable conditions,[532] to social security,[533] to an adequate standard of living including clothing, food and housing,[534] to the highest attainable standards of physical and mental health,[535] to education[536] and to the enjoyment of the benefits of cultural freedom and scientific progress.[537] Significantly, art. 2 outlines the legal obligations which are incumbent upon States parties under the Covenant to implement these rights, subject to its resources. In particular, states may implement its responsibilities through adoption of appropriate domestic legislation. Monitoring the implementation of the Covenant by States parties was the responsibility of the Economic and Social Council,[538] through the Committee on Economic, Social and Cultural Rights.[539]

International Covenant on Civil and Political Rights
The International Covenant on Civil and Political Rights addresses the State's traditional responsibilities for administering justice and maintaining the rule of law. Many of the provisions in the Covenant address the relationship between the individual and the State. In discharging these responsibilities, States must ensure that human rights of perpetrators and victims are respected. The civil and political rights defined in the Covenant include, inter alia, the right to self-determination,[540] the right to life,[541] liberty and security,[542]

---

[532] Art. 7 of the ICESCR 1966
[533] Art. 9 *Ibid*
[534] Art. 14
[535] Art. 12 (1)
[536] Art. 13
[537] Art. 15
[538] Articles 16-22
[539] ECOSOC Resolution 1985/17 of 28 May 1985
[540] Art. 1 (1) of the ICCPR 1966
[541] Art. 6 (1) *Ibid*
[542] Art. 9

freedom of movement including freedom to choose a place of residence and the right to leave the country,[543] freedom of thought, conscience, religion,[544] peaceful assembly[545] and association,[546] freedom from torture and other cruel and degrading treatment or punishment,[547] freedom from slavery and compelled labour,[548] freedom from arbitrary arrest or detention,[549] the right to a fair and prompt trial,[550] and the right to privacy.[551] There are also other provisions which protect members of ethnic, religious or linguistic minorities.[552] Under Art. 2, *all States Parties undertake to respect and take the necessary steps to ensure the rights recognized in the Covenant without distinction of any kind, such as race, colour, sex, language, religion, political or other opinion, national or social origin, property, birth or other status.*

The Covenant has two Optional Protocols. The first establishes the procedure for dealing with communications (or complaints) from individuals claiming to be victims of violations of any of the rights set out in the Covenant.[553] The second envisages the abolition of the death penalty.[554] The ICCPR authorizes a State to derogate from, or

---

[543] Art. 12
[544] Art. 18 (1)
[545] Art. 21
[546] Art. 22 (1)
[547] Art. 7
[548] Art. 8
[549] Art. 9 (1)
[550] *Ibid*
[551] Art. 17
[552] Art. 27
[553] Optional Protocol to the International Covenant on Civil and Political Rights General Assembly resolution 2200A (XXI) of 16 December 1966
[554] Second Optional Protocol to the International Covenant on Civil and Political Rights, aiming at the abolition of the death penalty Adopted and proclaimed by General Assembly resolution 44/128 of 15 December 1989

restrict, the enjoyment of certain rights in times of an official public emergency when an existential crisis prevails.[555] This extraordinary provision is subject to strict limitations[556] and must be reported to the other state parties through United Nations.[557] Even so, some provisions such as the right to life and freedom from torture and slavery may never be suspended. The Covenant provides for the establishment of a Human Rights Committee[558] to monitor implementation of the Covenant's provisions by States parties.[559]

International Convention on the Elimination of all Forms of Racial Discrimination

The phenomenon of racial discrimination was one of the concerns behind the establishment of the United Nations and has therefore been one of its major areas of attention. The International Convention on the Elimination of All Forms of Racial Discrimination was adopted by the General Assembly in 1965 and entered into force in 1969.[560] Art. 1 of the Convention defines the terms *racial discrimination* as:

> *"any distinction, exclusion, restriction or preference based on race, colour, descent, national or ethnic origin with the purpose or effect of nullifying or impairing the recognition, enjoyment or exercise, on an equal footing, of human rights in any field of public life, including political, economic, social or cultural life."*

It is notable that this definition encompasses wide range of grounds on which discrimination take place. The definition covers not only intentional discrimination, but also laws, norms and practices which may appear innocent. Parties to the Convention agree to

---

[555] Art. 4 (1) of the ICCPR 1966
[556] Art. 4 (2) *Ibid*
[557] Art. 4 (3)
[558] Art. 28 (1)
[559] Articles 40-42
[560] General Assembly resolution 2106 (XX) of 21 December 1965

eliminate discrimination in the enjoyment of civil, political, economic, social and cultural rights[561] and to provide effective remedies through national tribunals and State institutions.[562] States parties undertake not to refrain from racial discrimination against individuals, groups of persons or institutions, not to sponsor, defend or support racial discrimination by persons or organizations; to review government, national and local policies and to amend wherever appropriate, to prohibit and put a stop to racial discrimination and to encourage integration or multiracial organizations, movements etc.[563]

Convention on the Elimination of all Forms of Discrimination against Women

The Convention on the Elimination of All Forms of Discrimination against Women was adopted by the General Assembly in 1979 and entered into force in 1981. In addition to addressing the major issues pertaining to discrimination on lines of gender, the Convention also identifies a number of specific areas including participation in public life,[564] marriage,[565] family life and sexual exploitation.[566] It requires States parties to grant freedoms and rights to women on the same basis as men. It encourages parties to make use of positive measures, including preferential treatment, to advance the status of women and their ability to participate in decision making in all spheres of national life – economic, social, cultural, civil and political. States parties agree, inter alia, to integrate the principle of the equality of men and women into

---

[561] Art. 5 International Convention on the Elimination of all Forms of Racial Discrimination of 1965
[562] Art. 6 *Ibid*
[563] Art. 2 (1)
[564] Art. 7 (1) of the Convention on the Elimination of all Forms of Discrimination against Women of 1979
[565] Art. 16 *Ibid*
[566] Art. 6

national legislation,[567] to adopt legislative and other measures, including sanctions where appropriate,[568] to ensure through national tribunals and other public institutions the effective protection of women against discrimination.[569]

Convention against Torture and other Cruel, Inhuman or Degrading Treatment or Punishment

The adoption, on 10 December 1984 by the General Assembly, of the Convention against Torture and Other Cruel, Inhuman or Degrading Treatment or Punishment,[570] was the culmination of the codification process to combat the practice of torture. The Convention entered into force on 26 June 1987. Art. 1 defines *torture* as:

> *"any act by which severe pain or suffering, whether physical or mental, is intentionally inflicted on a person for such purposes as obtaining from him or a third person information or a confession, punishing him for an act he or a third person has committed or is suspected of having committed, or intimidating or coercing him or a third person, or for any reason based on discrimination of any kind, when such pain or suffering is inflicted by or at the instigation of or with the consent or acquiescence of a public official or other person acting in an official capacity."*

The overall objectives of the Convention are to prevent acts of torture and other acts prohibited under the Convention and to ensure that effective remedies are available to victims when such acts occur. More specifically, the Convention requires parties to take preventive action against torture such as the criminalization of

---

[567] Art. 16 (1) (f) *Ibid*
[568] Art. 2 (b)
[569] Art. 2 (c)
[570] General Assembly resolution 39/46 of 10 December 1984

acts of torture[571] and the establishment of laws to promote respect for human rights among its public servants for both victim and accused. It is to be noted that the provisions of this convention are applicable only with respect to action/inaction of public authorities and does not extend to private action.

Convention on the Rights of the Child

The Convention entered into force on 2 September 1990, within a year of its unanimous adoption by the General Assembly.[572] The Convention embodies four general principles for guiding implementation of the rights of the child:
  a) non-discrimination ensuring equality[573]
  b) State to prime consideration to the best interests of the child[574]
  c) Right to life and development shall include physical, mental, emotional, cognitive, social and cultural development and
  d) children should be free to express their opinions[575]

Other provisions of the Convention include, States parties agree that children's rights include: free and compulsory primary education,[576] protection from economic exploitation,[577] sexual abuse[578] and protection from physical and mental harm and neglect,[579] the right of the disabled child to special treatment[580] and

---

[571] Art 4 of the Convention against Torture and Other Cruel, Inhuman or Degrading Treatment or Punishment 1984
[572] General Assembly resolution 44/25 of 20 November 1989
[573] Articles 28, 29, 31 of the Child Rights Convention of 1989
[574] Art. 3 (1) *Ibid*
[575] Art. 12 (1)
[576] Art. 28 (1) (a)
[577] Art. 32 (1)
[578] Art. 34
[579] Art. 39
[580] Art. 23

protection of children affected by armed conflict.[581] Under art. 43 of the Convention, the Committee on the Rights of the Child was established to monitor the implementation of the Convention by States parties.

International Convention on the Protection of the Rights of all Migrant Workers and Members of their Families

The Convention was adopted by the General Assembly on 18 December 1990.[582] The Convention stipulates that persons who are considered as migrant workers under its provisions are entitled to enjoy their human rights throughout the migration process. This shall include preparation for migration, transit, stay and return to their State of origin or habitual residence. With regard to working conditions, migrant workers are entitled to conditions equivalent to those extended to nationals of the host States, including the right to join trade unions,[583] the right to social security[584] and the right to emergency health care. State parties are obliged to establish policies on migration, exchange information with employers and provide assistance to migrant workers and their families.[585] Similarly, the Convention stipulates that migrant workers and their families are obliged to comply with the law of the host State. The Convention distinguishes between legal and illegal migrant workers to eliminate illegal or clandestine movements and employment of migrant workers.[586]

Overlap of IHL and IHRL in Situations of Armed Conflict

IHRL deals with the inherent rights of the person to be protected at

---

[581] Art. 38 (1)

[582] General Assembly resolution 45/158 of 18 December 1990

[583] Art. 26 of the International Convention on the Protection of the Rights of all Migrant Workers and Members of their Families of 1990

[584] Art. 27 (1) and Art. 61 (3) *Ibid*

[585] Art. 65

[586] Art. 68

all times against abusive power of states and IHL regulates the conduct of parties to an armed conflict. Yet, there are a number of points of contact between the two bodies of law. These regimes overlap and it is necessary to apply them concurrently and to reconcile them. IHRL and IHL share a common ideal, protection of the dignity and integrity of the person, and many of their guarantees are identical, such as the protection of the right to life, freedom from torture and ill-treatment, the protection of family rights, economic, and/or social rights. Two main concepts central to their interaction are (a) the complementarity between norms and (b) that the more specific norm would prevail over the general norm when there is contradiction between the two. Procedural rights such as the right to a remedy and to reparation, which are more strongly enshrined in human rights law but have an increasing influence on international humanitarian law.

International Refugee Law
Throughout human history, people have moved from one place to another. While motivations and specific circumstances may vary, such movement are usually undertaken for a better life. When such movement is based on choice, it may be described as voluntary and when such movement is based out of compulsion and/or fear, it may be termed as *coerced movements*. In the latter category, specific circumstances that may prevail range from slavery, trafficking, climate, conflict etc. If movement is within a country, they may be described as internally displaced. Where such movement is across national boundaries, this may attract the application of international refugee law. International refugee law is a part of international human rights law. The term refugee connotes a legal status, that entails certain rights and protection under the law. At the outset, it is to be noted that there is no absolute right to refugee status under international law. Contemporary agreement between states inter se on this topic can be traced to the League of Nations period of the first of 20th Century. These efforts were intertwined with fear arising due to wars and collapse of European empires.

The Russian revolution leading to the collapse of the Romanovs, the Ottoman Wars, the impact of world war I on Austria and Germany were central to the mass exodus that took place during the 1920s. What started as efforts of non-governmental organizations and national humanitarian organizations gradually evolved into an intergovernmental institution. Of particular importance is the contribution of Norwegian explorer Fridtjof Nansen. The earliest travel documents issued to refugees providing them a degree of protection came to be known as the Nansen Passport which was valid for a year. First sanctioned to be issued in 1922 following the Intergovernmental Conference on Identity Certificates for Russian Refugees held at Geneva. Initially, this refugee travel document was sanctioned to address the protection status of Russian refugees. Following the demise of Nansen, under the auspices of the League of Nations, the Nansen International Office for Refugees was created and named in his memory and honor in the year 1930. The Nansen International Office for Refugees played a pivotal role in the adoption of the 1933 Refugee Convention. Limited to then 14 nation states, this Convention played a significant step to an international understanding of the legal status of refugees. Arguably the greatest contribution of the 1933 Convention to this branch of human rights law is the principle of *non-refoulement*. It is provided in Art. 3, wherein states are prohibited from the expulsion or return of a refugee, in the following manner

> *" Each of the Contracting Parties undertakes not to remove or keep from its territory by application of police measures, such as expulsions or non-admittance at the frontier (refoulement), refugees who have been authorized to reside there regularly, unless the said measures are dictated by reasons of national security or public order"*

The Office came to an end with the commencement of World War 2 and the League of Nations' inability to prevent the second great war. In 1938 the office of High Commissioner for Refugees was established. The second world war also bore witness to redrawing of political boundaries, turmoil and mass movement of people. The impasse over the handling of protection of Jews in Nuremberg and other places had a telling effect on the institutional resilience of the League of Nations and its principle office for refugees. After the end of second world war, two institutions were established under the United Nations. These are the United Nations Relief and Rehabilitation Administration created in the year 1944 and International Relief Organization in 1947. Later the Office of the United Nations High Commissioner for Refugees (UNHCR) was established as a subsidiary organ of the General Assembly by Resolution 319 (IV) of the United Nations General Assembly of December 1949.

As far as the evolution of refugee law is concerned, the 1948 UN GA Declaration on Human Rights titled Universal Declaration of Human Rights constitutes the next important step after the 1933 Refugee Convention. This declaration is per se an ideal and persuasive in nature and lack binding legal force. However, its provisions over time have helped lay down the foundations for a number of human rights instruments. Art. 14 of the UDHR 1948 states,

> *(1) Everyone has the right to seek and to enjoy in other countries asylum from persecution.*
> *(2) This right may not be invoked in the case of prosecutions genuinely arising from non-political crimes or from acts contrary to the purposes and principles of the United Nations.*

It may be pertinent to note that as such the UDHR of 1948 does not expressly mention the term *refugee*. The construct of the said provision and when read in light of Art. 15 which vests everyone with the right of nationality and effectively denying the state the option of arbitrary denial of nationality, gives rise to a variety of implications. At this juncture it is important to know the difference between *asylum seeker* and *refugee*. An asylum seeker is an individual who is seeking international protection. An asylum seeker is someone whose claim has not yet been finally decided on by the country in which he or she has submitted it. On the other hand, a refugee is defined under Art. 1 (2) of the Refugee Convention of 1951 in the following manner,

> *"owing to well-founded fear of being persecuted for reasons of race, religion, nationality, membership of a particular social group or political opinion, is outside the country of his nationality and is unable or, owing to such fear, is unwilling to avail himself of the protection of that country; or who, not having a nationality and being outside the country of his former habitual residence as a result of such events, is unable or, owing to such fear, is unwilling to return to it."*

Thus, the difference and relation between asylum seeker and refugee can be summarized by the words not every asylum seeker will ultimately be recognized as a refugee, but every refugee is initially an asylum seeker. The Refugee Convention of 1951, formally titled Convention Relating to the Status of Refugees was an important *attempt* at universalizing refugee protection. The temporal and geographical limits to the definition of refugee was addressed in 1967 by virtue of the Protocol Relating to the Status of Refugees. The word *attempt* is emphasized here, reason being a number of countries are yet to accede to the 1951 Convention. The last accession dates back to 2011 when Nauru became a state party bringing the tally of membership to 145. The International Covenant on Civil and Political Rights of 1966, in respect of refugee protections lays down, under Art. 12 that:

> *Everyone lawfully within the territory of a State shall, within that territory, have the right to liberty of movement and freedom to choose his residence.*
> *Everyone shall be free to leave any country, including his own.*
> *The above-mentioned rights shall not be subject to any restrictions except those which are provided by law, are necessary to protect national security, public order, public health or morals or the*

> *rights and freedoms of others, and are consistent with the other rights recognized in the present Covenant.*
>
> *No one shall be arbitrarily deprived of the right to enter his own country.*

Nearing 70 years since the inception of the 1951 Convention, substantial number of countries with significant population, owing to variety of reasons (no country is obliged to provide reasons for not acceding to a treaty) are yet to show interest. Such countries follow their municipal protection mechanisms. It remains a sovereign right of a country to decide whom to provide entry and residence. Over the years, owing to a combined reading of the 1951 Convention, the International Bill of Rights provisions and individual state practice, the following are widely considered as agreed norms of refugee protection, albeit to varying levels of practice:

- ➢ Right of non-refoulment[587] [588]
- ➢ Right not to be tortured or treated cruelly[589]
- ➢ Right to marry[590]
- ➢ Right to movement[591]
- ➢ Right to identity (including and id card)[592]
- ➢ Right of non-discrimination[593]
- ➢ Right to a fair trial[594]

---

[587] Art. 33 of the Refugee Convention of 1951
[588] Art. 3 of the United Nations Convention against Torture of 1987
[589] Art. 7 of the ICCPR of 1967
[590] Art. 23 (1) *Ibid*
[591] Art. 11 (1)
[592] Art. 27 of the Refugee Convention of 1951
[593] Art. 2 of the Universal Declaration of Human Right, Art. 2 and 26 of the ICCPR, Art. 2(2) ICESCR, Art. 2 Child Rights Convention, Art 5 Convention on the Elimination of Discrimination
[594] Art. 14 (1) of the ICCPR of 1966

- Family reunification[595]
- Right of Employment[596]
- Right of Housing[597]
- Right to Education
- Freedom of movement

---

[595] The Conference of Plenipotentiaries which adopted the 1951 United Nations Convention relating to the Status of Refugees recognized the significance of this principle for refugees when it approved, in its Final Act, the following recommendation:
"*The Conference, considering that the unity of the family, the natural and fundamental group unit of society, is an essential right of the refugee, and that such unity if constantly threatened, and Noting with satisfaction that, according to the official commentary of the Ad Hoc Committee on*
Statelessness and Related Problems (E/1618, p. 40) the rights granted to a refugee are extended to members of his family,
Recommends Governments to take the necessary measures for the protection of the refugee's family"

[596] Art. 18 of the Refugee Convention of 1951

[597] Art. 25 of the Universal Declaration of Human Rights 1948, Art. 11 of the International Covenant on Economic, Social and Cultural Rights, Art 21 of the Refugee Convention of 1951

12 The United Nations

> **Topics covered**
> - Overview of UN Charter
> - Sovereign equality of states
> - Non-use of force in international relations
> - Domestic jurisdiction clause
> - Membership to the UN
> - Observer status in the UN General Assembly
> - General Assembly & GA Revitalization
> - Security Council & Security Council Reform
> - Economic and Social Council
> - Trusteeship Council
> - ICJ: Jurisdiction, pending cases
> - India in the ICJ
> - Regional Arrangements
> - Secretariat and Secretary General
> - UN Peace Keeping
> - UN Peacebuilding
> - World Trade Organization and WIPO: A case study
> - Are International Organizations withering away?
> - US-China IPR differences on WTO and what it means for India

International organizations also called as intergovernmental organizations,[598] are organizations constituted by treaty or any other instrument governed by international law. They possess

---

[598] Art. 2(1) (i) Vienna Convention on the Law of Treaties of 1969

international legal personality.[599] International organizations are composed of, primarily, states, but may also include other subjects of International Law. The first and oldest intergovernmental organization is the International Telecommunication Union (founded in 1865).[600] The ITU was created on the lines of a specialized organization. In contrast, the League of Nations, created as part of the Treaty of Versailles 1919 was the worlds' first general international organization—addressing a variety of issues.

United Nations

It was in the backdrop of the second World War that the United Nations was formed. The forerunner of the United Nations was the League of Nations, conceived in similar circumstances during the previous great war, *to promote international cooperation and to achieve peace and security*.[601] The International Labor Organization was also created under the Treaty of Versailles as an affiliated agency of the League. The League of Nations ceased its activities after failing to prevent the Second World War. The name *United Nations*, coined by the then United States President Franklin D. Roosevelt was first used in the Declaration by United Nations of 1 January 1942, when representatives of 26 nations[602] pledged their Governments to

---

[599] Art. 2 (a) of the Draft articles on the Responsibility of International Organizations 2011
[600] International Telegraph Convention of 1865
[601] Preamble, The Covenant of the League of Nations 1920
[602] The original twenty-six signatories were: the United States of America, the United Kingdom of Great Britain and Northern Ireland, the Union of Soviet Socialist Republics, China, Australia, Belgium, Canada, Costa Rica, Cuba, Czechoslovakia, Dominican Republic, El Salvador, Greece, Guatemala, Haiti, Honduras, India, Luxembourg, Netherlands, New Zealand, Nicaragua, Norway, Panama, Poland, Union of South Africa, Yugoslavia. Subsequent adherents to the Declaration were (in order of signature): Mexico, Philippines, Ethiopia, Iraq, Brazil, Bolivia, Iran, Colombia, Liberia, France,

continue fighting together against the Axis Powers. The text of the Declaration is in the box below.

> *The Governments signatory hereto,*
> *Having subscribed to a common program of purposes and principles embodied in the Joint Declaration of the President of the United States of America and the Prime Minister of Great Britain dated August 14, 1941, known as the Atlantic Charter,*
> *Being convinced that complete victory over their enemies is essential to defend life, liberty, independence and religious freedom, and to preserve human rights and justice in their own lands as well as in other lands, and that they are now engaged in a common struggle against savage and brutal forces seeking to subjugate the world, Declare:*
> *(1) Each Government pledges itself to employ its full resources, military or economic, against those members of the Tripartite Pact and its adherents with which such government is at war.*
> *(2) Each Government pledges itself to cooperate with the Governments signatory hereto and not to make a separate armistice or peace*
> *The foregoing declaration may be adhered to by other nations which are, or which may be, rendering material assistance and contributions in the struggle for victory over Hitlerism.*

The next milestones on the journey towards the UN were the Moscow Conference of 30 October 1943 and the Tehran Conference of 1 December 1943. Signed in Moscow by Vyaches Molotov (Foreign Minister of the Soviet Union), Anthony Eden (Foreign Secretary of the United Kingdom), Cordell Hull (United States Secretary of State) and Foo Ping Shen, the Chinese Ambassador to the Soviet Union, the Declaration pledged further joint action in dealing with the enemies' surrender and proclaimed:

Ecuador, Peru, Chile, Paraguay, Venezuela, Uruguay, Turkey, Egypt, Saudi Arabia, Syria, Lebanon.

> That they recognize the necessity of establishing at the earliest practicable date a general international organization, based on the principle of the sovereign equality of all peace-loving states, and open to membership by all such states, large and small, for the maintenance of international peace and security[603]

A couple of months after the Declaration, US President Franklin Roosevelt, Premier of Soviet Union Josef Stalin and the Prime Minister of Great Britain Winston Churchill, meeting for the first time at Tehran declared that they had worked out concerted plans for final victory. For the period after the *final victory*, the three leaders declared as follows:

> And as to peace—we are sure that our concord will win an enduring peace. We recognize fully the supreme responsibility resting upon us and all the United Nations to make a peace which will command the good will of the overwhelming mass of the peoples of the world and banish the scourge and terror of war for many generations. With our diplomatic advisers we have surveyed the problems of the future. We shall seek the cooperation and active participation of all nations, large and small, whose peoples in heart and mind are dedicated, as are our own peoples, to the elimination of tyranny and slavery, oppression and intolerance. We will welcome them, as they may choose to come, into a world family of democratic nations. [604]

The Dumbarton Oaks Conference constituted the first important step taken to carry out paragraph 4 of the Moscow Declaration of 1943, which recognized the need for a post-war international organization to succeed the League of Nations. The representatives of China, Great Britain, the USSR and the United States met for a

---

[603] Clause 4 of the Moscow Declaration of 1943
[604] Declaration of the Three Powers, December 1, 1943

business-like conference at Dumbarton Oaks, a private mansion in Washington, DC and after discussions on October 7, 1944, they produced a proposal for the structure of the envisioned world organization.

The main elements of these proposals were as follows:

> *A Proposal for the World Organization*
> *Structure:* According to the Dumbarton Oaks proposals, four principal bodies were to constitute the organization to be known as the United Nations. There was to be a General Assembly composed of all the members. Then came a Security Council of eleven members. Five of these were to be permanent and the other six were to be chosen from the remaining members by the General Assembly to hold office for two years. The third body was an International Court of Justice, and the fourth a Secretariat. An Economic and Social Council, working under the authority of the General Assembly, was also provided for.
> *Roles and Responsibilities:* The essence of the plan was that responsibility for preventing future war should be conferred upon the Security Council. The General Assembly could study, discuss and make recommendations in order to promote international cooperation and adjust situations likely to impair welfare. It could consider problems of cooperation in maintaining peace and security, and disarmament, in their general principles. But it could not make recommendations on any matter being considered by the Security Council, and all questions on which action was necessarily had to be referred to the Security Council.
> *Method of Voting:* The actual method of voting in the Security Council, was left open at Dumbarton Oaks for future discussion.
> *Armed Forces in the Service of Peace:* Another important feature of the Dumbarton Oaks plan was that member states were to place armed forces at the disposal of the Security Council in its task of preventing war and suppressing acts of aggression. The absence

> of such force, it was generally agreed, had been a fatal weakness in the older League of Nations machinery for preserving peace.

One important gap in the Dumbarton Oaks proposals that had yet to be filled was the voting procedure in the Security Council. This was done at the Yalta Conference where Churchill, Roosevelt and Stalin, their foreign ministers and chiefs of staff, met. On February 11, 1945, the conference announced that this question had been resolved, and it summoned the San Francisco Conference. In 1945, representatives of 50 countries met in San Francisco at the United Nations Conference on International Organization to draw up the United Nations Charter. Those delegates deliberated on the basis of proposals worked out by the representatives of China, the Soviet Union, the United Kingdom and the United States at Dumbarton Oaks, United States in August-October 1944. The Charter was signed on 26 June 1945 by the representatives of the 50 countries. Poland, which was not represented at the Conference, signed it later and became one of the original 51 Member States. The United Nations officially came into existence on 24 October 1945, when the Charter had been ratified by China, France, the Soviet Union, the United Kingdom, the United States and by a majority of other signatories. United Nations Day is celebrated on 24 October each year.

Overview of UN Charter, Preamble & Purposes and Principles
The UN Charter has a Preamble, followed by chapters dealing respectively with: (a) Purposes and Principles[605] (b) Membership[606] (c) Organs[607] (d) The General Assembly[608] (e) The Security Council[609] (f) Pacific Settlement of Disputes (g) Action with Respect to Threats

---

[605] Art. 1 and 2 of the UN Charter of 1945
[606] Articles 3-6 *Ibid*
[607] Art. 7 and 8
[608] Articles 9-22
[609] Articles 23-54

to the Peace, Breaches of the Peace and Acts of Aggression, (h) Regional Arrangements (i) International Economic and Social Co-operation[610] (j) The Economic and Social Council[611] (k) Declaration regarding Non-Self-Governing Territories[612] (l) International Trusteeship System[613] (m) The Trusteeship Council[614] (n) The International Court of Justice[615] (o) The Secretariat[616] (p) Miscellaneous Provisions[617] (q) Transitional Security Arrangements[618] (r) Amendments[619] and (s) Ratification and Signature.[620] The Statute of the International Court of Justice is an integral part of the Charter. The Three Pillars of the United Nations are (a) human rights, (b) peace and security and (c) development. These three pillars are clearly captured in the Preamble of the UN Charter which begins with the words, *"We the peoples of the United Nations...."* The Preamble also captures the efforts towards establishing the two freedoms, namely freedom from want and freedom from fear. The respect[621] for the obligations arising from treaties and other sources of international law and the maintenance of international peace and security are the other important imperatives contained in the Preamble. As Hans Kelsen, rightly pointed out,[622] the Preamble is part of the Charter and has virtually the same legal validity, that is to say, the same binding force as the

---

[610] Articles 55-60
[611] Articles 61-72
[612] Art. 73 and 74
[613] Articles 75-85
[614] Articles 86-91
[615] Articles 92-96
[616] Articles 97-101
[617] Articles 102-105
[618] Art. 106 and 107
[619] Art. 108 and 109
[620] Art. 110 and 111
[621] Hans Kelsen, *The Preamble of the Charter: A Critical Analysis*, **The Journal of Politics** Vol. 8, No. 2 (May, 1946), pp. 134-159
[622] *Ibid*

other parts of the Charter. The Vienna Convention on the Law of Treaties of 1969[623] states that *"The context for the purpose of the interpretation of a treaty shall comprise, in addition to the text, including its preamble and annexes..."*[624] The Preamble concludes with the words, *"Accordingly, our respective Governments, through representatives assembled in the city of San Francisco...agreed to the present Charter of the United Nations and do hereby establish an international organization to be known as the United Nations."* This is interesting because the Preamble begins with *peoples* and concludes with *governments* which are not synonymous.

> The text of the Preamble of the UN Charter runs as follows:
> *We the peoples of the United Nations determined to save succeeding generations from the scourge of war, which twice in our lifetime has brought untold sorrow to mankind, and to reaffirm faith in fundamental human rights, in the dignity and worth of the human person, in the equal rights of men and women and of nations large and small, and to establish conditions under which justice and respect for the obligations arising from treaties and other sources of international law can be maintained, and to promote social progress and better standards of life in larger freedom, and for these ends to practice tolerance and live together in peace with one another as good neighbors, and to unite our strength to maintain international peace and security, and to ensure, by the acceptance of principles and the institution of methods, that armed force shall not be used, save in the common interest, and to employ international machinery for the promotion of the economic and social advancement of all peoples, have resolved to combine our efforts to accomplish these aims. Accordingly, our respective Governments, through representatives assembled in the city of San Francisco, who have exhibited their full powers found to be in good and due form, have agreed to the present Charter of the United Nations and do hereby establish an international organization to be known as the United Nations.*

---

[623] entry into force on 27 January 1980
[624] Art. 31 (2) of the Vienna Convention on Law of Treaties of 1969

The Purposes of the UN contained in Art. I of the Charter are four fold, namely: (a) to maintain international peace and security, (b) to develop friendly relations among nations, (c) achieve international co-operation in solving international problems of an economic, social, cultural, or humanitarian character, and in promoting and encouraging respect for human rights and for fundamental freedoms for all and (d) be a center for harmonizing the actions of nations in the attainment of these common ends. The seven principles of the UN are contained in Art. 2 and they are as follows:

(a) principle of the sovereign equality of all its Members;
(b) fulfilling in good faith the obligations assumed by the Members;
(c) settling international disputes by peaceful means;
(d) refrain from the threat or use of force against the territorial integrity or political independence of any state, or in any other manner inconsistent with the Purposes of the United Nations;
(e) assist the UN in any action it takes in accordance with the present Charter;
(f) states which are not Members of the United Nations to act in accordance with these Principles so far as may be necessary for the maintenance of international peace and security; and
(g) non-interference in matters which are essentially within the domestic jurisdiction of any state.

Sovereign Equality: In 1812, Judge John Marshall of US Supreme Court Justice emphasized *"full equality and absolute independence of the state"* in the *Schooner Exchange* Case.[625] The principle was reiterated in the revised edition of Oppenheim's International Law in the following manner; *"Equality is the extension of the foundation of*

---

[625] *The Schooner Exchange v. McFaddon*, 11 U.S. (7 Cranch) 116 (1812)

international law."[626] The UN Charter provides that *"the Organization is based on the principle of the sovereign equality of all its Members."*[627] Art. 78 reaffirms, *"...Members of the United Nations, relationship among which shall be based on respect for the principle of sovereign equality."* This essentially translates into one vote for each delegation at the UN. But there is a slight variation through the veto which is vested only in the permanent members of the UN Security Council.[628]

Non-use of force in international relations: Art. 2 (4) of the Charter prohibits the threat or use of force and calls on all Members to respect the sovereignty, territorial integrity and political independence of other States. However, there are two circumstances in which the prohibition does not apply: first, forcible measures may be taken or authorized by the Security Council[629] and second, force may be used in the exercise of the right of individual or collective self-defense.[630] Prior to the adoption of the Charter, the legitimacy of exercising self-defense was tested on the basis of the *Caroline* case: the necessity of force must be *"instant and overwhelming, and leaving no choice of means and no moment for deliberation."*[631]

Domestic jurisdiction clause: As Hans Kelsen has pointed out, the general provisions of the Charter conferring functions upon the UN and obligations upon its members are subject to important restrictions concerning matters of domestic jurisdiction[632] the right

---

[626] Robert Jennings, Arthur Watts, **Oppenheim's International Law: Volume 1 Peace** (9th Edition, Longman, London, 1992)
[627] Art. 2, para 1 of the UN Charter 1945
[628] Art. 27 of the UN Charter 1945
[629] Refer Chapter VII provisions of the Charter
[630] Art. 51 of the UN Charter 1945
[631] *The Caroline v. United States* 11 U.S. 496 (1813)
[632] Art. 2, Para 7 UN Charter 1945

of self-defense, and action[633] in relation to former *enemy states*.[634] Art. 2 (7) comprises two different rules: one broad prohibition against UN intervention in matters which are essentially within the domestic jurisdiction of any state; another releasing the members to submit such matters to settlement under the Charter.

Membership: Membership in the UN is open to all other peace-loving states which accept the obligations contained in the present Charter and, in the judgment of the Organization, are able and willing to carry out these obligations.[635] The admission of any such state to membership in the United Nations will be effected by a decision of the General Assembly upon the recommendation of the Security Council.[636] A Member state against which preventive or enforcement action has been taken by the Security Council may be suspended from the exercise of the rights and privileges of membership by the General Assembly upon the recommendation of the Security Council.[637] The exercise of these rights and privileges may be restored by the Security Council. A Member of the United Nations which has persistently violated the Principles contained in the present Charter may be expelled from the Organization by the General Assembly upon the recommendation of the Security Council.[638]

> *Observer status in the UN General Assembly*
> The United Nations General Assembly may grant non-member states, international organizations and other entities Permanent Observer Status. The UN Charter and the General Assembly Rules of Procedure have no provisions related to granting permanent

---

[633] Art. 51 *Ibid*
[634] Art. 53 and 107
[635] Art. 4 (1) *Ibid*
[636] Art. 4 (2)
[637] Art. 5
[638] Art. 6

> observer status.[639] The General Assembly decided that observer status would be confined to States and intergovernmental organizations whose activities cover matters of interest to the Assembly. The Sixth Committee of the General Assembly considers all applications for observer status before they are considered in the plenary session.[640] Permanent Observers may participate in the sessions and workings of the General Assembly and maintain missions at the UN Headquarters.

Principal organs of the United Nations
The main organs of the UN are the General Assembly, the Security Council, the Economic and Social Council, the Trusteeship Council, the International Court of Justice, and the UN Secretariat.[641] The principal organs were established in 1945 when the UN was founded.

General Assembly
All 193 Member States of the Organization are represented in the General Assembly,[642] to discuss and work together on a wide array of international issues covered by the Charter of the United Nations. The Assembly meets from September to December each year, and thereafter from January to September, as required, including to take up outstanding reports from the Administrative and Budgetary Committee and Legal Committee.[643] Also, during the resumed part of the session, the Assembly considers current issues of critical importance to the international community in the form of High-level Thematic Debates organized by the President of

---

[639] The process is described GA decision 49/426 of 9 December 1994 published in the 2008 United Nations Juridical Yearbook, p. 438, part B, paragraphs 8-11
[640] In para 2 of UN General Assembly Resolution 54/195
[641] Art. 7 of the UN Charter 1945
[642] Art. 9 (1) *Ibid*
[643] See Rule of Procedure of the UNGA A/520/Rev.18

the General Assembly in consultation with the membership. During that period, the Assembly traditionally also conducts informal consultations on a wide range of substantive topics as mandated by its resolutions.

> *Speaking order at the general debate every September*
> The general debate is held at the beginning of each session of the General Assembly, usually in September. Over time, certain customs have emerged during the general debate, including the custom of the order of the first few speakers. In current practice, after the opening of the meeting by the President of the General Assembly, the Secretary-General makes a statement, followed by the President of the General Assembly and then the representatives of Brazil (regardless of the level of representation) and the United States (as the host country, regardless of the level of representation). Since the 10th session in 1955, Brazil has spoken first and the United States has spoken second, with a few exceptions. At the 38th (1983) and 39th (1984) sessions, the United States spoke first and Brazil spoke second. At the 71st session, on 20 September 2016, Chad spoke second due to the delay in arrival of the President of the United States. At the 73rd session, on 25 September 2018, Ecuador spoke second due to the delay in arrival of the President of the United States.

The Assembly is empowered to make recommendations to States on international issues within its competence. It has also initiated actions—political, economic, humanitarian, social and legal— which have benefitted the lives of millions of people throughout the world. The landmark Millennium Declaration,[644] adopted in 2000, and the 2005 World Summit Outcome Document,[645] reflect the commitment of Member States:

---

[644] UNGA Resolution A/RES/55/2
[645] UNGA Resolution A/RES/60/1

(a) to reach specific goals to attain peace, security and disarmament along with development and poverty eradication;
(b) to safeguard human rights and promote the rule of law;
(c) to protect our common environment;
(d) to meet the special needs of Africa; and
(e) to strengthen the United Nations.

In September 2015, the Assembly agreed on a set of 17 Sustainable Development Goals,[646] contained in the outcome document of the United Nations summit for the adoption of the post-2015 development agenda.[647] According to the Charter of the United Nations, the General Assembly may:

(a) Consider and approve the UN budget and establish the financial assessments of Member States[648]

---

[646] The seventeen SDGs are as follows:
GOAL 1: No Poverty
GOAL 2: Zero Hunger
GOAL 3: Good Health and Well-being
GOAL 4: Quality Education
GOAL 5: Gender Equality
GOAL 6: Clean Water and Sanitation
GOAL 7: Affordable and Clean Energy
GOAL 8: Decent Work and Economic Growth
GOAL 9: Industry, Innovation and Infrastructure
GOAL 10: Reduced Inequality
GOAL 11: Sustainable Cities and Communities
GOAL 12: Responsible Consumption and Production
GOAL 13: Climate Action
GOAL 14: Life Below Water
GOAL 15: Life on Land
GOAL 16: Peace and Justice Strong Institutions
GOAL 17: Partnerships to achieve the Goal

[647] UNGA Resolution A/RES/70/1

[648] Art. 17 of the UN Charter 1945

(b) Elect the non-permanent members of the Security Council and the members of other United Nations councils and organs and,[649] on the recommendation of the Security Council, appoint the Secretary-General[650]

(c) Consider and make recommendations on the general principles of cooperation for maintaining international peace and security, including disarmament[651]

(d) Discuss any question relating to international peace and security and, except where a dispute or situation is currently being discussed by the Security Council, make recommendations on it[652]

(e) Discuss, with the same exception, and make recommendations on any questions within the scope of the Charter or affecting the powers and functions of any organ of the United Nations

(f) Initiate studies and make recommendations to promote international political cooperation, the development and codification of international law, the realization of human rights and fundamental freedoms, and international collaboration in the economic, social, cultural, educational and health fields[653]

(g) Make recommendations for the peaceful settlement of any situation that might impair friendly relations among countries[654]

(h) Consider reports from the Security Council and other United Nations organs[655]

---

[649] Art. 18 (2) *Ibid*
[650] Art. 97
[651] Art. 11
[652] *Ibid*
[653] Art. 13 (b) UN Charter 1945
[654] Art. 14 UN Charter 1945
[655] Art. 15 *Ibid*

The Assembly may also take action in cases of a threat to the peace, breach of peace or act of aggression, when the Security Council has failed to act owing to the negative vote of a permanent member. In such instances, according to its *Uniting for Peace Resolution* of 1950,[656] the Assembly may consider the matter immediately and recommend to its Members collective measures to maintain or restore international peace and security.

GA Revitalization: Strengthening the work of the General Assembly can help ensure that this *"chief deliberative, policymaking and representative organ of the United Nations"*[657] becomes a true, universal *parliament of nations*. Identified as a priority from the very outset of the Organization in 1946,[658] the General Assembly, at its 60th session and continuously since its 62nd session, has annually established an Ad Hoc Working Group on the revitalization of the work of the General Assembly (AHWG), in the context of which Member States consider the following broad thematic issues: (a) Role and authority of the General Assembly; (b) Working methods; (c) Selection and appointment of the Secretary-General and other executive heads; and (d) Strengthening the accountability, transparency and institutional memory of the Office of the President of the General Assembly.

Starting at its 62nd session, the AHWG elaborated an Inventory Chart reflecting the status of implementation of General Assembly revitalization resolutions.[659] This chart has subsequently been updated at the 63rd, 67th, 68th, 69th, 70th, 71st, 72nd and 73rd

---

[656] United Nations General Assembly Resolution A/RES/377(V)
[657] para. 149 of the World Summit Outcome Document 2005
[658] See generally the annexes to the UN General Assembly's Rules of Procedure
[659] (A/62/952/Add.1)

sessions[660] and continues to form a basis for the membership's deliberations under this item. Also based on the outcomes of the Assembly's consideration of ways to revitalize its work, the Assembly encouraged the holding of informal interactive debates on current issues of critical importance to the international community and invited the President of the General Assembly to propose themes for these interactive debates. It has also become an established practice for the Secretary-General to brief Member States periodically, in informal meetings of the General Assembly, on his recent activities and travels. These briefings have provided a well-received opportunity for exchange between the Secretary-General and Member States. The General Assembly has also encouraged its Presidents to continue with the practice of periodically briefing Member States on their activities, including official travel. As a result of the ongoing revitalization of its work,[661] the General Assembly now elects its President, Vice Presidents and Chairs of the Main Committees at least three months in advance of the start of the new session in order to further strengthen coordination and preparation of work among the Main Committees and between the Committees and the Plenary. It has also come to adopt the proposed program of work and timetable of five of its six Main Committees for the forthcoming session at the end of the main part of the session, thereby facilitating the planning and preparation of work for delegations, incoming chairs as well as the Secretariat. Similarly, the General Assembly now conducts the elections of the non-permanent members of the Security Council and the members of the Economic and Social Council, about six months before the elected members assume their responsibilities.

---

[660] See documents A/63/959, A/67/936, A/68/951, A/69/1007, A/70/1003, A/71/1007, A/72/896 and A/73/956 respectively

[661] Pursuant to Rule 30 UNGA Rules of Procedure

Security Council: Located in New York,[662] the Security Council has primary responsibility, under the UN Charter, for the maintenance of international peace and security.[663] Under the Charter, the functions and powers of the Security Council are: (a) to maintain international peace and security in accordance with the principles and purposes of the United Nations (b) to investigate any dispute or situation which might lead to international friction (c) to recommend methods of adjusting such disputes or the terms of settlement (d) to formulate plans for the establishment of a system to regulate armaments (e) to determine the existence of a threat to the peace or act of aggression and to recommend what action should be taken[664] (f) to call on Members to apply economic sanctions and other measures not involving the use of force to prevent or stop aggression[665] (g) to take military action against an aggressor[666] (h) to recommend the admission of new Members (i) to exercise the trusteeship functions of the United Nations in *strategic areas* and (j) to recommend to the General Assembly the appointment of the Secretary-General[667] and together with the Assembly, to elect the Judges of the International Court of Justice.[668]

---

[662] The Security Council held its first session on 17 January 1946 at Church House, Westminster, London. Since its first meeting, the Security Council has taken permanent residence at the United Nations Headquarters in New York City. It also travelled to many cities, holding sessions in Addis Ababa, Ethiopia, in 1972, in Panama City, Panama, and in Geneva, Switzerland, in 1990. A representative of each of its members must be present at all times at UN Headquarters so that the Security Council can meet at any time as the need arises.

[663] Art. 24 of the UN Charter 1945

[664] Art. 39

[665] Art. 41

[666] See generally Chapter VII powers of the UNSC under UN Charter 1945

[667] Art. 97 of the UN Charter 1945

[668] Art. 4 of the Statute of the ICJ 1946

The Security Council has 15 Members (5 permanent[669] and 10 non-permanent members).[670] Each Member has one vote. Under the Charter, all Member States are obligated to comply with Council decisions.[671] The Security Council takes the lead in determining the existence of a threat to the peace or act of aggression. It calls upon the parties to a dispute to settle it by peaceful means and recommends methods of adjustment or terms of settlement. In some cases, the Security Council can resort to imposing sanctions or even authorize the use of force to maintain or restore international peace and security. The Security Council has a Presidency, which rotates, and changes, every month.[672]

---

[669] The Republic of China, France, the Union of Soviet Socialist Republics, the United Kingdom of Great Britain and Northern Ireland, and the United States of America shall be permanent members of the Security Council

[670] Art. 23 (1)

[671] *When a complaint concerning a threat to peace is brought before it, the Council's first action is usually to recommend that the parties try to reach agreement by peaceful means. The Council may: (a) set forth principles for such an agreement; (b) undertake investigation and mediation, in some cases; (c) dispatch a mission; (d) appoint special envoys; or (e) request the Secretary-General to use his good offices to achieve a pacific settlement of the dispute. When a dispute leads to hostilities, the Council's primary concern is to bring them to an end as soon as possible. In that case, the Council may: (a) issue ceasefire directives that can help prevent an escalation of the conflict; or (b) dispatch military observers or a peacekeeping force to help reduce tensions, separate opposing forces and establish a calm in which peaceful settlements may be sought. Beyond this, the Council may opt for enforcement measures, including: (a) economic sanctions, arms embargoes, financial penalties and restrictions, and travel bans; (b) severance of diplomatic relations; (c) blockade; or (d) even collective military action. A chief concern is to focus action on those responsible for the policies or practices condemned by the international community, while minimizing the impact of the measures taken on other parts of the population and economy.*

[672] See generally Provisional Rules of Procedure of the United Nations Security Council

Security Council reform: The Security Council is not representative of the geopolitical realities of the modern world. Both Africa and Latin America lack a permanent seat on the Council, while Europe is over-represented and Asia is under-represented.[673] These problems are not easily addressed because the Permanent Five members (P5) of the Council do not want to see their power diminished. As a result, little progress has been made since 1993 in spite of the number of proposals that have been suggested. The central issues in Council reform are membership, transparency and working methods, and the veto. The P5 generally opposes any expansion of membership of the Council that would diminish their power though they occasionally support some countries bids. As negotiations are currently stalled over membership expansion, P5 countries have supported bids for membership by some countries.

Most recently, the US gave its support to India. France has backed Africa for a permanent seat. The G-4 countries have put themselves forward as the most serious candidates for permanent membership in the Council. Brazil, Germany, India and Japan have positioned themselves as leaders within the UN, but have failed to garner enough support - or quell the opposition - to ascend as permanent members. Other blocs of states have put forward reform proposals. During the 1990's, the *Coffee Club* opposed adding countries as permanent members, and instead proposed that members be elected on a regional basis to create more parity in representation. This effort was re-energized in the mid-2000's by Italy under the name Uniting for Consensus, and it has been actively working towards regionally based reform. Another group, self-identified as the Small Five (S-5)-which no longer exists, had put forward a series

---

[673] https://www.globalpolicy.org/security-council/security-council-reform/49885.html?itemid=1321; website visited on 29 April 2020

of proposals for Council reform as well.[674] The S-5 advocated for more transparency and coordination between the Security Council and the General Assembly and Economic and Social committees. The proposal also included some guidelines on the use of the veto. As a separate bloc, the African Union has put forward a suggestion to expand the Council, giving Africa and Latin America permanent seats and increasing representation for all regional areas. The expansion of the council would also include giving the power of the veto to new permanent members.

ECOSOC

The Economic and Social Council is the principal body for coordination,[675] policy review, policy dialogue and recommendations on economic, social, educational, cultural and health issues,[676] as well as implementation of internationally agreed development goals. It serves as the central mechanism for activities of the UN system and its specialized agencies in the economic, social and environmental fields, supervising subsidiary and expert bodies. It has 54 Members, elected by the General Assembly for overlapping three-year terms.[677] It is the United Nations' central platform for reflection, debate, and innovative thinking on sustainable development.

Trusteeship Council: The Trusteeship Council was established in 1945 by the UN Charter, under Chapter XIII, to provide international supervision for 11 Trust Territories that had been placed under the administration of seven Member States, and ensure that adequate steps were taken to prepare the Territories for self-government and independence. By 1994, all Trust Territories

---

[674] The S-5 Comprised of Costa Rica, Jordan, Lichtenstein, Singapore and Switzerland
[675] Art. 58 and 60 of the UN Charter 1945
[676] Art. 62 *Ibid*
[677] Art. 61

had attained self-government or independence.[678] The Trusteeship Council suspended operation on 1 November 1994. By a resolution adopted on 25 May 1994, the Council amended its rules of procedure to drop the obligation to meet annually and agreed to meet as occasion required by its decision or the decision of its President, or at the request of a majority of its members or the General Assembly or the Security Council.

International Court of Justice: ICJ is the principal judicial organ of the United Nations. Pursuant to the statute of the ICJ, its seat is at the Peace Palace in the Hague[679] (Netherlands).[680] The Court's role is to settle, in accordance with international law, legal disputes submitted to it by States[681] and to give advisory opinions on legal questions referred to it by authorized United Nations organs and specialized agencies.[682] (In more detail provided in this chapter)

Regional Arrangements: Chapter VIII of the Charter of the United Nations provides the constitutional basis for the involvement of regional organizations in the maintenance of international peace and security for which the Security Council is primarily responsible. Art. 52 provides for the involvement of regional arrangements or agencies in the peaceful settlement of disputes; Art. 53 allows such arrangements to take enforcement action, but only with explicit authorization by the Security Council. Art. 53, therefore, creates a mechanism that allows the Council to utilize regional arrangements to implement its enforcement measures. Finally, Art. 54 stipulates that regional arrangements or agencies

---

[678] The last Trust territory i.e. Palau in 1994 was delinked from council and later recognized as an independent member of the UN as the Republic of Palau

[679] Art. 22 of the Statute of the ICJ 1946

[680] All the other Principal Organs of the UN as based in the United States

[681] Art. 36 of the Statute of the ICJ 1946

[682] Art. 65 *Ibid*

shall inform the Council of their activities for the maintenance of international peace and security at all times.

Secretariat: The Secretariat comprises the Secretary-General and UN staff members[683] who carry out the day-to-day work of the UN as mandated by the General Assembly and the Organization's other principal organs. The Secretary-General is chief administrative officer of the Organization, appointed by the General Assembly on the recommendation of the Security Council[684] for a five-year, renewable term. While there is no limit as to the number of terms, practice so far has been two back to back tenures.[685] UN staff members are recruited internationally and locally, and work in duty stations and on peacekeeping missions all around the world. But serving the cause of peace in a violent world is a dangerous occupation. Since the founding of the United Nations, more than 3000 brave men and women have given their lives in its service.[686]

UN peacekeeping
Peacekeeping is not explicitly mentioned in the UN Charter and it is referred to as *Chapter Six and half powers* vested in the UN. Chapter Six of the UN Charter deals with peaceful settlement of disputes and Chapter Seven deals with measures to deal with threats to the peace, breaches of the peace and acts of aggression. There are three basic principles that continue to set UN peacekeeping operations apart as a tool for maintaining international peace and security. These three principles are inter-related and mutually reinforcing: (a) Consent of the parties; (b) Impartiality; and (c) Non-use of force except in self-defence and

---

[683] Art. 97 of the UN Charter 1945
[684] *Ibid*
[685] https://www.un.org/sg/en/appointment.shtml; website accessed on 29 April 2020
[686] https://peacekeeping.un.org/en/fatalities; website accessed on 29 April 2020

defence of the mandate. The Security Council determines the deployment of a new UN peace operation. If the Security Council determines that deploying a UN peace operation is the most appropriate step to take, it will formally authorize this by adopting a resolution. The resolution sets out the operation's mandate and size, and details the tasks it will be responsible for performing. The budget and resources are then subject to General Assembly approval. The Secretary-General normally appoints a Head of Mission (usually a Special Representative) to direct the peacekeeping operation. The Head of Mission reports to the Under-Secretary-General for Peace Operations at the UN Headquarters. The Secretary-General also appoints a peace operation's Force Commander and Police Commissioner, and senior civilian staff.

The Department of Peace Operations (DPO) and the Department of Operational Support (DOS) are then responsible for staffing the civilian components of a peace operation. The UN has no standing army or police force of its own, and Member States are asked to contribute military and police personnel required for each operation. Peacekeepers wear their countries' uniform and are identified as UN peacekeepers only by a UN blue helmet or beret and a badge. Civilian staff of peace operations are international civil servants, recruited and deployed by the UN Secretariat. The Secretary-General will then provide regular reports to the Security Council on the implementation of the mission mandate. The Security Council reviews these reports and briefings, and renews and adjusts the mission mandate, as required, until the missions are completed or closed. The first UN peacekeeping mission was established in May 1948, when the UN Security Council authorized the deployment of a small number of UN military observers to the Middle East to form the United Nations Truce Supervision Organization (UNTSO) to monitor the Armistice Agreement between Israel and its Arab neighbours. Over the past 70 years, more than 1 million men and women have served under the UN flag in more than 70 UN peacekeeping operations. More than

100,000 military, police and civilian personnel from 125 countries currently serve in 14 peacekeeping operations. There are currently 13 peacekeeping operations led by the Department of Peace Operations.

UN Peacebuilding

In the resolutions establishing the Peacebuilding Commission, resolution dated 20 December 2005,[687] the United Nations General Assembly and the Security Council mandated it:

- to bring together all relevant actors to marshal resources and to advise on and propose integrated strategies for post-conflict peacebuilding and recovery;
- to focus attention on the reconstruction and institution-building efforts necessary for recovery from conflict and to support the development of integrated strategies in order to lay the foundation for sustainable development;
- to provide recommendations and information to improve the coordination of all relevant actors within and outside the United Nations, to develop best practices, to help to ensure predictable financing for early recovery activities and to extend the period of attention given by the international community to post-conflict recovery.

General Assembly and Security Council[688] also stressed the importance of the Peacebuilding Commission to fulfil the following functions in this regard:

(a) To bring sustained international attention to sustaining peace, and to provide political accompaniment and advocacy to countries affected by conflict, with their consent;

(b) To promote an integrated, strategic and coherent approach to peacebuilding, noting that security, development and human rights are closely interlinked and mutually reinforcing;

---

[687] See Resolutions A/RES/60/180 and S/RES/1645 (2005)
[688] See Resolutions A/RES/70/262 and S/RES/2282 (2016)

(c) To serve a bridging role among the principal organs and relevant entities of the United Nations by sharing advice on peacebuilding needs and priorities, in line with the respective competencies and responsibilities of these bodies;

(d) To serve as a platform to convene all relevant actors within and outside the United Nations, including from Member States, national authorities, United Nations missions and country teams, international, regional and sub regional organizations, international financial institutions, civil society, women's groups, youth organizations and, where relevant, the private sector and national human rights institutions, in order to provide recommendations and information to improve their coordination, to develop and share good practices in peacebuilding, including on institution-building, and to ensure predictable financing to peacebuilding.

The UN Secretary-General's Peacebuilding Fund (PBF) is the organization's financial instrument of first resort to sustain peace in countries or situations at risk or affected by violent conflict. The PBF may invest with UN entities, governments, regional organizations, multilateral banks, national multi-donor trust funds or civil society organizations. From 2006 to 2017, the PBF has allocated $772 million to 41 recipient countries. Since inception, 58 member states contributed to the Fund, 33 in the present 2017-2019 Investment Plan. The Fund works across pillars and supports integrated UN responses to fill critical gaps; respond quickly and with flexibility to peace-building opportunities; and catalyze processes and resources in a risk-tolerant fashion.

75th anniversary of the United Nations
By a *modalities resolution* adopted by UN Member States on 14 June 2019, the UN will mark its 75th anniversary with a one-day high-level meeting of the UN General Assembly on Monday, 21 September 2020 on the theme, *The Future We Want, the UN We Need: Reaffirming our Collective Commitment to Multilateralism*. Also related

to the 75th anniversary commemoration, a Youth Plenary will be convened in conjunction with the 2020 ECOSOC Youth Forum and include a *youth-driven, global dialogue* on the theme of the commemoration event. The resolution also says Member States will commemorate the signing of the UN Charter on 26 June 2020 and UN Day on 24 October 2020 through observance ceremonies in New York, in addition to marking the anniversary in September.

International Court of Justice
History of international adjudication: **The creation of ICJ represented the culmination of a long process of developing methods for the pacific settlement of international disputes. Art. 14 of the Covenant of the League of Nations gave the Council of the League responsibility for formulating plans for the establishment of a Permanent Court of International Justice (PCIJ), which would be competent not only to hear and determine any dispute of an international character submitted to it by the parties to the dispute, but also to give an advisory opinion upon any dispute or question referred to it by the Council or Assembly of the League of Nations. The PCIJ met for the last time in October 1945 and resolved to transfer its archives and effects to the new International Court of Justice, which, like its predecessor, was to have its seat at the Peace Palace. The judges of the PCIJ all resigned on 31 January 1946, and the election of the first Members of the International Court of Justice took place on 6 February 1946, at the First Session of the United Nations General Assembly and Security Council. In April 1946, the PCIJ was formally dissolved, and the International Court of Justice, meeting for the first time, elected as its President Judge Jose Gustavo Guerrero (El Salvador), the last President of the PCIJ. The Court appointed the members of its Registry (largely from among former officials of the PCIJ) and held an inaugural public sitting on the 18th of that month. The first case was submitted in May 1947. It concerned incidents in the Corfu Channel and was brought by the United Kingdom against Albania.**

Members of the Court: The International Court of Justice is composed of 15 judges[689] elected to nine-year terms of office[690] by the United Nations General Assembly and the Security Council.[691] These organs vote simultaneously but separately.[692] In order to be elected, a candidate must receive an absolute majority of the votes in both bodies. This sometimes makes it necessary for a number of rounds of voting to be held. In order to ensure a degree of continuity, one third of the Court is elected every three years.[693] Judges are eligible for re-election. Should a judge die or resign during his or her term of office, a special election is held as soon as possible to choose a judge to fill the unexpired part of the term.

Judges must be elected from among persons of high moral character, who possess the qualifications required in their respective countries for appointment to the highest judicial offices, or are jurisconsults of recognized competence in international law.[694] The Court may not include more than one national of the same State.[695] Moreover, the Court as a whole must represent the main forms of civilization and the principal legal systems of the world.[696] The Court's *jurisdiction* is twofold: it decides, in accordance with international law, disputes of a legal nature that are submitted to it by States (*jurisdiction in contentious cases*); and it gives advisory opinions on legal questions at the request of the organs of the United Nations, specialized agencies or one related organization authorized to make such a request (*advisory jurisdiction*).

---

[689] Art. 3 (1) of the Statute of the ICJ
[690] Art. 13 *Ibid*
[691] Art. 4 (1)
[692] Art. 8 and Art. 10 (1)
[693] Art. 13
[694] Art. 2
[695] Art. 3
[696] Art. 9

Contentious Jurisdiction: In the exercise of its jurisdiction in contentious cases, the International Court of Justice settles disputes of a legal nature that are submitted to it by States in accordance with international law. An international legal dispute can be defined as a disagreement on a question of law or fact, a conflict, or a clash of legal views or interests. Only States may apply to and appear before the International Court of Justice. International organizations, other authorities and private individuals are not entitled to institute proceedings before the Court. Art. 35 of the ICJ Statute defines the conditions under which States may access the Court. While the first paragraph of that art. states that the Court is open to States parties to the Statute, the second is intended to regulate access to the Court by States which are not parties to the Statute. The conditions under which such States may access the Court are determined by the Security Council, subject to the special provisions contained in treaties in force at the date of the entry into force of the Statute, with the proviso that under no circumstances shall such conditions place the parties in a position of inequality before the Court. The Court can only deal with a dispute when the States concerned have recognized its jurisdiction. No State can therefore be a party to proceedings before the Court unless it has in some manner or other consented thereto.

Basis of jurisdiction: The jurisdiction of the Court in contentious proceedings is based on the consent of the States to which it is open. The form in which this consent is expressed determines the manner in which a case may be brought before the Court.

(a) Special agreement

Art. 36, para 1, of the Statute provides that the jurisdiction of the Court comprises all cases which the parties refer to it. Such cases normally come before the Court by notification to the Registry of an agreement known as a special agreement, concluded by the parties specially for this purpose. The subject of the dispute and the parties must be indicated.[697]

---

[697] Statute, Art. 40, para. 1; Rules, Art. 39

(b) Matters provided for in treaties and conventions
Art. 36, paragraph 1, of the Statute also provides that the jurisdiction of the Court comprises all matters specially provided for in treaties and conventions in force. Such matters are normally brought before the Court by means of a written application instituting proceeding; this is a unilateral document which must indicate the subject of the dispute and the parties[698] and, as far as possible, specify the provision on which the applicant founds the jurisdiction of the Court.[699]

A list of treaties and conventions governing the jurisdiction of the International Court of Justice in contentious cases is given in the *Treaties* section of the ICJ website. To these instruments must be added other treaties and conventions concluded earlier and conferring jurisdiction upon the Permanent Court of International Justice, for Art. 37 of the Statute of the International Court of Justice stipulates that whenever a treaty or convention in force provides for reference of a matter to a tribunal to have been instituted by the League of Nations, or to the Permanent Court of International Justice, the matter shall, as between the parties to the Statute, be referred to the International Court of Justice. In 1932, in its Collection of Texts governing the Jurisdiction of the Court[700] and subsequently in Chapter X of its Annual Reports[701] the Permanent Court reproduced the relevant provisions of the instruments governing its jurisdiction. By virtue of the art. referred to above, some of these provisions now govern the jurisdiction of the Court.

(c) Compulsory jurisdiction in legal disputes
The Statute provides that a State may recognize as compulsory, in relation to any other State accepting the same obligation, the

---

[698] Art. 40, para. 1 of the Statute of the ICJ
[699] Art. 38 *Ibid*
[700] PCIJ, Series D, No. 6 (fourth edition)
[701] PCIJ, Series E, Nos. 8-16

jurisdiction of the Court in legal disputes. Such cases are brought before the Court by means of written applications. The nature of legal disputes in relation to which such compulsory jurisdiction may be recognized are listed in Art. 36, paragraphs 2-5, of the Statute, which read as follows:

"2. The States parties to the present Statute may at any time declare that they recognize as compulsory ipso facto and without special agreement, in relation to any other State accepting the same obligation, the jurisdiction of the Court in all legal disputes concerning:
(a) the interpretation of a treaty;
(b) any question of international law;
(c) the existence of any fact which, if established, would constitute a breach of an international obligation;
(d) the nature or extent of the reparation to be made for the breach of an international obligation.
3. The declarations referred to above may be made unconditionally or on condition of reciprocity on the part of several or certain States, or for a certain time.
4. Such declarations shall be deposited with the Secretary-General of the United Nations, who shall transmit copies thereof to the parties to the Statute and to the Registrar of the Court.
5. Declarations made under Art. 36 of the Statute of the Permanent Court of International Justice and which are still in force shall be deemed, as between the parties to the present Statute, to be acceptances of the compulsory jurisdiction of the International Court of Justice for the period which they still have to run and in accordance with their terms."

The texts of these declarations can be found under the heading *Declarations Recognizing the Jurisdiction of the Court as Compulsory.*

(d) Forum prorogatum
If a State has not recognized the jurisdiction of the Court at the time when an application instituting proceedings is filed against it, that State has the possibility of subsequently accepting such jurisdiction to enable the Court to entertain the case: the Court thus has

jurisdiction as of the date of acceptance under the forum prorogatum rule.

(e) The Court itself decides any questions concerning its jurisdiction
Art. 36, paragraph 6, of the Statute provides that in the event of a dispute as to whether the Court has jurisdiction, the matter shall be settled by the decision of the Court. Art. 79 of the Rules lays down the arrangements for filing preliminary objections.

(f) Interpretation of a judgment
Art. 60 of the Statute provides that in the event of dispute as to the meaning or scope of a judgment, the Court shall construe it upon the request of any party. The request for interpretation may be made either by means of a special agreement between the parties or of an application by one or more of the parties (Rules, Art. 98).

(g) Revision of a judgment
An application for revision of a judgment may be made only when it is based upon the discovery of some fact of such a nature as to be a decisive factor, which fact was, when the judgment was given, unknown to the Court and also to the party claiming revision, always provided that such party's ignorance was not due to negligence (Statute, Art. 61, para. 1). A request for revision is made by means of an application (Rules, Art. 99).

Advisory Jurisdiction: Since States alone are entitled to appear before the Court, public (governmental) international organizations cannot be parties to a case before it. However, a special procedure, the advisory procedure, is available to such organizations and to them alone. This procedure is available to five United Nations organs, fifteen specialized agencies and one related organization. Though based on contentious proceedings, advisory proceedings have distinctive features resulting from the special nature and purpose of the advisory function. Advisory proceedings begin with the filing of a written request for an advisory opinion addressed to the Registrar by the United Nations Secretary-General or the director or secretary-general of the entity requesting the opinion. In urgent cases the Court may take all appropriate measures to speed up the proceedings. To assemble all the necessary information about the question submitted to it, the Court is empowered to hold written and oral proceedings. A few days after the request has been filed, the Court draws up a list of the States and international organizations that are likely to be able to furnish information on the question before the Court. Usually, the States listed are the member States of the organization requesting the opinion, while sometimes the other States to which the Court is open in contentious proceedings are also included. As a rule, organizations and States authorized to participate in the proceedings may submit written statements, followed, if the Court considers it necessary, by written comments on other's statements. These written statements are generally made available to the public at the beginning of the oral proceedings, if the Court considers that such proceedings should take place.

Basic documents of the ICJ: The International Court of Justice was established by the Charter of the United Nations, which provides that all Member States of the United Nations are ipso facto parties to the Court's Statute. The Statute, together with the Rules of Court, organizes the composition and functioning of the Court. Since October 2001, the Court has also issued Practice Directions for use by States appearing before it.

> *Charter of the United Nations*: The Charter of the United Nations, which was signed in San Francisco on 26 June 1945, is the foundational treaty of the United Nations. It is also the constitutive text of the International Court of Justice, which was created by the Charter.[702]

---

[702] Provisions on the Court can be found in Art. 7, para 1, Art. 36, paragraph 3, and Art. 92-96 (Chapter XIV) of the Charter

> *Statute of the Court*: The Statute of the International Court of Justice is annexed to the Charter of the United Nations, of which it forms an integral part. The main purpose of the Statute is to organize the composition and functioning of the Court. Like the Charter, the Statute can only be amended by a two-thirds majority vote in the General Assembly and ratification by two thirds of the States (Art. 69). Should the ICJ wish its Statute to be amended, it must submit a proposal to that effect to the General Assembly by sending a written communication to the Secretary-General of the United Nations (Art. 70). Hitherto, however, the Statute of the Court has never been amended.

> *Rules of Court*: Art. 30 of the Statute of the International Court of Justice provides that *"the Court shall frame rules for carrying out its functions."* These Rules are intended to supplement the general rules set out in the Statute and to make detailed provision for the steps to be taken to comply with them.

> *Practice Directions*: The Court adopted its first Practice Directions for use by States appearing before it in October 2001. Practice Directions supplement, rather than alter, the Rules of Court. They reflect the Court's ongoing review of its working methods. Once adopted by the Court, amendments to the Practice Directions are posted on the Court's website and published in the Court's Yearbook, with a note of any temporal reservations relating to their applicability.

> *Other Texts*: In addition to the Statute and the Rules of Court, other legal documents have been adopted by the Court or the United Nations, or concluded by the Court with the host country, and govern certain aspects of the Court's activities.

Pending cases: In light of the Covid-19 pandemic phenomenon, the ICJ issued a press release declaring suspension of judicial proceedings till 31 May 2020 [703] As of May 2020, the cases currently being heard, under deliberation or pending at the ICJ are:
(a) Gabcikovo-Nagymaros Project (Hungary/Slovakia); (b) Armed Activities on the Territory of the Congo (*Democratic Republic of the Congo v. Uganda*); (c) Question of the Delimitation of the Continental Shelf between Nicaragua and Colombia beyond 200 nautical miles from the Nicaraguan Coast (*Nicaragua v. Colombia*); (d) Alleged Violations of Sovereign Rights and Maritime Spaces in the Caribbean Sea (*Nicaragua v. Colombia*); (e) Maritime Delimitation in the Indian Ocean (*Somalia v. Kenya*); (f) Dispute over the Status and Use of the Waters of the Silala *(Chile v. Bolivia)*; (g) Immunities and Criminal Proceedings (*Equatorial Guinea v. France*); (h) Certain Iranian Assets (*Islamic Republic of Iran v. United States of America*); (i) Application of the International Convention for the Suppression of the Financing of Terrorism and of the International Convention on the Elimination of All Forms of Racial Discrimination (*Ukraine v. Russian Federation);* (j) Arbitral Award of 3 October 1899 (*Guyana v. Venezuela*); (k) Application of the International Convention on the Elimination of All Forms of Racial Discrimination (*Qatar v. United Arab Emirates*); (l) Appeal Relating to the Jurisdiction of the ICAO Council under Art. 84 of the Convention on International Civil Aviation (*Bahrain, Egypt, Saudi Arabia and United Arab Emirates v. Qatar*); (m) Appeal Relating to the Jurisdiction of the ICAO Council under Art. II, Section 2, of the 1944 International Air Services Transit Agreement (*Bahrain, Egypt and United Arab Emirates v. Qatar*); (n) Alleged violations of the 1955 Treaty of Amity, Economic Relations, and Consular Rights (*Islamic Republic of Iran v. United States of America*); (o) Relocation of the United States Embassy to Jerusalem (*Palestine v. United States of America*); (p) Guatemala's Territorial, Insular and Maritime Claim

---

[703] https://www.icj-cij.org/files/press-releases/0/000-20200407-PRE-01-00-EN.pdf ; website visited on 12 May 2020

(Guatemala/Belize); and (q) Application of the Convention on the Prevention and Punishment of the Crime of Genocide (*The Gambia v. Myanmar*); (r) Appeal Relating to the Jurisdiction of the ICAO Council under Art. 84 of the Convention on International Civil Aviation (*Bahrain, Egypt, Saudi Arabia and United Arab Emirates v. Qatar*) & (s) Appeal Relating to the Jurisdiction of the ICAO Council under Art. II, Section 2, of the 1944 International Air Services Transit Agreement (*Bahrain, Egypt and United Arab Emirates v. Qatar*).

India in ICJ cases: India has been a party to cases at the ICJ on 6 occasions.

a) *Case about Right of Passage over Indian Territory*[704]

Portugal filed a case in 1955 at the ICJ claiming that Portugal had a right of passage through the territory of India to ensure communications between its territory of Daman (coastal Daman) and its enclaved territories of Dadra and Nagar-Haveli. Portugal argued that this right of passage comprises transit of persons and goods and passage of representatives & armed forces necessary to exercise the sovereignty of its territories. India on its part contended that the events that took place in Dadra on 21st & 22nd July 1954 overthrew Portuguese authority in these enclaves creating tension in the surrounding Indian territory. India further contended that suspension of passage became necessary because of the abnormal situation in Dadra and the tension created in surrounding Indian territory. The ICJ did not find fault with India and ruled that India has not acted contrary to its obligations.

b) *Appeal regarding the Jurisdiction of ICAO*[705]

India filed a case against Pakistan in 1971 contending that

---

[704] *Portugal v India*, [1960] ICJ Rep 6
[705] *India v. Pakistan*, 1971 I.C.J. 347 (Order of Sept. 16)

the Council of the International Civil Aviation Organization (ICAO) had no jurisdiction on an application & compliant filed by Pakistan. India further contended that any issue between the two countries is governed by the *Special Regime of 1966*. The ICJ while rejecting Pakistan's objection that ICJ has no jurisdiction to entertain India's appeal also held that the ICAO is indeed competent to entertain the complaint made to it by Pakistan. At the same time, the ICJ also mentioned that the ICAO was in need of guidance and pointed out multiple procedural lapses made by the ICAO.

c) *Case concerning the trial of Pakistani Prisoners of War*[706]
Pakistan filed a case in the ICJ in 1973 for instituting proceedings against India in the case of the charges of genocide against 195 Pakistani nationals, prisoners of war or civilian internees in the Indian custody. In 1973, Pakistan had informed the ICJ that both India & Pakistan governments held discussions and came to an agreement on the issue. Pakistan also informed the court that they are not going ahead with the proceedings in this case.

d) *Aerial Incident of 1999*[707]
Pakistan had filed a case at the ICJ in 1999 regarding a dispute relating to the destruction of a Pakistani aircraft by India in 1999. Pakistan contended that the ICJ had jurisdiction in this issue. India on the other hand contested the jurisdiction of ICJ in the issue saying that Pakistan's application to the ICJ did not refer to any treaty or convention in force between the two countries. The court in its decision in 2000 rejected Pakistan's contention that the Shimla Accord provides for disputes between the two countries to be submitted to the ICJ. ICJ concluded that it

---

[706] *Pakistan Vs India* 1973 I.C.J. 328
[707] *Pakistan Vs India* 2000 I.C.J. 12

had no jurisdiction to entertain the application filed by Pakistan. At the same time, the court requested both the countries to settle their disputes by peaceful means.

e) *Case about the obligation of negotiations about cessation of Nuclear Arms Race*[708]

The Republic of the Marshall Islands had instituted proceedings at the ICJ in 2014 against all nuclear weapon states, including India, contending breach of customary law obligations on nuclear disarmament (from Art. VI of the NPT). India contended that the ICJ had no jurisdiction in this case. In 2016, the court ruled that it does not have any jurisdiction on the issue in the absence of a dispute between the two countries. The court further ruled that it cannot proceed to the merits of the case because of the lack of jurisdiction.

f) *Jadhav case*[709]

These proceedings were instituted on 8 May 2017 by the filing in the Registry of an Application by the Republic of India against the Islamic Republic of Pakistan, alleging violations of the Vienna Convention on Consular Relations of 24 April 1963 with regard to the detention, since March 2016, and trial of an Indian national, Mr. Kulbhushan Sudhir Jadhav, who was accused of performing acts of espionage and terrorism on behalf of India, and sentenced to death by a military court in Pakistan in April 2017. In particular, India contended that Pakistan acted in breach of its obligations under Art. 36 of the Vienna Convention (i) by not informing India, without delay, of the detention of Mr. Jadhav; (ii) by not informing Mr. Jadhav of his rights under Art. 36; and (iii) by

---

[708] *Marshall Islands Vs India* I.C.J. Reports 2016, p. 255
[709] *India v. Pakistan* ICGJ 515 (ICJ 2017), [2017] ICJ GL No 168

denying consular officers of India access to Mr. Jadhav. The Court found in July 2019 that the Islamic Republic of Pakistan, in the matter of the detention and trial of an Indian national, Mr. Kulbhushan Sudhir Jadhav, had acted in breach of the obligations incumbent on it under Art. 36 of the Vienna Convention on Consular Relations.

World Trade Organization and WIPO: A Case study
The World Trade Organization (WTO) is the only global international organization dealing with the rules of trade between nations. Located in Geneva, Switzerland, the WTO was established on 1 January 1995 and created by the Uruguay Round negotiations (1986-94) of the GATT. Its current membership comprises 164 members representing 98 per cent of world trade. At the heart of the Organization are the WTO agreements, negotiated and signed by the bulk of the world's trading nations and ratified in their parliaments. The current body of trade agreements comprising the WTO consists of 16 different multilateral agreements (to which all WTO members are parties) and two different plurilateral agreements (to which only some WTO members are parties). The goal is to ensure that trade flows as smoothly, predictably and freely as possible. The WTO has many roles: it operates a global system of trade rules, it acts as a forum for negotiating trade agreements, it settles trade disputes between its members and it supports the needs of developing countries.

Main functions: The main functions of the WTO are (a) administering WTO trade agreements; (b) being a forum for trade negotiations; (c) handling trade disputes; (d) monitoring national trade policies; (e) technical assistance and training for developing countries; and (f) cooperation with other international organizations.

Intellectual property: The WTO's Intellectual Property Agreement contains rules for trade in ideas and creativity. The rules state how copyrights, patents, trademarks, geographical names used to identify products, industrial designs and undisclosed information such as trade secrets – *intellectual property* – should be protected when trade is involved.

Dispute settlement: The WTO's procedure for resolving trade conflicts under the Dispute Settlement Understanding is vital for enforcing the rules and therefore for ensuring that trade flows smoothly. Governments bring disputes to the WTO if they think their rights under the WTO agreements are being infringed. Confidence in the system is borne out by the number of cases brought to the WTO – more than 500 cases since the WTO was established compared with the 300 disputes dealt with during the entire life of the GATT (1947-94). On 10 December 2019, the Dispute Settlement Body ceased to function because of the refusal by the administration of US President Donald Trump to allow re-appointments to the DSB panel. Then in January 2020, 17 WTO members including Switzerland, the EU and China agreed to create a temporary mechanism to settle international trade disputes by invoking Art. 25 of the WTO Dispute Settlement Understanding.

World Intellectual Property Organization
WIPO is the global forum for intellectual property (IP) services, policy, information and cooperation. We are a self-funding agency of the United Nations, with 193 member states. Its mission is to lead the development of a balanced and effective international IP system that enables innovation and creativity for the benefit of all. Its mandate, governing bodies and procedures are set out in the WIPO Convention, which established WIPO in 1967. Governing Bodies which have been established by the WIPO Convention are WIPO's highest decision-making bodies. They traditionally meet in September/October each year in either ordinary or extraordinary session. Any of the Governing Bodies can constitute committees as required. For example: (a) Program and Budget Committee (PBC); (b) Committee on Development and Intellectual Property (CDIP);

(c) Intergovernmental Committee on Intellectual Property and Genetic Resources, Traditional Knowledge and Folklore (IGC); and (d) Advisory Committee on Enforcement (ACE). If one of the Standing or Permanent Committees determines that sufficient progress has been made to move towards treaty adoption, the General Assembly can decide to convene a Diplomatic Conference. This is a high-level meeting of member states, convened with the sole purpose of finalizing negotiations on a new treaty. The most recent have included: (a) Diplomatic Conference for the Adoption of a new Act of the Lisbon Agreement - The Geneva Act of the Lisbon Agreement on Appellations of Origin and Geographical Indications; (b) Diplomatic Conference to Conclude a Treaty to Facilitate Access to Published Works by Visually Impaired Persons and Persons with Print Disabilities; and (c) Diplomatic Conference on the Protection of Audiovisual Performances.

WIPO administers 26 treaties including the WIPO Convention. The first general group of treaties defines internationally agreed basic standards of intellectual property (IP) protection in each country and includes;
(1) Beijing Treaty on Audiovisual Performances;
(2) Berne Convention;
(3) Brussels Convention;
(4) Madrid Agreement (Indications of Source);
(5) Marrakesh VIP Treaty;
(6) Nairobi Treaty;
(7) Paris Convention;
(8) Patent Law Treaty;
(9) Phonograms Convention;
(10) Rome Convention;
(11) Singapore Treaty on the Law of Trademarks;
(12) Trademark Law Treaty;
(13) Washington Treaty;
(14) WIPO Copyright Treaty (WCT); and
(15) WIPO Performances and Phonograms Treaty (WPPT)

The second general group, known as the global protection system treaties, ensures that one international registration or filing will have effect in any of the relevant signatory States. The services provided by WIPO under these treaties simplify and reduce the cost of making individual applications or filings in all the countries in which protection is sought for a given IP right. These treaties include
(1) Budapest Treaty
(2) Hague Agreement
(3) Lisbon Agreement
(4) Madrid Agreement (Marks)
(5) Madrid Protocol and
(6) Patent Cooperation Treaty (PCT)

The third and final general group is the classification treaties, which create classification systems that organize information concerning inventions, trademarks and industrial designs into indexed, manageable structures for easy retrieval. These treaties include
(1) Locarno Agreement;
(2) Nice Agreement;
(3) Strasbourg Agreement and
(4) Vienna Agreement.

Are International Organizations withering away?
In recent years, the question of the withering away of post-World War Two multilateralism has been debated in academic and governance circles. Without doubt there is a crisis of confidence with the United Nations and a host of other international bodies. The lack of reforms in the World Bank and the IMF have been used by countries like China, India and others in the developing world to criticize the Western led approach. However, the most potent challenge to multilateralism and by association, international organizations, is from the approach of the US Administration under President Donald Trump. On the other hand, the content of

multilateralism is being re-defined by the Belt and Road Initiative of the People's Republic of China. Take the case of human rights. As is well known, Human Rights Day is observed by the international community every year on 10 December. It commemorates the day in 1948 the United Nations General Assembly adopted the Universal Declaration of Human Rights. The formal inception of Human Rights Day dates from 1950, after the Assembly passed resolution 423 (V) inviting all States and interested organizations to adopt 10 December of each year as Human Rights Day. When the General Assembly adopted the Declaration, with 48 states in favor and eight abstentions, it was proclaimed as a *common standard of achievement for all peoples and all nations*. That *common standard* lies in tatters today. The US President Donald Trump's decision in July 2018 to withdraw from the UN Human Rights Council in Geneva is a major challenge for the post World War II international order. The US Permanent Representative to the UN in New York at that time Ms. Nikki Haley described the Human Rights Council as a "*hypocritical and self-serving organisation*" that displayed "*unending hostility towards Israel*". US Secretary of State Mike Pompeo denounced the Council as "*a protector of human rights abusers.*"

In the second half of 2019, the withering away of the promise of human rights protections and mechanisms had played out in multiple ways. The Hong Kong Human Rights and Democracy Act of 2019 which was passed by the US Congress on 15 November 2019 addresses Hong Kong's status under U.S. law and imposes sanctions on those responsible for human rights violations in Hong Kong. The Department of State shall certify annually to Congress as to whether Hong Kong warrants its unique treatment under various treaties, agreements, and U.S. law. The analysis shall evaluate whether Hong Kong is upholding the rule of law and protecting rights enumerated in various documents, including (1) the agreement between the United Kingdom and China regarding Hong Kong's return to China, and (2) the Universal Declaration of

Human Rights.[710] Predictably the reaction from the Chinese Government was strong with the spokesperson of their Foreign Ministry warning that they were ready to *retaliate with determination* and with Chinese Foreign Minister Wang Yi describing the US legislation as *madness* that will damage the bilateral relationship. Just as Venezuela started dropping off the radar of the human rights watchers, the situation in Chile and Bolivia deteriorated. The Amnesty International's recent report on Chile observed that security forces have engaged in widespread and indiscriminate attacks against protesters over the last month. The eye injuries to protesters have been of particular concern. In Bolivia, former President Evo Morales made allegations of genocide being perpetrated. There is a genuine fear that political interests are pushing human rights to the back-burner and worse still being used as a tool to promote political ends and undermine opponents. Iran has forcefully refuted reports about the death toll in the recent protests after a decision by authorities to ration gasoline and substantially increase the fuel price. It has accused US Secretary of State Mike Pompeo's tweet in which he supported the protests and described the protesters as *"the people of Iran."*

The fact that the UN Security Council is divided especially on human rights related issues is evident in the recent positions of the members on the US change in stance regarding the status of Israeli settlements. Before a meeting of the Security Council on 20 November 2019, five European allies of the United States — Britain, France, Germany, Belgium and Poland — reiterated in a joint statement that *"all settlement activity is illegal under international law"* and also reiterated concern *"about the calls for a possible annexation of*

---

[710] https://www.congress.gov/bill/116th-congress/house-bill/3289; website accessed on 29 April 2020

areas in the West Bank."[711] In this regard, the sharp divisions on Syria also came to a head in September 2019 when Russia cast its thirteenth of U.N. Security Council action on the Syrian conflict, blocking a demand for a truce in northwest Syria because it does not include an exemption for military offensives against U.N. blacklisted militant groups. The crisis on the global trade front is equally, if not more, disconcerting. The issue at hand is the end of the WTO's dispute settlement body mechanism. The World Trade Organizations' (WTO) highest dispute-resolution body ceased to function after the administration of US President Donald Trump blocked reappointments to its panel. Without a working appeals system, international trade disputes may never see resolution and could quickly evolve into tit-for-tat tariff wars that spiral out of control. Additionally, the Trump administration has also ratcheted up its pressure on the World Trade Organization by raising the possibility of blocking the approval of the institution's biennial budget and effectively halting its work starting 2020. This is indeed quite a big fall for a mechanism which was described as the "most active in the dispute settlement system since the establishment of the organization" with a total of 488 disputes having been brought to the WTO by 2014.[712] In terms of immediate impact of the impending winding down of the DSB, a Reuters report notes,

> *"WTO adjudicators are facing weighty decisions on the US-China tariff tussle, on metal duties imposed by Trump since 2018 and on conflicts between Japan and South Korea and between Qatar and its neighbors. However, those decisions may carry no legal weight because of U.S. steps to disable the appeals process. In a future with no functioning Appellate Body, any party unhappy with an initial*

---

[711]https://upnorthlive.com/news/nation-world/un-security-council-members-rebuke-us-on-israel-settlements; website accessed on 29 April 2020

[712]https://www.wto.org/english/thewto_e/20y_e/dispute_brochure20y_e.pdf; website accessed on 29 April 2020

ruling could simply file an appeal into a void."[713]

This development occurred immediately after the refusal of India to join the RCEP [Regional Comprehensive Economic Partnership]. Spelling out the Government of India's reasons, Commerce and Industry Minister Piyush Goyal in a written reply to the House said that during the third RCEP Leaders Summit on November 4, 2019 in Bangkok, India stated that the current structure did not reflect its guiding principles or address the outstanding issues and concerns of India, in the light of which India did not join the agreement. He said that RCEP had provisions on trade remedies which also covers anti-dumping rules. *"Moreover, India was seeking an automatic trigger safeguard mechanism (ATSM) for tackling import surges,"* he added.[714]

Only time can pronounce on the impact of this development especially given the fact that India is today a large consumer market with a total GDP of more than US$ 2.6 trillion. In essence however, the crisis in multilateralism is also a manifestation of the changing international situation. China's determined push to occupy top positions in international organizations is a symptom. A Foreign Policy art. of October 2019 notes that Chinese nationals now head four of the 15 specialized agencies of the United Nations, namely Food and Agriculture Organization, International Civil Aviation Organization, International Telecommunication Union and the UN Industrial Development Organization.[715] So even as China pushes

---

[713] https://www.reuters.com/article/us-wto-trade/global-trade-umpire-the-next-casualty-of-trumps-tariff-war-idUSKBN1XS1T0; website accessed on 29 April 2020

[714] https://economictimes.indiatimes.com/news/economy/foreign-trade/rcep-did-not-address-outstanding-issues-concerns-of-india-piyush-goyal/articleshow/72144050.cms; website accessed on 29 April 2020

[715] https://foreignpolicy.com/2019/10/23/china-united-states-fao-kevin-moley/; website accessed on 29 April 2020

ahead with its international outreach through the Belt and Road Initiative and its attendant efforts, the USA is receding from the pole position in multilateral affairs. There are no credible solutions in sight. National interests are running rough shod over international cooperation. The coming years could well represent the nadir of multilateralism.

The increasing coherence of public international law
In the past few decades, especially after the end of the Cold War, the various elements of public international law have become more inter-connected. The subjects themselves have evolved on the one hand and on the other hand new mechanisms and modalities for their inter-linkages have been fleshed out. Such developments have made public international law truly multi-disciplinary. In this chapter the inter-connectedness of two sets of topics are explored from a contemporary perspective.

Part Two: Impact of US-China IPR related differences on WTO jurisprudence and what it means for India
After almost 15 years[716] of negotiations[717] and with the acceptance by 142 member-states of the World Trade Organization, the People's Republic of China became the 143rd member of the global body on 11 December 2001.[718] In the process, China agreed to undertake a series of important commitments to open and liberalize its regime in order to better integrate in the world economy and offer a more predictable environment for trade and foreign investment in accordance with World Trade Organization rules.[719]

---

[716] Official Communication from the People's Republic of China to GATT titled **China's Status as A Contracting Party**, L/6017 14 July 1986
[717] https://www.wto.org/english/thewto_e/acc_e/a1_chine_e.htm; WTO official website, accessed on 7 May 2020
[718] **WTO Accession of The People's Republic of China,** WT/L/432, 2001
[719] WTO News, *"WTO successfully concludes negotiations on China's Entry"*, Press/243, 17 September 2001

Specifically, on protection of intellectual property rights, China agreed to implement the TRIPS Agreement in full from the date of accession.[720]

The promise of 2001 sours

In spite of the promise that China's entry into the World Trade Organization generated, very soon, one of the primary enablers, namely the United States started voicing misgivings. Then US Deputy Secretary of State Robert Zoellick captured his country's angst in his famous ***"responsible stakeholder"*** speech in New York city on 21 September 2005 in the following words[721],

> *"...a responsible major global player shouldn't tolerate rampant theft of intellectual property and counterfeiting, both of which strike at the heart of America's knowledge economy. China's pledges – including a statement just last week by President Hu in New York – to crack down on the criminals who ply this trade are welcome, but the results are not yet evident."*

The US Government stated almost a decade later, in 2014, that China did not follow through on commitments including at summit meeting between President Obama and President Xi Jinping;

> *"that foreign companies are free to base technology transfer decisions on business and market considerations and to independently negotiate and decide whether and under what circumstances to assign or license intellectual property rights to affiliated or unaffiliated enterprises."*[722]

Later, in September 2015, Obama and Xi reached a Cyber

---

[720] *Ibid*

[721] Robert Zoellick, *"Whither China? From Membership to Responsibility,"* Remarks to the **National Committee on U.S.-China Relations,** 21 Sep 2005

[722] **2018 Report to Congress on China's WTO Compliance,** United States Trade Representative, February 2019

Agreement[723], under which the two sides agreed, amongst other things, to *"refrain from conducting or knowingly supporting cyber-enabled theft of intellectual property."* In this regard, a 2018 assessment[724] by National Counterintelligence and Security Center observed that China will continue to be a threat to US proprietary technology and intellectual property through cyber-enabled means or other methods. A Council on Foreign Relations backgrounder on Made in China 2025 pin-pointed the ten-year program of the Chinese Government to use government subsidies, mobilize state-owned enterprises, and pursue intellectual property acquisition to catch up with—and then surpass—Western technological prowess in advanced industries.[725] It *red-flagged* forced transfer agreements imposed on foreign companies to enter into joint ventures with Chinese firms under terms that require them to share sensitive intellectual property and advanced technological know-how and noted the impact of these terms on acquisition of technologies ranging from high-speed rail to electric vehicle batteries.[726] Successive US Administrations have also been prolific in taking China to the dispute settlement process of the World Trade Organization. According to one tabulation in March 2019, over the last 16 years, US officials have challenged Chinese practices 23 times in the World Trade Organization; the win-loss record is 19-0, with four cases pending.[727] In the matter concerning *Measures*

---

[723] The White House Press Release, *President Xi Jinping's State Visit to the United States*, Office of the Press Secretary, 25 September 2015

[724] Report titled **Foreign Economic Espionage in Cyberspace 2018**, National Counterintelligence and Security Center, Annual Report submitted pursuant to Sec 1637, National Defense Authorization Act 2015

[725] James McBride and Andrew Chatzky, *"Is 'Made in China 2025' a Threat to Global Trade?,"* Council on Foreign Relations, 13 May 2019

[726] *Ibid*

[727] Jeffrey J. Schott and Euijin Jung, *"In US-China Trade Disputes, the WTO Usually Sides with the United States,"* **Trade and Investment Policy Watch**, Pieterson Institute for International Economics, March 12, 2019

Affecting the Protection and Enforcement of Intellectual Property Rights, the World Trade Organization panel report adopted on 20 March 2009 upheld some but not all US claims and subsequently China announced it has fully complied with the World Trade Organization ruling in March 2010. On 23 March 2018, the US requested for consultations on *Certain Measures Concerning the Protection of Intellectual Property Rights* and a World Trade Organization panel was composed in January 2019. European concerns have also been along similar lines and articulated as frequently and forcefully as the Americans. A European Commission report[728] of March 2018 concluded that China continues to be the top priority for the European Union because of persistent and longstanding problems on the protection and enforcement of intellectual property rights; China remains the origin of most counterfeit and pirated goods arriving in the European Union; and that more than 80% of the seizures of counterfeit and pirated goods come from China or Hong Kong. Chinese writings have noticed the greater willingness of the European Union to work in tandem in recent years on World Trade Organization actions.[729] Another important actor, namely Japan requested to join the consultations at the World Trade Organization on the complaint brought by the US on 23 March 2018 concerning certain measures pertaining to the protection of intellectual property rights. Similarly, Japan joined with the European Union on the latter's complaint on June 2018 concerning certain measures imposed by China pertaining to the transfer of foreign technology into China. Bilaterally speaking, the mechanism of choice is the

---

[728] Commission Staff Working Document, European Commission, **Report on The Protection and Enforcement of Intellectual Property Rights in Third Countries,** SWD (2018) 47 dated 21 Feb 2018

[729] *"What the EU and US WTO IP Disputes Reveal About Trade Diplomacy,"* **The China IPR**, 13 June 2018

China-Japan joint IP Working Group.[730] In this regard, a Harvard Business Review art.[731] of October 2019 notes that there appears to be potential discrimination against foreigners during the patent examination processes at the European Patent Office and Japanese Patent Office. The Chinese position on the IPR issues is comprehensively covered in its White Paper of June 2018 titled, *"China and the World Trade Organization."* The White Paper[732] identifies four aspects of its IPR protection regime:

   (a) strengthening IPR protection on China's own initiative
   (b) building a full-fledged legal system on IPR protection
   (c) continuously strengthening law enforcement on IPR protection
   (d) attaining notable results in IPR protection.

It pointed out that China has set up three IPR courts in Beijing, Shanghai and Guangzhou, and special judicial organs at 15 intermediate courts in Nanjing, Suzhou, Wuhan, Xi'an and other cities to handle cross-regional IPR cases, including those related to patents. Further, testifying to its own efforts to push the boundaries in its pursuit of the targets in Made in China 2025, the White Paper observed that according to the World Intellectual Property Organization, 51,000 patent applications filed from China through

---

[730] 7th Meeting of the Japan-China Joint IP Working Group was held in Tokyo in January 2019 during which both sides, *"...exchanged views concerning a variety of issues involving IP protection so as to address the current situation where problems involved in IP protection have been becoming complex, widespread and sophisticated as illustrated by the distribution of counterfeit and pirated products online."* Official Press Release https://www.meti.go.jp/english/press/2019/0124_005.html website visited on 6 December 2019

[731] Dan Prud'homme, *"Three Myths About China's IP Regime,"* **Harvard Business Review**, 23 October 2019

[732] White Paper titled *"China and the World Trade Organization,"* The State Council Information Office of the People's Republic of China, June 2018

the Patent Cooperation Treaty were accepted in 2017, second only to the US. In their defense, Chinese state media argue that the LEGO Group's successes in IP action in the mainland is an indication of the robustness of both its IPR protection regime and for judicial integrity. In October 2017, the LEGO Group won a case against BELA, a Chinese toy manufacturer, for infringing the copyrights of the LEGO Group and for unfair competition. In another case decided earlier in July 2017, the LEGO logo and the LEGO word mark were recognized by the Beijing Higher Court as *"well-known"* trademarks in China. As recent as November 2018, the Guangzhou Yuexiu District Court ruled[733] that four companies had *"infringed multiple copyrights of the LEGO Group and conducted acts of unfair competition…"*

Most Western countries have used a combination of domestic legislative actions, bilateral dialogue mechanisms and referral to the World Trade Organization (as already captured) in trying to force China to protect IPRs. However, these countries have not met with success in these endeavors. In this context, the Belt and Road Initiative of Xi Jinping has added newer complications. To put in simple terms, by creating a parallel system,[734] China is trying to rationalize and expand its essentially non-economic model into parts of Central Asia, Southeast Asia and Africa. Xi Jinping's emphasis on high quality development and strengthening IPR protection and cooperation should be understood in this light. In this scenario, the attempt by US President Donald Trump to front load economic and trade issues onto the US-China dispute framework is significant. It flows from the firm belief that almost two decades after China pledged to support the World Trade Organization's multilateral trading system, China has not

---

[733] *"Toymaker Lego wins court case against Chinese copycats,"* **Reuters** (Copenhagen), 6 November, 2018

[734] Zhao Xinying, *"IPR protection efforts thriving along Belt, Road,"* **China Daily,** 29 April, 2019

embraced open, market-oriented policies.[735] The state remains in control of China's economy, and it heavily intervenes in the market to achieve industrial policy objectives.[736] On the other hand, the Chinese Government White Paper of June 2019 titled, *"China's Position on the China-US Economic and Trade Consultations"* described the country as *"a highly-sophisticated civilization"* that *"contributed significantly to human progress over the course of 5,000 years"*[737] and selectively referred to statements by former World Intellectual Property Organizations' Director General Arpad Bogsch, US Chamber of Commerce and American Chamber of Commerce in China. As the experience with the Made in China 2025, Belt and Road Initiative and the various Chinese domestic laws including those related to national security and cyber security showed, the Western pushback has been lacking in scope and determination.

A new and aggressive US campaign
In a statement dated 5 April 2018, US President Donald Trump announced that a USTR investigation under Sec. 301 of the Trade Act of 1974 had found that China has repeatedly engaged in practices to unfairly obtain America's intellectual property; that these practices had destroyed thousands of American factories and millions of American jobs; and that the US side had decided on approximately US$ 50 billion in tariffs on imports from China as an initial means to obtain the elimination of policies and practices identified in the USTR investigation.[738] At a World Trade Organization meeting in May 2018, US envoy Dennis Shea alleged

---

[735] **2018 Report to Congress on China's WTO Compliance,** United States Trade Representative, February 2019

[736] *Ibid*

[737] White Paper on **China's Position on the China-US Economic and Trade Consultations**, The State Council Information Office of The People's Republic of China, June 2019

[738] Statement from President Donald J. Trump on "**Additional Proposed Section 301 Remedies**", Whitehouse Release dated 5 April 2018

that China's forced technology transfers and licensing and administrative rules were violative of the rule of law. In dramatic fashion he added, *"Fundamentally, China has made the decision to engage in a systematic, state-directed, and non-market pursuit of other (World Trade Organization) members' cutting-edge technology in service of China's industrial policy."*[739] In their rebuttal the Chinese envoy flatly rejected the criticism and retorted that the US Trade Representative's office had failed to produce a single piece of evidence, and that some of its claims were *"pure speculation"*, adding that the USTR saw Chinese M&A activity as a Chinese government conspiracy.[740] As of 26 November 2019, the total US tariffs applied exclusively to Chinese goods was US $ 550 billion and the total Chinese tariffs applied exclusively to US goods was US $ 185 billion.[741] According to latest news reports[742], fresh guidelines issued by the Chinese Government in end November 2019 raises the penalties on violations of IPRs and leaves the door open for lowering the thresholds for criminal punishments for those who steal IP. China has said that it seeks to curb IPR infringement and the costs associated with protecting intellectual property by 2022, and for Chinese *social satisfaction* around IPR protections to *maintain a high level* by 2025. The directive also prioritizes strengthening protections around trade secrets and other intellectual property and their source codes.[743] The US and China agree on two elements, first that intellectual property issues

---

[739] Statements by the United States at the Meeting of the WTO Dispute Settlement Body Geneva, 28 May, 2018

[740] Tom Miles, "*U.S. and China clash over technology transfer at WTO,*" **Reuters** dated 29 May 2018

[741] Dorcas Wong and Alexander Chipman Koty, "*The US-China Trade War,*" **China Briefing** dated 28 Nov 2019

[742] "*China to Raise Penalties on IP Theft in Trade War Compromise,*" **Bloomberg News** dated 24 November 2019

[743] **The Guideline on Strengthening Intellectual Property Rights Protection 2019;** Joint Directive issued by Communist Party of China Central Committee and the State Council

constitute fundamental differences between them and second that these issues have to be addressed in their entirety in the second phase. However, there exists a wide chasm in their respective understandings of the problem including the quantum of loss for US companies, the strength and independence of Chinese judiciary, administrative requirements as well as Chinese governments programs.[744] In so far as the IPR basket is concerned, the two sides are testing each other's intentions and staring at a deep dialogue on systemic matters. These problems are exacerbated by the position adopted by the Trump Administration towards the World Trade Organization's dispute settlement body.[745] With the US Administration blocking re-appointments to the panel, the once successful mechanism will be reduced to a pale shadow of its former self. Further, the Trump Administration has also expressed its unhappiness by raising the possibility of blocking the approval of the World Trade Organization's biennial budget and effectively halting its work starting 2020. US President Trump has been determined in his use of national security clauses to stop IPR abuses by Chinese entities. While the Huawei case takes the top spot, the manner in which ZTE Corporation was forced to pay a US $ 1.2 billion fine to the US Bureau of Industry and Security, revamp its top leadership, and hire compliance officials picked by the U.S. government for exporting U.S. products to North Korea and Iran are also instructive.[746] In May 2019, an executive order signed by the US President declaring a national emergency and barring US companies from using telecommunications equipment made by

---

[744] Jane Cai, "*Trade war: why US and China remain so far apart on intellectual property rights,*" **South China Morning Post**, dated 30 Sep, 2018

[745] Sunod Jacob, "*Will December 2019 represent the Nadir of Multilateralism and Human Rights,*" **Modern Diplomacy** dated 23 November 2019

[746] *Secretary Ross Announces $1.4 Billion ZTE Settlement; ZTE Board, Management Changes and Strictest BIS Compliance Requirements Ever,* Official Press Release by US Department of Commerce, 7 June 2018

companies posing a national security risk was passed.[747] Later, in November 2019, the US Federal Communications Commission (FCC) voted 5-0 to designate China's Huawei and ZTE as national security risks, barring their rural carrier customers in the US from tapping an $ 8.5 billion government fund to buy equipment or services.[748] The US Justice Department charges against Huawei and its chief financial officer, Meng Wanzhou outlined a decade-long attempt by the company to steal trade secrets, obstruct a criminal investigation and evade economic sanctions on Iran.[749] The use of national security clause to try and thwart Huawei's 5G ambitions is the most dramatic escalation of the trade war between US and China. In another case, the Justice Department accused Huawei of stealing trade secrets, wire fraud and obstructing justice for allegedly stealing robotic technology from carrier T-Mobile to test smartphones' durability.[750] In its push back, Huawei issued a White Paper[751] in June 2019 titled, *"Respecting and Protecting Intellectual Property: The Foundation of Innovation"* wherein Huawei elaborated on its practices in and contributions to innovation and the

---

[747] **Executive Order on Securing the Information and Communications Technology and Services Supply Chain**, May 15, 2019; Order passed pursuant to **International Emergency Economic Powers Act** (50 U.S.C. 1701 et seq.) (IEEPA), the **National Emergencies Act** (50 U.S.C. 1601 et seq.), and section 301 of title 3, **United States Code**

[748] Federal Communications Commission order titled **Protecting Against National Security Threats to the Communications Supply Chain Through FCC Programs**, DA/FCC #: FCC-19-121; Docket/RM: 18-89, 19-351, 19-352

[749] David E. Sanger, Katie Benner and Matthew Goldstein, *"Huawei and Top Executive Face Criminal Charges in the U.S,"* **The New York Times**, dated Jan. 28, 2019

[750] Alex Lockiejan, *"US calls Huawei and CFO Meng national security threats, indicts with fraud, IP theft charges,"* **The Business Insider**, 29 January, 2019

[751] Huawei White Paper on Innovation and Intellectual Property titled *"Respecting and Protecting Intellectual Property: The Foundation of Innovation,"* June 27, 2019

protection of IPR. The report stressed that Huawei had made sustained investment in R&D and open innovation, submitted more than 60,000 technical contributions to international standards organizations, respects third parties' Intellectual Property and trade secrets, entered into more than 100 patent license agreements, executed more than 10 outbound license agreements through amicable negotiations, respects international rules of legally implementing third parties' Intellectual Property through cross licensing or by paying licensing fees and royalties to third party Intellectual Property holders; and promotes legislative reform by providing its suggestions on and inputs to IP protection legislation and its amendment, as well as policy-making in major jurisdictions worldwide. Chief Legal Officer of Huawei Dr. Song Liuping's statement[752] at the Huawei Press Conference on the occasion of unveiling of this White Paper emphasized, inter alia, in the past 30 years, no court has ever concluded that Huawei engaged in malicious IP theft, and that they had never been required by the court to pay damages for this. Further, Dr. Song mentioned that;

> *"Huawei fully supports the IPR protection system, both globally and in the United States. IP is private property, defined by the US Constitution. If politicians use IP as a political tool, they will destroy confidence in the patent protection system. If some governments selectively strip companies of their IP, it will break the foundation of global innovation."*

The challenges by Huawei in the UK lower court cases of ***Unwired Planet v. Huawei***[753] and ***Conversant S.a.r.l v. Huawei***[754] expected to be pronounced upon by the Supreme Court in 2020 will be watched with rapt attention. The outcome is unpredictable, but many experts believe the lower court decisions have a fair chance

---

[752] https://www.huawei.com/en/press-events/news/2019/speeches/dr-songliuping-statement-june27; website accessed on 7 May 2020

[753] [2017] EWHC 711 (Pat)

[754] [2019] EWCA Civ 38

of being upheld.⁷⁵⁵ Similarly, the response by Western Governments to Huawei's 5G push has been followed closely around the world. In the case of India, the Central Government has permitted Huawei to conduct 5G testing in early 2019, but with the caveat that such a permission, however, is no guarantee that India will welcome 5G. With this background, we move to the third and concluding section of the assessment.

Impact of US-China IPR differences on India: India is also a target of US actions on the Intellectual Property Rights front with a total of 8 cases,⁷⁵⁶ albeit of a lesser degree compared to Peoples' Republic of China with 23; though none are in the IPR field.⁷⁵⁷ According to the latest Special 301 report of the USTR on Intellectual Property Protection and Review of Notorious Markets for Piracy and Counterfeiting issued in April 2019, India was among the 11 on the

---

⁷⁵⁵ Michael T. Renaud, James Wodarski and Matthew S. Galica, *Key Considerations for Global SEP Litigation*, **Lexology**, 5 November 2019

⁷⁵⁶ These eight cover the following: Patent Protection for Pharmaceutical and Agricultural Chemical Products (initiated in July 1996 by the US and implementation report filed by India in April 1999); Quantitative Restrictions on Imports of Agricultural, Textile and Industrial Products (initiated in July 1997 and implementation report filed by India in April 2001); Measures Affecting Trade and Investment in the Motor Vehicle Sector (initiated in June 1999 and implementation report filed by India in November 2002); Additional and Extra-Additional Duties on Imports from the United States (initiated in March 2007 and implementation report filed in November 2008); Measures Concerning the Importation of Certain Agricultural Products (initiated in March 2012); Certain Measures Relating to Solar Cells and Solar Modules (initiated in February 2013); Export Related Measures (initiated in March 2018 and panel report is under appeal); and Additional duties on certain products from the United States (initiated in July 2019).

⁷⁵⁷ https://www.wto.org/english/tratop_e/dispu_e/dispu_by_country_e.htm; website accessed on 6 December 2019

Priority Watch List. The USTR found that

> "India has yet to take steps to address long-standing patent issues that affect innovative industries. Companies across different sectors remain concerned about narrow patentability standards, the potential threat of compulsory licensing and patent revocations, as well as overly broad criteria for issuing such licenses and revocations under the India Patents Act. Furthermore, patent applicants face costly and time-consuming patent opposition hurdles, long timelines for receiving patents, and excessive reporting requirements."

Specifically, in terms of the impact of the US-China IPR differences on India, three broad dimensions can be identified. The first one pertains to the World Trade Organization regime and other regional trade arrangements. This is a more generalized dimension. USA's stance on the DSB and its approach to funding the World Trade Organization in the future have already been covered. As rightly point out in a recent ORF paper[758] on this aspect, as the fifth most active participant of the World Trade Organization's dispute settlement system, India had recognized the impasse in appellate body member appointments with concern and aims to support reforms of the World Trade Organization. With India facing its highest number of complaints in 2019, the revival of the dispute settlement system is essential to a swift resolution to these trade disputes. It is also pertinent to mention that groups of developing countries have taken initiatives to break the deadlock at the World Trade Organization. This is happening in the backdrop of the creation of the AfCFTA [African Continental Free Trade Area]. At the 12th extraordinary session of the Assembly of the African Union held in Niamey, Niger in July 2019, African leaders welcomed the entry into force of the AfCFTA on 30 May

---

[758] Aarshi Tirkey, *The WTO Dispute Settlement System: An Analysis of India's Experience and Current Reform Proposals*, **ORF Occasional Paper**, September 2019

2019 and launched its operational phase.[759] As the World Economic Forum[760] rightly analyses the AfCFTA will be the world's largest free trade area by number of countries once it's fully up and running after overcoming infrastructure logjam and bureaucracy as well as harmonizing regulations. The WEF further states,

> "As global trade rules are being eroded in other regions, with China and the United States spiraling into a trade war and protectionism tightening its grip in many countries, Africa has the opportunity to create a trade buffer for itself."

As the preparations for the 12th World Trade Organization Ministerial Conference in Kazakhstan in June 2020 gets underway, India and China have hosted separate mini-Ministerial to sort out the contentious issues, albeit with very limited success. In a recent NITI Aayog report[761] on Free Trade Agreements, the authors argued that; "*Given India's inability to negotiate a good service deal in the past, RCEP negotiations especially with China need a second thought. Indian industry will have more to lose than gain if it agrees to a liberal tariff elimination schedule specially w.r.t China*" ….and recommended among other measures…. "*Before getting into any multilateral trade deal India should firstly, review and assess its existing FTAs in terms of benefits to various stakeholders like industry and consumers, trade complementarities and changing trade patterns in the past decade.*" This report preceded the decision by India to walk away from the RCEP negotiations in Bangkok. The recent UNCTAD report[762] on *Trade*

---

[759] Decisions & Declarations by Assembly of The African Union, Twelfth Extraordinary Session (Niamey) Ext/Assembly/AU/Dec.1-3(XII), 7 July 2019

[760] Kim Cloete, "*Africa's new free trade area is promising, yet full of hurdles*", **World Economic Forum on Africa,** 6 Sep 2019

[761] Dr. V.K. Saraswat, Prachi Priya and Aniruddha Ghosh, *A Note on Free Trade Agreements and Their Costs*, **NITI AAYOG** Report on FTA 2019

[762] Alessandro Nicita, "*Trade and trade diversion effects of United States tariffs on China*", UNCTAD Research Paper No. 37 UNCTAD/SER.RP/2019/9 November 2019

and trade diversion effects of United States tariffs on China, India gained about $755 million in additional exports, mainly of chemicals, metals and ore, to the US in the first half of 2019 due to the trade diversion effects of Washington's tariff war with China and as such does not find any IPR implications.

Secondly, India needs to brace for further action at the World Intellectual Property Organization and on the larger question of what US withdrawal from multilateral trade bodies means for the international community. India's engagement with the WIPO has intensified over the years even as its domestic measures especially since the adoption of the National IPR Policy in 2016 has led to considerable reduction in pendency of IP applications and increase in disposal and examination due to large-scale augmentation of manpower in Indian IP offices. India has acceded to five IPR treaties administered by WIPO[763] in the 12-month period ending September 2019. The organization of major events in India, like the Global Digital Content Market and the PCT Roving Seminars, has helped progressively build on our cooperation with WIPO. In fact, the recent launch of the 2019 report of the Global Innovation Index in New Delhi was a significant step, as it was the first time; the report was being launched in a developing country. India has witnessed a substantial jump of 29 places in the rankings since 2015, and this showcases the importance of innovation in the fastest growing major economy in the world. India is also one of the applicants for hosting an External Office of WIPO in its national capacity and has given assurances to the other Member States that opening of an EO in India will only strengthen the IP ecosystem

---

[763] These include the WIPO Copyright Treaty, WIPO Performances and Phonograms Treaty, Nice Agreement concerning the International Classification of Goods and Services for the purposes of registration of marks, Locarno Agreement establishing an International classification for industrial designs & Vienna Agreement establishing an International Classification of the figurative elements of marks.

globally, by ushering in innovative thinking and focus on IP. However, the immediate and indeed perhaps the long-term challenge for the WIPO ecosystem is how it will adjust to the US withdrawal from multilateral bodies under the Trump Administration. As Colum Lynch writes[764] in Foreign Policy,

> *"Beijing has its sights on leading the global organization that is supposed to protect IP, and which sets international standards for patents, trademarks, and copyrights."*

In November 2019, China nominated Wang Binying, its national who currently serves as deputy director-general for WIPO's Brands and Designs Sector, to succeed the agency's Australian Director-General, Francis Gurry, after he steps down in September 2020, having served for 12 years on the job. The election is scheduled to take place March 5 and 6 of 2020. The US is supposedly supporting Daren Tang, the head of Singapore's Intellectual Property Office. If the election results for the FAO in mid-2019 when a Chinese national easily won against other rivals including the Indian candidate and the Georgian candidate who was supported by the USA is any indication, the outcome for the WIPO election is also swinging the Chinese way.

Thirdly, Indian Government and companies need to try and leverage the opportunities that may be created by China's reforms in the IPR field including the Pilot Free Trade Zone at Shanghai. China's National Intellectual Property Administration (CNIPA) is the coordinating ministry for the Patent Law of 1984 (amended in 1992, 2000 and 2008) and the Trademark Law of 1982 (amended in 1993, 2001, 2014, and 2019). National Copyright of Administration and Copyright Protection Centre of China is responsible for the Copyright Law, 1990; amended in 2001 and 2010 and PRC Tort

---

[764] Colum Lynch, *"China Bids to Lead World Agency Protecting Intellectual Property"* **Foreign Policy,** 26 November, 2019

Liability Law, 2009. State Administration for Market Regulation is responsible for Anti-Unfair Competition Law, 1993; amended in 2017 and 2019 and Administrative Licensing Law, 2003; amended in 2019. By 2014, three specialized IP courts were established in Beijing, Shanghai, and Guangzhou. From 2017, 18 specialized IP tribunals were set up. In October 2018, the Standing Committee of the People's National Congress approved the pilot program of the Supreme People's Court on the establishment of a specialized appellate tribunal to hear appeals in civil and administrative cases of technology-related IP disputes across the country; it began operations January 1, 2019. While the Beijing, Shanghai, and Guangzhou IP courts and the IP tribunal of the Supreme People's Court can only adjudicate civil and administrative IP cases, the specialized regional IP tribunals can adjudicate civil, administrative and criminal IP cases. In April 2019, the Supreme People's Court announced that the number of IP-related cases heard by courts at all levels across the country had increased significantly in 2018 – and with a high rate of settlement.[765]

With the improvement in bilateral relations since the *Wuhan spirit* and *Chennai Connect*, the two Governments of Indian and China have decided to address longstanding economic issues. Indian companies must make use of this opportunity to push for their space in the IP field, even though their experience with market access for Indian pharma and software products have not been too encouraging. Companies must make use of the new provisions for the Shanghai Pilot FTZ pertaining to arbitration and alternate dispute settlement mechanisms. According to a recent assessment[766] when these new provisions are fully implemented,

---

[765] Frank Ka-Ho Wong, *Intellectual Property in China: Laws and Registration Procedures,* **China Briefing,** 14 November, 2019

[766] Martin Rogers, Noble Mak (Davis Polk & Wardwell LLP) *"Foreign Administered Arbitration in China: The Emergence of a Framework Plan for the Shanghai Pilot Free Trade Zone,"* Kluwer Arbitration Blog, 6 Sep 2019

and foreign arbitration institutions begin to operate directly in mainland China, Shanghai will likely become a much more important arbitration hub than it is currently. These would be in addition to the new explorations that were made in industrial forecasting, protection of intellectual property rights, information disclosure, scientific and technological innovation, and a talent service system under this latest Pilot FTZ.[767] Combined with the increasing attraction of the China International Import Expo, there would be new avenues for Indian corporates to encash on the recent developments.

---

[767] Guangwen Meng and Douglas Zhihua Zeng, "*Structural transformation through free trade zones: the case of Shanghai*", **Transnational Corporations** (UNCTAD Publications) Volume 26, 2019, Number 2

Select Bibliography

1. Jeremy Bentham, **Introduction to the Principles of Morals and Legislation,** 1780; Subsequent version printed for W. Pickering and E. Wilson, London, 1823
2. E. Vattel, **The Law of Nations: Or, Principles of the Law of Nature Applied to the Conduct and Affairs of Nations and Sovereigns,** 1758
3. Christian Baldus, **Vestigia pacis- The Roman Peace Treaty: Structure or Event?** (First edition, Cambridge University Press, 2004)
4. The San Francisco Conference 1945
5. UNGA Resolution 174 (II) of 21 November 1947
6. JG Starke, **Introduction to International Law** (10th Edition, Butterworth -Heinemann, 1989)
7. John Austin, The **Province of Jurisprudence Determined** (1832 Edited by Rumble W. E, Cambridge University Press, 1995)
8. DJ Harris, **Cases and materials on International law** (5th edition, Sweet & Maxwell, London, 1998) p. 6
9. *Philippines v. China* (PCA case number 2013–19)
10. Statement of the Ministry of Foreign Affairs of the People's Republic of China on the Award of 12 July 2016 of the Arbitral Tribunal in the South China Sea Arbitration Established at the Request of the Republic of the Philippines
11. UN Charter 1945
12. North Atlantic Treaty 1949
13. Charter of the International Military Tribunal for the Far East 1945
14. Ulrich Huber, **De Conflictu Legum** (edited by Ernest G. Lorenzen 1919)
15. Paras Diwan and Peeyushi Diwan, **Private International Law Indian and English** (14th edition, Deep & Deep Publications, New Delhi, 1998)

16. P.M. North and J.J. Fawcett, **Cheshire and North's Private International Law**, (12th edition, Butterworths, 1992) p. 14
17. **Reparation** of **Injuries** Suffered in Service of the UN, Advisory Opinion, 1949 ICJ 174 (Apr. 11)
18. S.K. Verma, **An Introduction to Public International Law** (Eastern Economy, 1998) p. 113
19. UN General Assembly A/RES/3237 (XXIX)
20. UN General Assembly A/RES/52/250
21. UN General Assembly A/RES/58/314
22. The Charter of 1943
23. International Military Tribunal for Nuremberg, Judgment, 1 October 1946, p. 41
24. General Assembly resolution 95 (1) of 11 December 1946
25. General Assembly resolution 177(II) of 21 November 1947
26. The Covenant of the League of Nations 1919
27. John Humphrey, "The International Law of Human Rights in the Middle Twentieth Century," (International Law Association, London, 1973)
28. MEA document titled, *Guidelines/SoP on the conclusion of International Treaties in India*
29. United Nations Audio Visual Library of International Law, Lecture by J. Antonio Augusto Cançado Trindade on *Statute Of The International Court Of Justice*; https://legal.un.org/avl/pdf/ha/sicj/sicj_e.pdf; website accessed on 17 March 2020
30. Additional Protocol to the Child Rights Convention
31. United Nations Audio Visual Library of International Law, Lecture by J. Christopher Greenwood on *Sources of International Law: An Introduction*; https://legal.un.org/avl/pdf/ls/greenwood_outline.pdf; website accessed on 17 March 2020
32. *France v. Turkey* PCIJ (ser. A) No. 10 (1927)
33. ICJ GL No 95, [1996] ICJ Rep 226, ICGJ 205 (ICJ 1996), 8th July 1996
34. Columbian Peruvian Asylum Case 1950 ICJ

35. North Sea Continental Shelf cases (1969)
36. ICJ Reports 1996 (I), pp. 254-255
37. ICJ GL No 169, ICGJ 534 (ICJ 2019), 25th February 2019
38. *Portugal v India* Right of Passage over Indian Territory ICJ 1960
39. Case Concerning Barcelona Traction, Light, and Power Co., Ltd (*Belgium v. Spain*) [1970] ICJ 1
40. *Temple of Preah Vihar* case ICJ Reports (1962)
41. *Eastern Greenland* case (1933), PCIJ, Ser. A/B. no. 53
42. Diversion of Water from the Meuse Case (*Netherlands v. Belgium*) [1937], PCIJ (Ser. A/B) No. 70
43. Nuclear Test cases ICJ Rep. 1974
44. *Blaskic,* (ICTY Trial Chamber) IT-95-14-T. 3 March 2000
45. **South West African Cases**
46. Judgment in the Application of the Convention on the Prevention and Punishment of the Crime of Genocide case
47. Statute of the ICJ
48. Advisory Opinion on Nuclear Weapons (1996)
49. Questions of Interpretation and Application of the 1971 Montreal Convention arising from the Aerial Incident at Lockerbie (*Libyan Arab Jamahiriya v United Kingdom*) [1992] ICJ Rep 3
50. *Prosecutor v. Dusko Tadic* (Appeal Judgement), IT-94-1-A
51. https://legal.un.org/avl/pdf/ls/greenwood_outline.pdf
52. *Bosnia and Herzegovina v Serbia and Montenegro* [2007] ICJ 2
53. Rome Statute of the International Criminal Court, 2002
54. *Prosecutor v. Furundžija*, International Criminal Tribunal for the Former Yugoslavia, 2002, 121 International Law Reports 213 (2002)
55. Case Concerning the Arrest Warrant of 11 April 2000 (*Democratic Republic of the Congo v. Belgium*) ICJ Reports 2002
56. *Jones v. Ministry of Interior Al -Mamlaka Al -Arabiya AS. Saudiya (the Kingdom of Saudi Arabia)* [2006] UKHL 26
57. Montevideo Convention of 1933
58. *UN welcomes South Sudan as 193rd Member State,* **UN News**,

dated 14 July 2011;
59. UN General Assembly resolution A/RES/60/264
60. https://sheir.org/edu/theories-for-state-recognition/
61. *Recognition in International Law: A Functional Reappraisal,* **The University of Chicago Law Review**, Vol. 34, No. 4 (Summer, 1967), pp. 857-883
62. Hans Kelsen, **Principles of International Law**, (1952)
63. Dionisio Anzilotti, Cours de droit international (1929)
64. Heinrich Triepel, Völkerrecht und Landesrecht, By. Leipzig: C. L. Hirschfeld, 1899; reprint by Scientia Antiquariat Aalen, 1958 p. 102
65. Henry Wheaton, **Elements of International Law**; edited with notes by Richard Henry Dana (8th edition, Little, Brown and Company, Boston, 1866)
66. Oppenheim, **International Law: A Treatise** 109 (1905)
67. Hans Kelsen, *Recognition in International Law: Theoretical Observations,* **The American Journal of International Law**, Vol. 35, No. 4 (Oct., 1941), pp. 605-617
68. *Recognition in International Law: A Functional Reappraisal;* **The University of Chicago Law Review**, Vol. 34, No. 4 (Summer, 1967), pp. 857-883
69. James Leslie Brierly, **The Law of Nations**, (6th edition revised by Sir Humphrey Waldock, Oxford: Clarendon Press, 1963) p. 140
70. John Basset Moore, **International Law Digest** (Washington, 1906)
71. Chen Ti-chiang, The International Law of Recognition; Edited by L.C. Green (Stevens and Sons, 1951)
72. Josef L. Kunz, *"Identity of States Under International Law,"* **AJIL** Vol. 49, Issue 1, Jan 1955, pp. 68-76
73. Herbert W. Briggs, *"Recognition of States: Some Reflections on Doctrine and Practice,"* **AJIL** Vol. 43, Issue 1 Jan 1949
74. Arbitration Commission of the Peace Conference on Yugoslavia 1991
75. The Tinoco Arbitration Award (*Great Britain v. Costa Rica*) 1

U.N. Rep. Int'l Arb. Awards 369 (1923) Note: Non-
76. Digest of the United State Practice in International Law, 1976, pp. 19-20
77. Malcolm N. Shaw, **International Law** (Eight edition, Cambridge University Press, 2017)
78. JG Starke, **Introduction to International Law** (Tenth Edition, Butterworth -Heinemann, 1989) P. 125
79. Charles L. Cochran, *De Facto and De Jure Recognition: Is there a Difference?*, **The American Journal of International Law**, Vol. 62, No. 2 (Apr., 1968), pp. 457-460
80. Jorge Castaneda, **Mexico and the United Nations** (First Edition, Manhattan Publishing, 1958) p. 185
81. Palacios Trevino, Jorge. **La Doctrina Estrada y el Principio de la No-Intervención** (1937)
82. *The Mukden Incident of 1931 and the Stimson Doctrine,* US Office of the Historian Release, https://history.state.gov/milestones/1921-1936/mukden-incident; website accessed on 17 March 2020
83. Rhodesia's Unilateral Declaration of Independence, 1965
84. UN Security Council Resolution 216 and 217 S/RES/216 (1965)
85. UN General Assembly Resolution RES/63/3 (A/63/L.2) of 8 October 2008
86. International Law of the Unilateral Declaration of Independence in Respect of Kosovo, Advisory Opinion, ICJ Reports 2010, p. 403
87. UN GA Resolution 64/298
88. http://opiniojuris.org/2019/07/18/recognition-of-governments-legitimacy-and-control-six-months-after-guaido/; website visited on 6 April 2020
89. Relocation of the United States Embassy to Jerusalem (*Palestine v. United States of America*) 2018 https://www.icj-cij.org/en/case/176; website visited on 6 April 2020
90. Declaration on the Granting of Independence to Colonial Countries and Peoples; General Assembly resolution 1514

(XV) of 14 December 1960
91. https://www.oxfordbibliographies.com/view/document/obo-9780199796953/obo-9780199796953-0031.xml; website accessed on 6 April 2020
92. Factory at Chorzow, *Germany v Poland*, Judgment, Claim for Indemnity, Merits, Judgment No 13, (1928) PCIJ Series A No 17
93. UN ILC Special Rapporteur R Ago, '*Report on State Responsibility*' [1963] para. 5
94. https://opil.ouplaw.com/view/10.1093/law:epil/9780199231690/law-9780199231690-e1093#law-9780199231690-e1093-div1-2 website accessed on 6 April 2020
95. ILC Draft Articles of 1996
96. *Ethiopia v South Africa; Liberia v South Africa*
97. South West Africa/Namibia [Advisory Opinions and Judgments]
98. Claim for Indemnity, Merits, Judgment No 13, (1928) PCIJ Series A No 17, ICGJ 255 (PCIJ 1928),
99. *Germany v. Poland* PCIJ Series A. No 7
100. *United Kingdom of Great Britain and Northern Ireland v. Albania* ICJ Reports 1948
101. Corfu Channel case, Judgment ICJ Reports 1949,
102. *Bosnia and Herzegovina v Serbia and Montenegro* [2007] ICJ 2
103. *The Gambia v. Myanmar* 23 Jan 2020 General List No. 178
104. Application of the Convention on the Prevention and Punishment of the Crime of Genocide (*Bosnia and Herzegovina v. Yugoslavia*) Preliminary Objections, Judgment, ICJ Reports 1996(II), p.615, para.31
105. Federica Paddeu, **Countermeasures, in Justification and Excuse in International Law: Concept and Theory of General Defences** (Cambridge University Press, 2018) pp. 225–284
106. Case Concerning the Air Services Agreement of 27 March 1946 *(US vs France)* 1978 Volume XVIII pp. 417-493
107. E. Zoller, **Peacetime Unilateral Remedies: An Analysis of**

Countermeasures (Transnational Publishers, New York, 1984) p. 131
108. Gabčikovo-Nagymaros Project, *Hungary v Slovakia* ICGJ 65 (ICJ 1997)
109. *Carlos Ghosn: Japan presses for ex-Nissan boss's extradition from Lebanon*, https://www.bbc.com/news/business-51010128; website accessed on 5 March 2020
110. https://mea.gov.in/leta.htm
111. US Constitution 1787
112. https://definitions.uslegal.com/d/doctrine-of-specialty/
113. *United States v. Rauscher*, 119 U.S. 407 (US 1886)
114. https://www.unodc.org/pdf/model_treaty_extradition.pdf
115. https://www.icij.org/investigations/collateraldamage/post-911-renditions-extraordinary-violation-international-law/
116. *Honduras v. Brazil*, Order of 12 May 2010, ICJ Reports 2010, p. 303
117. Pact of Bogota 1948
118. Vienna Convention on Diplomatic Relations 1961
119. ICJ case concerning *Status vis-à-vis the Host State of a Diplomatic Envoy to the United Nations* 2006
120. https://legal.un.org/avl/ha/vccr/vccr.html ; website accessed on 10th April 2020
121. *Breard v. Greene* 523 US 371, 1988
122. Vienna Convention on Consular Relations of 1963 reads;
123. Advisory Opinion of the Inter-American Court of Human Rights: Due Process of Law is a Fundamental Right (OC-16/99), para. 82
124. *Germany v. United States of America* Judgment Jurisdiction, Admissibility, Merits, ICJ GL No 104, [2001] ICJ Rep 466, (2001) 40 ILM 1069, ICGJ 51 (ICJ 2001), 27th June 2001
125. Case Concerning Avena and Other Mexican Nationals (*Mexico v. United States of America*) Judgment, ICJ Reports 2004, 12 General List No. 128
126. Catherine M. Amirfar, "*The Avena Case in the International Court of Justice,*" **German Law Journal**, No. 4, April, 2004

127. *India v. Pakistan* ICGJ 515 (ICJ 2017), [2017] ICJ GL No 168
128. https://www.un.org/en/sections/issues-depth/oceans-and-law-sea/index.html; website accesses on 11 April 2020
129. Hugo Grotius, **Mare Liberum, sive de jure quod Batavis competit ad Indicana commercia dissertation** (Lodewijk Elzevir, 1609)
130. John Selden, **Mare Clausum** (London, John Stansby, 1635)
131. Eric G. M. Fletcher; Transactions of the Grotius Society, Vol. 19, Problems of Peace and War, Papers Read before the Society in the Year 1933 (Cambridge University Press, 1933), pp. 1-12
132. Cornelis van Bijnkershoek, **De Dominio Maris** (The Hague, 1703)
133. The Truman Proclamation 1945
134. **Policy of the United States with Respect to the Natural Resources of the Subsoil and Sea Bed of the Continental Shelf,** Presidential Proclamation No. 2667 of 28th September, 1945
135. **Policy of the United States with Respect to Coastal Fisheries in Certain Areas of the High Seas**, Presidential Proclamation No. 2668 of 28th September, 1945
136. Satya Nanda, "*The Exclusive Economic Zone: a historical perspective*" [1987] available at FAO Website http://www.fao.org/docrep/s5280T/s5280t0p.htm; website visited on 11 April 2020
137. Geneva Convention on Law of Seas 1958
138. United Nations Convention on the Law of the Sea 1982
139. Agreement relating to the implementation of Part XI of the United Nations Convention on the Law of the Sea of 10 December 1982 adopted by UNGA Resolution A/RES/48/263
140. Annex II to the United Nations Convention on the Law of the Sea 1982
141. https://legal.un.org/avl/ha/gclos/gclos.html; website accessed on 16 April 2020

142. Donald Rothwell, Alex G. Oude Elferink, Karen Nadine Scott, Tim Stephens, **The Oxford Handbook of the Law of the Sea** (Oxford University Press, Oxford, 2015) p.16
143. https://wcl.american.libguides.com/c.php?g=563260&p=3877789; website accessed on 16 April 2020
144. UNGA Resolution Resolution 1307 (XIII) of 10 December 1958
145. A/CONF.19/L.15
146. James Kraska, **Maritime Power and the Law of the Sea: Expeditionary Operations in World Politics** (Oxford University Press, New York, 2011) p. 137
147. **Essays in Memory of Jean Carroz: The Law and the Sea** (Food and Agriculture Organization of the United Nations, 1987) p. 177
148. Committee on the Peaceful Uses of the Sea Bed and the Ocean Floor Beyond the Limits of National Jurisdiction (1970)
149. Shigeru Oda, **Fifty Years of the Law of the Sea** (Kluwar Law International, Hague, 2003) p. 477
150. Declaration of The Meeting of Ministers on The Territorial Sea, Patrimonial Sea, And Continental Shelf, 1972
151. Agenda item 92, UNGA 22nd Session, First Committee, 1515th Meeting, 1967
152. Third United Nations Conference on the Law of the Sea, December 1973
153. Milenko Milic, Third United Nations Conference on the Law of the Sea, 8 **Case Western Reserve Journal of International Law** 168 (1976)
154. United Nations Convention on the Law of the Sea, 1982
155. Aldo Chircop, Norman Letalik, Ted, McDorman, Susan Rolston, **The Regulation of International Shipping: International and Comparative Perspectives** (Martinus Njhoff Publishers, Boston, 2012)
156. Jessica E. Tauman, *"Rescued at Sea, but Nowhere to Go: The Cloudy Legal Waters of the Tampa Crisis,"* 11 **Pac. Rim L &**

Pol'y J. 461 (2002)
157. *"The Three-Mile Limit: Its Juridical Status"* 6 **Val. U. L. Rev.** 170 (1972) pp. 170-182
158. HSK Kent, *"The Historical Origins of the Three-Mile Limit,"* **The American Journal of International Law**, Vol. 48, No. 4 (Oct., 1954), pp. 537-553
159. *The Republic of Philippines v. The People's Republic of China)- The question of 'historic rights'*
160. Deliberations of Second Committee at the UN Conference on Law of Sea 1973
161. Dispute concerning Delimitation of the Maritime Boundary between Bangladesh and Myanmar in the Bay of Bengal between The People's Republic of Bangladesh Case No. 16 Judgement dated 14 March 2012
162. William Wertenbaker, *"The Law of the Sea"* **The New Yorker**, Vol. 59, Part 4 p. 59
163. The United Nations Convention on the Law of the Sea: A historical Perspective (Division of Ocean Affairs and the Law of Sea, 1998)
164. Baldeo Sahai, **Indian Navy, A perspective: From the Earliest Period to Modern Times** (Ministry of Information and Broadcasting of India Publications Division, New Delhi, 2006) p. 120
165. Rand McNally, **Atlas of The Oceans** (Rand McNally & Company, Chicago, 1987) p. 165
166. Pew Trust Factsheet on The Clarion-Clipperton Zone Dec 2017; https://www.pewtrusts.org/en/research-and-analysis/fact-sheets/2017/12/the-clarion-clipperton-zone; website accessed on 17 April 2020
167. General Assembly resolution 2749 (XXV) of 17 December 1970
168. https://www.isa.org.jm/frequently-asked-questions-faqs; website accessed on 17 April 2020
169. Charles Chernor Jalloh, Olufemi Elias, **Shielding Humanity: Essays in International Law in Honour of**

Judge Abdul G Koroma (Koninklijke-Brill, Leiden, 2015) p. 143

170. Clifford E. Griffin, **The Race for Fisheries and Hydrocarbons in the Caribbean Basin** (Ian Randle Publishers, Kingston, 2007) p. 40

171. The United Nations Convention on the Law of the Sea: A historical Perspective (Division of Ocean Affairs and the Law of Sea, 1998)

172. UNCLOS at 30 (United Nations, New York, 2012)

173. of the United Nations Convention on the Law of the Sea of 1982

174. Yoshifumi Tanaka, **The International Law of the Sea** (Third Edition, Cambridge University Press, Cambridge, 2019)

175. Rules of the Tribunal

176. Agreement between The International Seabed Authority and The Government of Jamaica Regarding The Headquarters Of The International Seabed Authority

177. Rules of Procedure of The Assembly of The International Seabed Authority 1994

178. https://ran-s3.s3.amazonaws.com/isa.org.jm/s3fs-public/files/documents/council1996-2020-i.pdf website accessed on 12 April 2020

179. https://www.isa.org.jm/member-states; website accessed on 12 April 2020

180. ISA Secretary-General Michael W Lodge, *Strengthening the participation of women and girls in ocean science to achieve the Sustainable Development Goals,"* **ISA Opinion Pieces,** 10 February 2020

181. Voluntary Commitments Registered at the 2017 Ocean Conference

182. Decision of the Council relating to an environmental management plan for the Clarion-Clipperton Zone 2012, ISBA/18/C/22

183. Annex II, Commission on The Limits of The Continental

Shelf, UNCLOS III 1982
184. United Nations Convention on the Law of the Sea of 1982
185. Annex II, Commission on The Limits of The Continental Shelf, UNCLOS III 1982
186. Rules of Procedure of the Commission on the Limits of the Continental Shelf of 2008
187. Treaty on Principles Governing the Activities of States in the Exploration and Use of Outer Space, including the Moon and Other Celestial Bodies; Adopted by the General Assembly in its resolution 2222 (XXI)
188. Agreement on the Rescue of Astronauts, the Return of Astronauts and the Return of Objects Launched into Outer Space; Adopted by the General Assembly Resolution 2345 (XXII)
189. Convention on International Liability for Damage Caused by Space Objects; Adopted by the General Assembly Resolution 2777 (XXVI)
190. Convention on Registration of Objects Launched into Outer Space; Adopted by General Assembly Resolution 3235 (XXIX)
191. Agreement Governing the Activities of States on the Moon and Other Celestial Bodies; Adopted by General Assembly Resolution 34/68
192. GA resolution 1962 (XVIII) of 13 December 1963
193. GA resolution 37/92 of 10 December 1982
194. GA resolution 41/65 of 3 December 1986
195. GA resolution 47/68 of 14 December 1992
196. General Assembly resolution 51/122 of 13 December 1996
197. https://fas.org/nuke/control/ost/intro.htm
198. UNGA Resolution 2222 (XXI)
199. https://www.unoosa.org/oosa/en/ourwork/spacelaw/treaties/introouterspacetreaty.html
200. https://fas.org/nuke/control/ost/intro.htm
201. https://www.armscontrol.org/factsheets/outerspace
202. UN GA Resolution 2345 (XXII)

203. The Outer Space Treaty and the Liability Convention have their roots in a prior international covenant: the 1944 Convention on International Civil Aviation, more commonly known as the Chicago Convention.
204. UNGA Resolution 2777 (XXVI)
205. General Assembly Resolution 3235 (XXIX)
206. Resolution 1721B (XVI) of December 1961
207. UNGA Resolution A/RES/72/78
208. UNGA Resolution A/RES/68/74
209. UNGA Resolution A/RES/62/101
210. UNGA Resolution A/RES/59/115
211. UNGA Resolution A/RES/55/122
212. UNGA Resolution RES 1721 (XVI)
213. UNGA Resolution ST/SPACE/49
214. UNGA Resolution A/AC.105/934
215. https://edition.cnn.com/2013/10/22/world/international-space-station-fast-facts/index.html
216. https://aerospace.org/sites/default/files/policy_archives/Space%20Station%20Intergovernmental%20Agreement%20Jan98.pdf
217. https://www.reuters.com/article/us-india-satellite-tests-factbox/factbox-anti-satellite-weapons-rare-high-tech-and-risky-to-test-idUSKCN1R80UW
218. https://www.cfr.org/backgrounder/chinas-anti-satellite-test
219. Lee Paddock, Du Qun, Louis J. Kotzé, David L. Markell, Kenneth J. Markowitz, Durwood Zaelk **Compliance and Enforcement in Environmental Law: Toward More Effective Implementation** (Edward Elgar Publishing, Northampton, 2011)
220. https://www.un.org/ruleoflaw/thematic-areas/land-property-environment/environmental-law/
221. 27th Session of UNEP Governing Council/Global Ministerial Environment Forum 2013
222. The United Nations Conference on the Human

Environment 1972 A/CONF.48/14/REV.1
223. Report of the World Commission on Environment and Development: Our Common Future Transmitted to the General Assembly as an Annex to document A/42/427
224. United Nations Conference on Environment & Development 1992 A/CONF.151/26
225. World Summit on Sustainable Development 2002
226. Anne Burnett, International Environmental Law (ASIL, 2015) p. 4
227. https://guides.ll.georgetown.edu/InternationalEnvironmentalLaw website accessed on 29 April 2020
228. https://unfccc.int/process-and-meetings/the-convention/what-is-the-united-nations-framework-convention-on-climate-change website accessed on 29 April 2020
229. https://unfccc.int/kyoto_protocol website accessed on 29 April 2020
230. http://www.unece.org/fileadmin//DAM/env/lrtap/welcome.html; website accessed on 29 April 2020
231. http://www.imo.org/en/OurWork/Environment/LCLP/Pages/default.aspx; website accessed on 29 April 2020
232. https://www.cites.org/eng/disc/what.php; website accessed on 29 April 2020
233. http://www.basel.int/TheConvention/Overview/tabid/1271/Default.aspx
234. The Convention concerning the Protection of the World Cultural and Natural Heritage of 1975
235. Conference for the Establishment of the United Nations Educational, Scientific and Cultural Organization, held at the Institute of Civil Engineers, London, November, 1945 ECO/CONF/29
236. UNGA Resolution Res. 3.342
237. UNGA Resolution Res 3.412
238. United Nations Convention to Combat Desertification in Those Countries Experiencing Serious Drought and/or

Desertification, Particularly in Africa 1994
239. Annex I Regional Implementation for Africa of 1994
240. The Future Strategic Framework Of The Convention Decision 7/COP.13 ICCD/COP(13)/21/Add.1
241. ICJ Application instituting proceedings filed in the registry of the Court on 4 May 2006 Pulp Mills on the River Uruguay (*Argentina v. Uruguay*) 2006 General List No. 135
242. Treaty between the Argentine Republic and the Eastern Republic of Uruguay of 7 April 1961 concerning the Boundary Constituted by the River Uruguay United Nations, Treaty Series, Vol. 635, No. 9074
243. Pulp Mills on the River Uruguay (*Argentina v. Uruguay*), Judgment, ICJ Reports 2010, p. 14
244. Functions of CARU, The River Uruguay Executive Commission Comisión Administradora Del Rio Uruguay; http://www.caru.org.uy/web/pdfs_publicaciones/The-River-Uruguay-executive-commission-Uruguay-Paysandu.pdf website accessed on 14 April 2020
245. Certain Activities Carried Out by Nicaragua in the Border Area (*Costa Rica v. Nicaragua*) and Construction of a Road in Costa Rica along the San Juan River (*Nicaragua v. Costa Rica*), Judgment, I.C.J. Reports 2015, p. 665
246. James Harrison, "*Significant International Environmental Law Cases: 2017–18*" **Journal of Environmental Law**, 2018 Vol. 30, pp. 527–541
247. Application instituting proceedings filed in The Registry of the Court on 31 May 2010 Whaling in The Antarctic (*Australia V. Japan*) 2010 General List No. 148
248. Whaling in the Antarctic (*Australia v. Japan: New Zealand intervening*), Judgment, ICJ Reports 2014, p. 226
249. UN Charter 1945
250. http://www.gutenberg.org/ebooks/41046 website accessed on 23 March 2020
251. https://ihldatabases.icrc.org/applic/ihl/ihl.nsf/Treaty.xsp?action=openDocument&documentId=85EE9A58C871B072C

12563CD002D6A15 website accessed on 23 March 2020
252. https://archive.org/details/Arthasastra_English_Translation; website accessed on 23 March 2020
253. https://sites.ualberta.ca/~enoch/Readings/The_Art_Of_War.pdf website accessed on 23 March 2020
254. https://ebooks.adelaide.edu.au/m/machiavelli/niccolo/m149p/complete.html website accessed on 23 March 2020
255. http://www.clausewitz.com/readings/OnWar1873/TOC.htm website accessed on 23 March 2020
256. http://www.systemicpeace.org/warlist/warlist.htm website accessed on 23 March 2020
257. Annual Reports and International Review of Red Cross for Humanitarian efforts https://international-review.icrc.org/
258. ICTY, *The Prosecutor v. Dusko Tadic*, Decision on the Defence Motion for Interlocutory Appeal on Jurisdiction, IT-94-1-A, 2 October 1995, para. 70
259. ICTY, *The Prosecutor v. Fatmir Limaj*, Judgment, IT-03- 66-T, 30 November 2005, para. 135-170
260. Rogier Bartels, *"The Relationship between International Humanitarian Law and the Notion of State Sovereignty,"* **Journal of Conflict and Security Law**, Volume 23, Issue 3, Winter 2018, pp. 461–486
261. St. Petersburg Declaration of 1868
262. Convention on the Prohibition of the Development, Production, Stockpiling and Use of Chemical Weapons and on their Destruction 1992;
263. Protocol IV of the 1980 Convention on Certain Conventional Weapons
264. Convention on the Prohibition of the Development, Production and Stockpiling of Bacteriological (Biological) and Toxin Weapons and on their Destruction 1972
265. Agreement on Ending the War and Restoring Peace in Vietnam 27 Jan 1973
266. Instrument of Surrender of Pakistan forces in Dacca, 16 December 1971

267. Jann Kleffner, *"Scope of Application of International Humanitarian Law"*, in Dieter Fleck (ed.), **The Handbook of International Humanitarian Law** (3rd edition, Oxford University Press, Oxford, 2013) 4
268. *The Republic of Nicaragua v. The United States of America* 1986 I.C.J. 14
269. Additional Protocol (I) 1977
270. Convention (II) with Respect to the Laws and Customs of War on Land and its annex: Regulations concerning the Laws and Customs of War on Land. The Hague, 29 July 1899
271. Convention (IV) respecting the Laws and Customs of War on Land and its annex: Regulations concerning the Laws and Customs of War on Land. The Hague, 18 October 1907
272. Protocol Additional to the Geneva Conventions of 12 August 1949, and relating to the Protection of Victims of International Armed Conflicts (Protocol I), 8 June 1977
273. Protocol additional to the Geneva Conventions of 12 August 1949, and relating to the Adoption of an Additional Distinctive Emblem (Protocol III), 8 December 2005
274. Hague Convention for the Protection of Cultural Property in the Event of Armed Conflict 1954
275. Protocol Additional to the Geneva Conventions of 12 August 1949, and relating to the Protection of Victims of International Armed Conflicts; June 8, 1977
276. Vienna Convention on the Law of Treaties 1969
277. Draft articles on the Responsibility of International Organizations 2011
278. Moscow Declaration of 1943
279. Declaration of the Three Powers, 1943
280. Hans Kelsen, *The Preamble of the Charter: A Critical Analysis*, **The Journal of Politics** Vol. 8, No. 2 (May, 1946), pp. 134-159
281. Vienna Convention on Law of Treaties of 1969
282. *The Schooner Exchange v. McFaddon*, 11 U.S. (7 Cranch) 116 (1812)

283. Robert Jennings, Arthur Watts, **Oppenheim's International Law: Volume 1 Peace** (9th Edition, Longman, London, 1992)
284. GA decision 49/426 of 9 December 1994 published in the 2008 United Nations Juridical Yearbook, p. 438, part B, paragraphs 8-11
285. UN General Assembly Resolution 54/195
286. Rule of Procedure of the UNGA A/520/Rev.18
287. UNGA Resolution A/RES/55/2
288. UNGA Resolution A/RES/60/1
289. UNGA Resolution A/RES/70/1
290. United Nations General Assembly Resolution A/RES/377(V)
291. World Summit Outcome Document 2005
292. Annexes to the UN General Assembly's Rules of Procedure
293. UNGA Resolution A/62/952/Add.1
294. UNGA Resolution A/63/959
295. UNGA Resolution A/67/936
296. UNGA Resolution A/68/951
297. UNGA Resolution A/69/1007
298. UNGA Resolution A/70/1003,
299. UNGA Resolution A/71/1007
300. UNGA Resolution A/72/896
301. UNGA Resolution A/73/956
302. UNGA Rules of Procedure
303. Provisional Rules of Procedure of the United Nations Security Council
304. https://www.globalpolicy.org/security-council/security-council-reform/49885.html?itemid=1321; website visited on 29 April 2020
305. https://www.un.org/sg/en/appointment.shtml; website accessed on 29 April 2020
306. https://peacekeeping.un.org/en/fatalities; website accessed on 29 April 2020
307. UNGA Resolutions A/RES/60/180

308. UNGA Resolution S/RES/1645 (2005)
309. Resolutions A/RES/70/262 and S/RES/2282 (2016)
310. Reports of International Arbitral Awards Vol XXIX, pp.125-134
311. Statute of the ICJ 1946
312. Certain activities carried out by Nicaragua in the Border Area (*Costa Rica v. Nicaragua*) and Construction of a Road in Costa Rica along the San Juan River (*Nicaragua v. Costa Rica*) Summary 2015/3 16 December 2015; (ICJ Reports 2010 (I)
313. Lavanya Rajamani, "*Ambition and Differentiation in the 2015 Paris Agreement: Interpretative Possibilities and Underlying Politics*", 65 **INT'L&COMP. L. Q.** 493 (2016)
314. Peel, J., & Lin, J. "*Transnational Climate Litigation: The Contribution of the Global South*" **American Journal of International Law,** Volume 113, Issue 4 679-726.
315. *Massachusetts v. Environmental Protection Agency*, 549 U.S. 497 (2007)
316. *Urgenda Foundation v. The Netherlands* [2015] HAZA C/09/00456689 (June 24, 2015)
317. *Juliana v. United States*, 339 F. Supp. 3d 1062 (D. Or. 2018)
318. Laura Parker, "*Support is surging for teens' climate change lawsuit*", **National Geographic (Environment)** 5 March 2019
319. https://time.com/person-of-the-year-2019-greta-thunberg/ website accessed on 17 December 2019
320. *M C Mehta. Vs. Union of India and Others*, Writ Petition (civil) 4677 of 1985
321. Official Communication from the People's Republic of China to GATT titled *China's Status as A Contracting Party*, L/6017 14 July 1986
322. https://www.wto.org/english/thewto e/acc e/a1 chine e. htm; WTO official website, visited on 12 Dec 2019
323. WTO Accession of The People's Republic of China, WT/L/432, 2001
324. WTO News, "*WTO successfully concludes negotiations on

China's Entry", Press/243, 17 September 2001
325. Robert Zoellick, *"Whither China? From Membership to Responsibility"*, Remarks to the National Committee on U.S.-China Relations, 21 Sep 2005
326. 2018 Report to Congress on China's WTO Compliance, United States Trade Representative, February 2019
327. The White House Press Release, *President Xi Jinping's State Visit to the United States*, Office of the Press Secretary, 25 September 2015
328. Report titled *Foreign Economic Espionage in Cyberspace 2018*, National Counterintelligence and Security Center, Annual Report submitted pursuant to Sec 1637, National Defense Authorization Act 2015
329. James McBride and Andrew Chatzky, *"Is 'Made in China 2025' a Threat to Global Trade?"*, Council on Foreign Relations, 13 May 2019
330. Jeffrey J. Schott and Euijin Jung, *In US-China Trade Disputes, the WTO Usually Sides with the United States*, **Trade and Investment Policy Watch**, Pieterson Institute for International Economics, March 12, 2019
331. Commission Staff Working Document, European Commission, *Report on The Protection and Enforcement of Intellectual Property Rights in Third Countries*, SWD (2018) 47 dated 21 Feb 2018
332. *"What the EU and US WTO IP Disputes Reveal About Trade Diplomacy,"* **The China IPR**, 13 June 2018
333. 7th Meeting of the Japan-China Joint IP Working Group was held in Tokyo in January 2019 Official Press Release
334. Dan Prud'homme, *"Three Myths About China's IP Regime"*, **Harvard Business Review**, 23 October 2019
335. White Paper titled *"**China and the World Trade Organization**,"* The State Council Information Office of the People's Republic of China, June 2018
336. *"Toymaker Lego wins court case against Chinese copycats"*, **Reuters** (Copenhagen), 6 November, 2018

337. Zhao Xinying, "*IPR protection efforts thriving along Belt, Road,*" **China Daily,** April 29, 2019
338. *2018 Report to Congress on China's WTO Compliance*, United States Trade Representative, February 2019
339. White Paper on *China's Position on the China-US Economic and Trade Consultations*, The State Council Information Office of The People's Republic of China, June 2019
340. Statement from US President Donald J. Trump on *Additional Proposed Section 301 Remedies*, Whitehouse Release dated 5 April 2018
341. Statements by the United States at the Meeting of the WTO Dispute Settlement Body Geneva, 28 May, 2018
342. Tom Miles, "*U.S. and China clash over technology transfer at WTO*", **Reuters** dated 29 May 2018
343. Dorcas Wong and Alexander Chipman Koty, "*The US-China Trade War*", **China Briefing** dated 28 Nov 2019
344. "*China to Raise Penalties on IP Theft in Trade War Compromise*", **Bloomberg News** dated 24 November 2019
345. **The Guideline on Strengthening Intellectual Property Rights Protection 2019;** Joint Directive issued by Communist Party of China Central Committee and the State Council
346. Jane Cai, "*Trade war: why US and China remain so far apart on intellectual property rights*", **South China Morning Post**, dated 30 Sep, 2018
347. Sunod Jacob, "*Will December 2019 represent the Nadir of Multilateralism and Human Rights*", **Modern Diplomacy** dated 23 November 2019
348. *Secretary Ross Announces $1.4 Billion ZTE Settlement; ZTE Board, Management Changes and Strictest BIS Compliance Requirements Ever*, Official Press Release by US Department of Commerce, dated 7 June 2018
349. **Executive Order on Securing the Information and Communications Technology and Services Supply Chain**, May 15, 2019; Order passed pursuant to **International**

Emergency Economic Powers Act (50 U.S.C. 1701 et seq.) (IEEPA), the National Emergencies Act (50 U.S.C. 1601 et seq.), and section 301 of title 3, United States Code
350. Federal Communications Commission order titled **Protecting Against National Security Threats to the Communications Supply Chain Through FCC Programs**, DA/FCC #: FCC-19-121; Docket/RM: 18-89, 19-351, 19-352
351. David E. Sanger, Katie Benner and Matthew Goldstein, *"Huawei and Top Executive Face Criminal Charges in the U.S,"* **The New York Times**, dated Jan. 28, 2019
352. Alex Lockiejan, *"US calls Huawei and CFO Meng national security threats, indicts with fraud, IP theft charges,"* **The Business Insider**, January 29, 2019
353. Huawei White Paper on Innovation and Intellectual Property titled *"Respecting and Protecting Intellectual Property: The Foundation of Innovation,"* June 27, 2019
354. *Unwired Planet v. Huawei* [2017] EWHC 711 (Pat)
355. *Conversant S.a.r.l v. Huawei* [2019] EWCA Civ 38
356. Michael T. Renaud, James Wodarski and Matthew S. Galica, *Key Considerations for Global SEP Litigation*, **Lexology** dated 5 November 2019
357. Patent Protection for Pharmaceutical and Agricultural Chemical Products (initiated in July 1996 by the US and implementation report filed by India in April 1999)
358. Quantitative Restrictions on Imports of Agricultural, Textile and Industrial Products (initiated in July 1997 and implementation report filed by India in April 2001)
359. Measures Affecting Trade and Investment in the Motor Vehicle Sector (initiated in June 1999 and implementation report filed by India in November 2002)
360. Additional and Extra-Additional Duties on Imports from the United States (initiated in March 2007 and implementation report filed in November 2008)
361. Measures Concerning the Importation of Certain Agricultural Products (initiated in March 2012)

362. Certain Measures Relating to Solar Cells and Solar Modules (initiated in February 2013)
363. Export Related Measures (initiated in March 2018 and panel report is under appeal)
364. Additional duties on certain products from the United States (initiated in July 2019).
365. https://www.wto.org/english/tratop_e/dispu_e/dispu_by_country_e.htm; website visited on 6 December 2019
366. Aarshi Tirkey, *The WTO Dispute Settlement System: An Analysis of India's Experience and Current Reform Proposals*, **ORF Occasional Paper**, September 2019
367. Decisions & Declarations by Assembly of The African Union, Twelfth Extraordinary Session (Niamey) Ext/Assembly/AU/Dec.1-3(XII), 7 July 2019
368. Kim Cloete, "*Africa's new free trade area is promising, yet full of hurdles*", **World Economic Forum on Africa,** 6 Sep 2019
369. Dr. V.K. Saraswat, Prachi Priya and Aniruddha Ghosh, *A Note on Free Trade Agreements and Their Costs*, **NITI AAYOG** Report on FTA 2019
370. Alessandro Nicita, "*Trade and trade diversion effects of United States tariffs on China*", UNCTAD Research Paper No. 37 UNCTAD/SER.RP/2019/9 November 2019
371. These include the WIPO Copyright Treaty, WIPO Performances and Phonograms Treaty, Nice Agreement concerning the International Classification of Goods and Services for the purposes of registration of marks, Locarno Agreement establishing an International classification for industrial designs & Vienna Agreement establishing an International Classification of the figurative elements of marks.
372. Colum Lynch, "*China Bids to Lead World Agency Protecting Intellectual Property*" **Foreign Policy,** dated November 26, 2019
373. Frank Ka-Ho Wong, *Intellectual Property in China: Laws and*

Registration Procedures, **China Briefing,** 14 November, 2019

374. Martin Rogers, Noble Mak (Davis Polk & Wardwell LLP) *"Foreign Administered Arbitration in China: The Emergence of a Framework Plan for the Shanghai Pilot Free Trade Zone,"* Kluwer Arbitration Blog, 6 Sep 2019

375. Guangwen Meng and Douglas Zhihua Zeng, *"Structural transformation through free trade zones: the case of Shanghai",* **Transnational Corporations** (UNCTAD Publications) Volume 26, 2019, Number 2

376. International Covenant of Civil and Political Right 1966

377. International Covenant on Economic, Social and Cultural Right 1966

378. Convention on the Right to a Child 1989

379. Universal Declaration of Human Rights 1948

380. UN Convention against Torture 1987

381. Convention Relating to the International Status of Refugees 1933

382. Convention Relating to the Status of Refugees 1951

383. Protocol Relating to the Status of Refugees 1967

384. UN General Assembly Resolution 319 (IV)

385. International Covenant on Economic, Social and Cultural Rights 1976

386. https://www.ngdc.noaa.gov/mgg/global/etopo1_ocean_volumes.pdf; website accessed on 21 April 2020

387. EA Alpers, **The Indian Ocean in World History** (Oxford University Press, 2013)

388. A. Johnson, **The British empire in the Indian Ocean, Geopolitical Orientations, Regionalism and Security in the Indian Ocean** (South Asian Publishers, New Delhi, 2004)

389. H. V. Bowen, **Britain's Oceanic Empire: Atlantic and Indian Ocean Worlds** (Cambridge University Press, New York, 2012)

390. TT Poulose, **Indian Ocean Power Rivalry** (Young Asia Publications, New Delhi, 1974) p. 201

391. Akhilesh Pillalamarri, "*A Brief History of the US Navy in the Indian Ocean,*" **The Diplomat** dated 14 October 2015
392. Bertil Lintner, **The Costliest Pearl: China's Struggle for India's Ocean** (Hurst Publishers, London, 2019)
393. Jean Tournadre, "*Anthropogenic pressure on the open ocean: The growth of ship traffic revealed by altimeter data analysis*" 2014 **Geophysical Research Letters** Vol. 41 No. 22 pp. 7924-7932
394. Vijay Sakhuja and Kapil Narula, **Maritime Safety and Security in the Indian Ocean** (National Maritime Foundation, Gandhinagar, 2016)
395. H. Lyman Stebbins, **British Imperialism in Qajar Iran: Consuls, Agents and Influence in the Middle East** (Bloomsbury Academic, London, 2017)
396. Thanet Aphornsuvan, **Rebellion in Southern Thailand: Contending Histories** (East West Center, Washington DC, 2007)
397. https://www.lki.lk/wp-content/uploads/2019/05/Navigating-Challenges-and-Prospects-in-the-Indian-Ocean-Towards-a-shared-understanding.pdf; website accessed on 22 April 2020
398. Speech by Shivshankar Menon titled *The New Asian Geopolitics* at Institute for Human Sciences (IWM), Vienna 29 Sep 2019
399. Sustainable Sri Lanka 2030 Vision and Strategic Path (Presidential Expert Committee) 2019
400. Report of US Energy Information Administration titled, *World Oil Transit Chokepoints*, July, 2017
401. Key note address by Vice Chief of Indian Navy, Ashok Kumar at International Conference on India and the Indian Ocean Region: Dynamics of Geopolitics, Security, and Global Commons (The Peninsula Foundation), 12 July 2019
402. https://www.maritime-executive.com/editorials/seaman-guard-ohio-crew-acquitted; website accessed on 22 April 2020

403. Chapsos, Ioannis & Holtom, Paul, *"Stockpiles at Sea: Floating Armories in the Indian Ocean"* Weapons and the World - Small Arms Survey Yearbook 2015
404. Sunod Jacob, *"Withering away of World War II era Multilateralism,"* **Modern Diplomacy** dated 14 December 2019
405. Amy L. Catalinac, *"Why New Zealand Took Itself out of ANZUS: Observing Opposition for Autonomy' in Asymmetric Alliances,"* **Foreign Policy Analysis** (2010) 6, pp. 317–338
406. https://www.mofa.go.jp/files/000430632.pdf; website accessed on 28 March 2020
407. **A Free and Open Indo-Pacific Advancing A Shared Vision**, US Department of State, 4 Nov 2019
408. Prime Minister of India's Keynote Address, Shangri La Dialogue, 1 June 2018
409. Shared Vision of India-Indonesia Maritime Cooperation in the Indo-Pacific, **India-Indonesia Bilateral Joint Statement**, 30 May 2018
410. Prime Minister of India's Statement at the East Asia Summit, 4 November 2019
411. Lloyd Alexander M. Adducul, *"The Indo-Pacific Construct in Australia's White Papers: Reflections for ASEAN-Australia Future Strategic Partnership"* **Center for International Relations and Strategic Studies Commentary, Foreign Service Institute**, Vol. V, No. 6, March 2018
412. Australian Government Foreign Policy White Paper, 2017
413. Cary Huang, *"US, Japan, India, Australia ... is Quad the first step to an Asian NATO?"* **South China Morning Post**, 25 Nov, 2017
414. Derek Grossman, *"How the U.S. Is Thinking About the Quad"*, **Australian Strategic Policy Institute Commentary** 7 February 20
415. Sunod Jacob, **Post Millennium Trends in the Global Energy Security Architecture** (BV, 2020)

416. A Gnanasagaran, *"Is the Quad still relevant?"* **The Asean Post**, 5 December 2018; See also: Mark J. Valencia, *"The Quad: Whistling by Its Grave – Analysis,"* **Eurasia Review**, 20 March 2019
417. Vision and Actions on Energy Cooperation in Jointly Building Silk Road Economic Belt and 21st-Century Maritime Silk Road, (BRI Official Document) 2017
418. Office of the Leading Group for the Belt and Road Initiative, **Building the Belt and Road: Concept, Practice and China's Contribution,** (Foreign Languages Press, Beijing, 2017)
419. *"Belt and Road forum: China's 'project of the century' hits tough times,"* **The Guardian**, 25th April 2019
420. https://www.fmprc.gov.cn/nanhai/eng/snhwtlcwj_1/t1380 615.htm; website accessed on 28 March 2020
421. Annex 1 to the Charter of The Indian Ocean Rim Association (as Amended in November 2018)
422. https://www.mfa.gov.lk/iora_wg-_eng/; accessed on 28 March 2020
423. https://www.navy.gov.au/ions; website accessed on 22 April 2020
424. *Portugal v India*, [1960] ICJ Rep 6
425. *India v. Pakistan*, 1971 I.C.J. 347 (Order of Sept. 16)
426. *Pakistan v. India* 1973 I.C.J. 328
427. *Pakistan v. India* 2000 I.C.J. 12
428. *Marshall Islands v. India* I.C.J. Reports 2016, p. 255
429. http://www.icrc.org/eng/assets/files/other/what_is_ihl.pdf ; website visited on 1/05/2020
430. Christopher Harland's views on *'Human Dignity'*, **Basic Documents on International Humanitarian Law- South Asia Collection** (Second Edition, ICRC, New Delhi, 2011)
431. Michael Schmitt, *"Wound, Capture, or Kill"*, **E.J.I.L.** 2013, 24(3), pp. 855-861
432. VS. Mani, **Handbook of International Humanitarian Law in South Asia** (Oxford University Press, New Delhi, 2007)

433. World Report 2013, Human Rights Watch
434. Gareth Evans, *Remembering Sri Lanka's Killing Fields*, **Project Syndicate** (Worldwide Distribution), 26 October 2012
435. http://www.theguardian.com/world/2013/oct/18/drone-strikes-us-violate-law-un; website visited on 1/05/2020
436. The Report of the Special Rapporteur on the Promotion and Protection of Human Rights and Fundamental Freedoms while Countering Terrorism
437. Statement by Ambassador Masood Khan, Permanent Representative of Pakistan to UN [Doc: A/C.3/68/L.61/Rev.I]
438. National Assembly of Pakistan Resolution dated 10/12/2013
439. https://www.theguardian.com/world/2009/sep/06/sri-lanka-expels-unicef-official; website visited on 1/05/2020
440. Nepal-UCPN-M, Action Plan, December 2009
441. http://www.un.org/apps/news/story.asp?NewsID=33696&Cr=Nepal&Cr1#.UqqKreQjL9k; website visited on 1/05/2020
442. *Advocate Raja Ram Dhakal v. Prime Minister of Nepal*; Writ No 2942, 2059 of year 2004
443. https://www.dhakatribune.com/bangladesh/2020/04/12/bangabandhu-killer-majed-hanged; website visited on 1/05/2020
444. Criminal Appeal Nos.24-25 of 2013 (Appeal against ICT-BD No.2, judgment dated 5.2.2013)
445. http://www.thehindu.com/news/international/south-asia/bangladesh-sc-upholds-jamaat-leaders-death-penalty/article5451053.ece; website visited on 1/05/2020
446. *"Bangladesh: ICRC honored for helping victims of 1971 conflict"*; http://www.icrc.org/eng/resources/documents/feature/2012/bangladesh-feature-2012-04-19.htm; website visited on 1/05/2020

447. Sri Lanka's Killing Fields; documentary aired by Channel 4 on14 June 2011
448. Women, Peace and Security", UNSC Resolution 1325 (2000)
449. Dominic McGoldrick, A.P.V. Rogers, *"Assassination and Targeted Killing - The Killing of Osama Bin Laden"*, **I.C.L.Q.** 2011, 60(3), pp. 778-788
450. David Axe, *"Why South Asia loves Peacekeeping,"* **The Diplomat**, dated 20 December 2010
451. https://peacekeeping.un.org/sites/default/files/02_country_ranking_21.pdf; website visited on 2/05/2020
452. Marco Sassoli, *The Implementation of International Humanitarian Law: Current and Inherent Challenges*, **Yearbook of International Humanitarian Law**, 10, 2007, pp. 45-73
453. "International Humanitarian Law and the Challenges of Contemporary Armed Conflicts", Report by the International Committee of the Red Cross, October 2011
454. Sandesh Sivakumaran, *"Re-envisaging the International Law of Internal Armed Conflict"*, **E.J.I.L.** 2011, 22(1), pp. 219-264
455. Micaela Frulli, *"The Criminalization of Offences against Cultural Heritage in times of Armed Conflict: The Quest for Consistency"*, **E.J.I.L.** 2011, 22(1), pp. 203-217
456. Additional Protocol II to Hague Convention on Protection of Cultural Property in Times of Armed Conflict;1954
457. UNEP, Ground Contamination Assessment Report: Military Waste Storage Site, Astana, Afghanistan, December 2006
458. ICRC Commentary on Additional Protocol I
459. David Luban, *"Military Necessity and the Cultures of Military Law"*, **L.J.I.L.** 2013, 26(2), pp. 315-349
460. Geneva Convention relative to the Protection of Civilian Persons in Time of War, 1949
461. Armed Forces Special Powers Act 1958
462. Armed Forces Special Powers Act (Assam & Manipur) 1958

463. Armed Forces Special Powers Act (Punjab & Chandigarh) 1983
464. UN Peacekeeping: The Next 5 Years, Report by NYU Centre on International Cooperation, 2012
465. Jardine, David. A Reading on the Use of Torture in the Criminal Law of England (Baldwin and Cradock, London, 1837) pp. 10–12.
466. Jeffrey M. Perl, "A Dictatorship of Relativism?" 2007 Common Knowledge, Vol. 13, Issue 2-3, p. 276
467. Sec. 5 of (Scottish) Treason Act 1708
468. Stephens, Lt. Col. RGW Hoare, Oliver (ed.). **Camp 020: MI5 and the Nazi Spies: The Official History of MI5's Wartime Interrogation Centre** (Public Records Office, 2000)
469. *Factor v. Laubenheimerl*, 290 US 276 (1933)
470. *Kelly v. Griffin*, 241 US 6 (1916)
471. Dvorak, Petula, *"World War II secret interrogators break their silence,"* **Washington Post**, dated 20th August 2006
472. Ullstein Berlin, **Tapping Hitler's Generals: Transcripts of Secret Conversations 1942-1945** (Frontline Books, 2007)
473. Optional Protocol to the International Covenant on Civil and Political Rights General Assembly resolution 2200A (XXI) of 16 December 1966
474. Second Optional Protocol to the International Covenant on Civil and Political Rights, aiming at the abolition of the death penalty Adopted and proclaimed by General Assembly resolution 44/128 of 15 December 1989
475. General Assembly resolution 39/46 of 10 December 1984
476. Convention against Torture and Other Cruel, Inhuman or Degrading Treatment or Punishment 1984
477. General Assembly resolution 44/25 of 20 November 1989
478. International Telegraph Convention of 1865

www.ingramcontent.com/pod-product-compliance
Lightning Source LLC
Chambersburg PA
CBHW052341220526
45465CB00003BA/904